Secret of the Darwin's Code

By

Henrik Hirsimaa

Table of Contents

Chapter 1: Professor Edmond Grant

I ran in the drizzle with a dark brown leather bag in my hand along the cobblestones slippery with wet oak leaves towards the University of Cambridge. There, my intention was to enrol in the Faculty of Geology. I was late for our meeting and hoped to myself that Professor John Henslow had not yet arrived. After all, starting my studies here was his idea. I laughed to myself as I remembered how frightened I was at his suggestion of university studies. On the other hand, at least this is a natural science, unlike that dreary deaconry degree that I finally got finished. If I get into university, how do I finance my studies? I won't go to work, and my father would hardly be willing to support me financially for the third time when I hadn't been more successful before. Fortunately, I know professor Henslow. He is a great man. With Henslow, I can get some meaningful work in the future even without a university degree. Despite all my problems, I wanted to see positive signs in my future. When I opened the front door of the university, that same familiar warm moist stale air struck my face, bringing back stark memories of my recent studies. I quickly expelled them from my mind, leaping quickly along the hallway toward the secretariat. As I opened the door, instead of professor Henslow, I came across Professor Edmond Grant.

He smiled kindly at me, more familiar than usual. He immediately inquired about my affiliation and asked me to have lunch right away with him. I declined because I wanted to get through the registration bureaucracy as soon as possible. Grant said he would take care of all the paperwork for me in good time if there were any need for it after our discussion. I wondered by his unusually great interest in me. Professor Grant promised to tell me about the good news at lunch, as long as I was smart enough to go with him right away, so we went out to eat at a nearby restaurant. The waitress guided us to Grant's reserved table near the window. After we sat down, Grant said he had been on leave for half a year and would soon be moving to the University of London to become a professor. He briefly mentioned that he had recently been studying "the science of the future" on his own, as he put it.

"What exactly is such science?" I asked enthusiastically.

He ignored my question, continuing: "Look, Charles, we are on the threshold of a new era where change will be drastic for all nations. In the next century, we will be able to determine for ourselves what our future will be like. It is made possible by tremendous developments in technology and the various sciences. In your college year, you must have noticed how the progressive winds of the Enlightenment are already blowing our island at full blast.

As a result, our perceptions of morality will change. We will form our own new values in the future, and those will liberate us. This development requires us to develop our minds. As a nation, we must renew our world of thought. I have met your father a few times, and we have discussed these things. You have an important part to play in our plans."

I didn't answer as I was very surprised by his visions of the future. Now he was finally admitting he knew my father. At the same time, like a lightning strike, I remembered a snippet from my father's diary that I had secretly read. In it, my father wrote that Grant was visiting our home.

"When have you met my father?"

"A couple of years ago, on one occasion." He continued carelessly.

"On what occasion?"

"I won't answer that yet." Grant replied coolly.

"What plans do you have for me?"

Grant leaned back on his chair, laughing, and saying: "My dear Charles, not just for you, but for all of mankind! This ideology will permanently change the thinking and morals of all people. It will change the lifestyle of the whole world."

Grant apparently thought his speech would get me excited, but I was only even more confused because I didn't understand anything of his visions.

"Are these plans of yours related to my deacon's studies?" I asked naively.

Grant burst out laughing. When he had calmed down, he continued: "You can completely forget those Christian things. This matter has nothing to do with wretched deaconry work."

"Why is that food taking so long?" I tried to change the subject.

"Charles, at the turn of the year, a research ship will leave for South America. During the exploration, you will explore local nature and wild Indian tribes. I know the captain of the ship, and he asked me if I knew any young man who had studied natural science. I suggested you to him. You have a good reputation, and you are from a wealthy family. Think about it. You could go on expeditions to the virgin nature of South America that no one has explored before. You will be digging there and looking for evidence of an already extinct species. We also need evidence that different animal species have transformed into new species over millions of years, so bring back as much research material as you can that we can use as evidence. In addition, you will make detailed notes of all your observations along the way, which you can then write a book on when you return to England. This is the opportunity of your life! If you don't go, someone else will be sent anyway. This development cannot be stopped!"

Grant was immensely excited about his matter. He stressed his words, waving his hands in the air like a swordsman. I replied that I had not studied a single day of science. I didn't understand anything about animals or Indians, and even if I agreed to go on an exploration, who would fund it?

Grant raised his hand, interrupting my protest, saying money is not a problem. Investors have already promised to pay most of our expenses, and my father had promised to take care of the rest.

"My father? Why is he involved in this? Will he pay part of the cost even if I don't go on the exploration you suggested?" I asked in surprise.

"Your father is a patriot, as you surely know, so he thinks the best of our country. I don't want to elaborate further on his motives. You had better discuss it with

each other." Grant replied calmly.

"Who are the other investors, and how do they relate to this?"

Grant didn't say their names, nor did he reveal any more background. I continued to grill Grant by asking about the duration of the exploration. Again, Grant didn't want to say any exact time but only provisionally thought it would take about a year.

"Well, Charles, are you leaving?" Grant, in turn, began grilling me.

I replied that I did not yet dare to give my firm consent, but I said I was interested. Grant rushed to say he wanted my consent as soon as possible. He said he would tell me more if he got my word first. I suggested meeting at the same restaurant at the end of the week. It suited him. Finally, the waitress brought our food. We ate fast and didn't talk about it anymore. After the meal, we went out for a walk, during which Grant vehemently swore me not to talk about it to anyone, especially to Professor Henslow. I promised not to tell. We said goodbye to each other, and I walked to my apartment. I thought about our conversation all night. I would have a few days to think about how I would respond to Grant's proposal. If I went along with his suggestion, that decision could turn my hitherto boring life around forever. I wouldn't have time to go home to ask my father more about the expedition, and an inquiry by letter would also take too long. If I were to go on a sea voyage, then I wouldn't have to start studying geology. That reason should also be good enough for Professor Henslow as well. The trip would solve many problems at once. Who would miss me? No one. What options did I have? Only that pathetic deacon's work or study, and neither of those options interested me anymore. I wouldn't lose anything when I left for the trip. Instead, I could gain a reputation as a naturalist, as Grant had promised.

On Friday night, I met Professor Grant in the restaurant yard. I immediately told him I would participate in their plan. "I knew you would join. You haven't told anyone about this?" He said, delighted.

"I have not."

"Good. The ship's captain is Robert FitzRoy. You will meet him in London at the Whitehall Admiralty. There you can discuss the voyage arrangements, schedules, and more. Here is the address and a letter of recommendation from me. I hope you can go to London as soon as possible so that he won't take somebody else in your place." Grant continued calmly.

I said I would go as soon as next week. Finally, I told him of my desire to attend the inauguration of the graduates as deacons.

"Charles, after this exploration, you won't need any useless deacon degree. You will never even think about such pathetic things again. Believe in me." Grant said, looking straight into my eyes from under his thick brows, smiling like a father. He also gave me a couple of books that dealt with the "science of the future," as he called it. As I walked into my rental apartment, I wondered about the challenges of the forthcoming exploration and where I would have ended up without my father's continued financial help. Probably at work, like my fellow students used to say.

Chapter 2: Captain Robert FitzRoy

I left for London with excitement but great enthusiasm. Upon arrival, I immediately went to the address given by Grant to meet with the ship's captain. I expected forward to an interesting meeting. I felt excitement within my stomach because my entire future might depend on this meeting. I wondered how I could convince the captain that it was worth having me on a voyage. I arrived at the agreed time, and I felt nervous, but I stiffly knocked on the door. Soon an older man opened the door. I hastily told my name and asked if he was Captain FitzRoy. He smiled kindly, saying there wasn't, but he asked me to enter the room so that he could introduce me to the captain. I thanked him politely and stepped into the office. I took off my coat and followed this gentleman further. We arrived in a room where a man in a dark uniform of a naval officer was examining some papers on the table with his back to us. The senior gentleman introduced me to Commander Captain Robert FitzRoy, after which we formally shook hands. To my surprise, I found him to be a naval officer. Based on Grant's speeches, I had thought FitzRoy was an ordinary ship captain, but he was Commander captain of the navy. I hastily gave him Grant's letter of recommendation. FitzRoy did not open the letter but carelessly threw it on the table next to his maps.

FitzRoy seemed quite a stressed-out young man, and he didn't look like a traditional captain at all. Admittedly, I didn't know what a ship's captain should look like, but FitzRoy, with its bushy sideburns, looked more like some aristocratic writer. He asked me in a slightly arrogant tone about my studies and was greatly amazed when I told him that I had studied divinity school for two years instead of the natural sciences. The captain replied to me in a loud voice sarcastically: "Seems like Grant had already lost the best candidates when he sent the missionary on a naval expedition!"

I blushed. I felt ashamed of my studies. I tried to justify myself by telling him about my extensive collections of bugs, but they didn't interest him. Instead, he asked a new question.

"Well, have you sailed the oceans before?"

Of course, I hadn't, which made him laugh. Our cooperation did not start well. I apparently didn't make a good impression on him because he went on with scornful questions: "You must be from a rich family when you can afford to travel around the globe? Surely Grant said we don't pay you a salary? We had many better-qualified candidates for this exploration than you. But they refused to work without pay."

Of course, Grant hadn't said that. I lied to the captain as I prepared for an unpaid voyage.

In the end, he shocked me by saying we would share the same cabin all the way. I was already starting to suspect I had bitten too much, but I had no tolerable alternative in my life other than to go on this sailing trip. I didn't want to tell the captain that fact. I asked the captain about the departure date and duration of the trip. He muttered:" We are leaving Plymouth from the end of the year, and the exploration will take at least three years, so be prepared for that in terms of clothing as well."

I left the office with uncertain thoughts. I was a little worried about the captain's attitude. He treated me like a journey boy, even though he was only a few years older than me. As I walked anxiously to the shabby hotel, I wondered what trouble I had put my head into. Is the money enough for three years or more? What were the requirements of the trip funders regarding the trip? I still spent in London the next day watching the sights. As I walked towards the Natural History Museum, I got the great idea of cancelling my participation in that expedition. The more I thought about leaving myself out of the trip, the more attractive it started to feel. After leaving London, I decided not to agree to go bouncing for years to that nasty and malicious under Mr. Commander-in-Chief into that pathetic little ship. Let them acquire another fool as their companion. I decided to tell Grant of my decision when I got back to Cambridge.

When I returned, I immediately went to the university to meet Professor Grant. I walked briskly upwind across the university yard toward the entrance. I felt great confidence inside me, encouraging myself to defend my freedom of choice. Nobody won't treat me with contempt. If someone wants to cooperate with me, they have to show me respect and kindness. I was already old enough to decide for myself where I left and what I wanted out of my life. I leaped up the stairs, rushing between the students towards Grant's office. Without knocking, I slammed the door open, and I stepped inside the room without asking permission. To my shock, Grant discussed it with my father. I was terrified of the situation so badly that I couldn't even apologize for the disturbance. My father looked at me in dismay. On the other hand, Grant took over the situation smoothly, asking with delight the results of my meeting. I said hurriedly that I might not be able to take part in the expedition anyway. Before Professor Grant had time to ask a follow-up question, my father quickly got up from his chair and walked defiantly straight in front of me. He shouts in front of my face asking his questions:" Can't you commit to anything? Why are you such a coward? Why do you always stop everything in the middle? What do you want from your life? What do you think about doing for a living?"

I felt in horror how my stomach twisted, and my heart pounded with fear. I tried to say something quickly, but I didn't dare answer anything. Words just stuck in my throat. In a panic, I took turns looking at Grant and my father. My father kept staring into my eyes angrily all the time, and Grant sat behind his desk with a serious face and arms crossed overlapped on his chest. Finally, I said that the captain seemed unfriendly. He probably won't want me to be his companion on the ship. My father responded with an even louder voice and told me to stop blaming others and take responsibility for my own life. He said contemptuously with a laugh that I would die as a poor deacon in a small village in the north of England if I did not agree with their plans. That awful fact made me change my mind. I stammered to them in a quiet voice that it must be better for me to go on a sailing trip. I apologized for the disturbance I had caused and turned to leave the room. My father said he would later send me money for the trip and told me to go away. I left embarrassed Grant's study.

Chapter 3: Professor John Henslow

As I walked down the aisle, I remembered my promise to Professor John Henslow to start studying geology, so I continued straight to his office. I had planned to tell him I wasn't going to start studying. I just didn't know how I would present my refusal to him. I wouldn't want to lose his help in any future life challenges. Fortunately, Henslow was, as usual, friendly. He had a gentle look and an almost feminine beautiful smile.

"Good afternoon, Charles. How are you? I didn't see your name on the list. Did you already enroll in the faculty as a geology student?"

"Good afternoon, Professor Henslow. That's what I really had to talk about. I can't start those studies. I will be going on a research trip to South America."

I answered in a hurried way. Before I had time to continue, Henslow interrupted me.

"Hopefully, this is not one of those Grant's plans?"

"Yes, this is. How did you know?"

"For the last six months, he has been trying to catch my best students to that exploration. What did he promise you?"

"Nothing. He only said this is an important journey that will revolutionize the world of thought of all humankind."

Henslow laughed sarcastically.

"Really? The whole world of humankind thoughts. For a man has a megalomaniac and evil plans. Don't believe him. I've heard he's involved in some ancient pagan, occult, pantheistic nature religion movement. I recommend you stay away from that gang."

"I didn't know that."

"When are you leaving, and who is funding the exploration trip?" He continued his questions in interrogation style.

"At the end of the year from Plymouth. Grant has raised funding for the trip, and my father will pay the rest." I answered hurriedly.

"Do you receive any compensation for this trip?" Henslow looked seriously at me, straight into my eyes.

"No, but I can write a book about my findings," I explained in an uncertain voice.

"Charles, I encourage you to find out about the funders of the exploration trip and their motives before making a final decision."

"I've already made my decision. I've had enough of being bored with the theoretical nonsense of the university. I want to decide for myself my own life and get something done. It doesn't matter to me who finances the trip and what their motives have. The main thing is that the journey comes true."

"Fine, Charles, but let's keep in touch. When you make some new scientific findings, do you write about them?" Henslow asked conciliative.

"I promise to write, although Grant asked me not to share my findings with anybody else than him at this point."

"When do you return to England?"

"I do not know the exact time, but the ship's captain said the trip would last at least three years."

"It's a long time, Charles. During that time, the thoughts of a young man your age will change a lot. Are you still interested in the work of a deacon?"

"I haven't thought about it. I want to use all my energy for this expedition." I replied to him nervously, looking at the floor.

As we resigned, Henslow wished me a good journey and said he would pray for me. I thanked him for all the help and said goodbye to him. I left for home in confused thoughts. As I walked, I pondered Henslow's claim to Grant's occult background when I suddenly remembered the awful memory of a gloomy autumn evening a few years ago when my father wasn't home. I had gone to my father's working room without permission, where I saw his diary opened on the table. After closing the door silently, I walked behind my father's desk. I usually kept my fingers off my dad's things, but that night I couldn't resist the temptation.

I realized how something outside force was forcing me to grab his diary. I browsed it with excitement, and just as if from the strange spiritual guidance, I ended up on an interesting page. My breathing stopped as I read the text. Professor Grant had been on the visit for two days in my home at the same time as I had begun my studies as a deacon at Christ College, Cambridge. The diary also had the names of other acquaintances of my father that I did not know. At the end of the page was written a strange, intricate foreign language text and ancient pagan symbols that I did not understand. The questions were hurled in my head then. Why had they gathered in our home? What had they discussed?

There was cold weather in Plymouth when I got there. The wind blew so hard I could almost hardly even walk. There would be only a few days left to the expedition. My feelings were confused and tense. I couldn't comprehend why miraculously we set off in the winter. I knew nothing about the future challenges of the trip. Would this change my boring life for the better? I took a microscope, a compass, a telescope, a shovel, notes, a Spanish dictionary, a rifle, bullets, various shoes, tobacco, and lots of liquor for the expedition. I had reserved clothes for every season. I also brought cheap glasspearls and trinkets. These with liquor would be needed when we meet wild Indians.

After seeing me carrying my big bags, Captain FitzRoy burst out laughing. He asked vividly between his laughter.

"Has Pastor Darwin left on an exploration trip for the rest of his life?"

"Mr. Captain, it's probably easier to prepare for the stress of a trip before leaving than at sea," I replied, panting.

"You're right. I was just kidding. Come here, and I'll show you our common cabin." He continued with a grin.

I left my stuff outside the ship and followed him onto the ship. Hell, how much I was ashamed of my deacon degree. It would be of no use on this exploration trip. As I walked into the hold following the captain, pleasant odours drifted into my nostrils. First, the smell of fresh wood came up, and in the longer distance corridor, it changed to the smell of food. At the back of the hallway was the kitchen, and next to it was our room. With great expectations, I stepped into the cabin after FitzRoy, but I felt severely disappointed as I looked around the small dim room, yet without showing my feelings. In the centre of the cabin was one small table with a large Tilley lamp in the centre and lots of large candles giving light. The opposite walls had narrow, ascetic beds. There was a bookshelf on the end wall where the captain kept his maps on the roll. Our cabin room was approximately twenty feet deep, fifteen feet wide, and the height was barely seven feet.

When we got back on the deck, the captain was commanding a couple of sailors to help me to carry my stuff. I left my most important stuff in our room and took the rest to a nearby warehouse. We continued walking on the ship. Same time, I wondered, was this little ship suitable enough for an expedition? I thought the ship looked far too small for ocean sailing. The mast was painted, and the deck was being finished. At the end of the round, he introduced me to the other crew members. In all, there were about fifty men on board. There was a minority of sailors, and they were quite a colourful gang. In particular, the gaze of the cleaner remained in my mind. He was an old, skinny, serious, and nasty-looking man. Most of the crew were soldiers and were commanded by a couple of officers. Looking at them, I wondered for myself the purpose of the trip. We are embarking on a scientific research trip, so why is the ship full of soldiers instead of scientists?

On the evening of our original departure day, I was reading a book I had received from Professor Grant in my bed when commander captain FitzRoy came into the cabin. He tapped the cover of my book with a bottle of whiskey and dropped it directly on my face.
"It's a hard storm outside. We can't leave for at least the next couple of days, so let's drink the bottle empty and get to know each other.

Time passes more relaxed as you drink, as you probably know." The captain suggested with a smile.

"Thanks for the offer, but I don't really drink alcohol at all."

"What is a man who doesn't drink alcohol?"

"Well, if now, this one time, I might take one little sip."

"That's what I thought. I don't think a sober man can be a fun and good companion. Liquor triggers the atmosphere and makes it easier to get acquainted. I won't spoil a good drink with water. I hope you don't either. Cheers, Darwin."

"Cheers, Mr. Captain."

We drank at once to our empty glasses. I hadn't tasted alcohol in a while, so there was a burning feeling in my throat. FitzRoy, on the other hand, drank whiskey like water.

"Did you get upset by my comments in London?"

"No," I answered cautiously.

"Well, that's good. I want to be outspoken from the beginning. I will be under alot of pressure as a ship captain, and I might say nasty things when I am nervous. I am responsible for this ship, cargo, and crew."

"Of course, I understand."

Soon he was already pouring more for both of us. I asked him to slow down, but he wasn't even listening to me. The captain sat in his chair and quickly glanced at the book I had placed on the table.

"What does that book all about?"

"It tells about the differences between human races. I got it from Professor Grant."

"I should have guessed. Did you take any Bibles with you?"

"No. I didn't even think about it." I replied in embarrassment.

"You're a weird priest when you don't drag the Bible with you. During this journey, you have a great opportunity to convert an entire Indian tribe to a new religion. What do you think about it?"

"I don't know. That work doesn't seem to be for me. Nature interests me much more." I felt a blush rise on my cheeks.

"Well, if you come to other thoughts, I might have one Bible in that closet. As you may have noticed, there are a few black wild people on this ship."

"As a matter of fact, I didn't notice. Where did you get them?"

"We didn't get them anywhere but robbed them on our first trip. It was much safer for us to move there when they were our hostages. We forced them to walk in front of us by ropes tied together. It prevented other Indians from attacking us."

"Why did you take them on board?"

"I was thinking about the possibility of educating them. You will find that the Indians have already learned a little about our civilized customs. Of course, they cannot be fully civilized, but even a little. From one thing to another, were you thinking of writing a diary during our trip?"

"Yes, because Professor Grant asked me to write down all my scientific observations."

"What does he do with your notes?"

"I don't know."

"By the way, do you know the real purpose of this trip?" FitzRoy asked, looking serious.

"Grant said that my job is to study the local nature and the natives," I replied sincerely.

The captain slowly turned his head, looking at the floor, laughing cynically.

"Isn't this a scientific research trip?" I asked naively.

"No, Charlie boy. Not at all. The purpose of this voyage is to map the sea routes for our glorious fleet and identify new potential bases as well. I want to avoid the fate of my predecessor, and that's why you got on this journey. You must keep me in a good mood, and that's your only job on this expedition. You are my unpaid companion. Did you understand?" The captain explained to me, waving his finger.

I was silent after hearing the captain's response. My stomach ached, and panic took over my mind. I asked myself, had I wanted this trip to keep company for him? After wiping the deep disappointment out of my mind, I made my counter-comment to the captain.

"Grant promised me that this would be a scientific research trip, during which evidence would be sought for the development of different animal species," I explained startled.

"Really? Is that what he had promised you? Well, you can, of course, study an example like of the life of worms, if you want, but that's not your main job, as I said." The captain said and slapped an empty glass on the table.

"Did Grant lie to me?"

"Well, I don't know what he promised you, but knowing him, I think he's told you a slightly modified piece of truth, as he used to say," FitzRoy explained, laughing contemptuously.

I sank for a moment into my own thoughts, thinking about my future on this ship. I felt myself a weak, depressed fool who was mercilessly exploited by people. I couldn't escape this situation, or my dad would make me disinherited, so I decided to submit to my fate. The captain glared at me and started mocking me, intoxicated.

"Sounds like you know nothing about anything. You look like an insecure sissy-boy. Don't you have opinions on any issues? Based on your character, you seem like a loose guy!"

I didn't comment on his character analysis because he was partly right about it. The captain stood up and walked straight in front of my face. He stared at me with the drunken man's cultivated eyes, shouting:

"Has Mr. Darwin doubted my knowledge of humans?"

"I have no doubt about that, but could you judge me by the trip? I'm not challenging you for anything, so, please, could we sit down?"

"I'm calm. We sailors have a harder sense of humour than you land lobsters. Besides, I won't learn to know you if I don't make you nervous. I am not interested in your motives for this trip. You study what you study. Take more whiskey once it seems to be left. Give me that cup. Have you been abroad before?"

"I once visited France with my brother. I didn't like that country. The French are probably the most vanity and proud people in the world. They couldn't even speak English. The much-praised French cuisine did not make a positive impression on us. I think English food is just as good as French. No wonder we British have fought against them so many times. By the way, where else have you sailed?"

"Despite my young age, I have sailed on all seven seas. On this ship, this is my second voyage of exploration. I was on the first voyage as an assistant to the then captain. That journey took more than four years. Our mission was to help a larger vessel explore the east coast of South America. The voyage was difficult, and it became even more difficult when our captain shot himself in the stomach. Can you imagine what a fool he was? When you want to finish your days by your own hand, then you must shoot in the head!

He was tormented in his bed for two weeks. Eventually, he died, and I became the captain of the ship."

"That's awful. Why did he shoot himself?"

"Didn't tell me, but he was probably depressed by loneliness. Under my leadership, we arrived back in England last year. This year, major alterations were made to this ship. Now those are nearing completion, as you saw yourself. Thanks to it, we have new and the best measuring devices that can befound in the world." Skipper explained proudly.

I dug deep into my thoughts, trying to get something positive out of this situation. I thought about my mission on the coming journey. So, a captain designed me as his companion. Well, that's his problem. There is no worse entertainer than me in this world. Why didn't he get a young woman here to entertain himself? Even the thought of it bothered me. At the same time, I looked at the captain with a side-eye. He seemed to calm down as he got to talk about himself, burping, farting, and mocking others. His temperament seems to be of inherently low quality, and there would also be an improvement in his sense of humor. In his aristocratic way, he wants tobe omniscient in every matter. I couldn't help but think of Professor Grant either. I considered him a moral man, but he lied to me in the face.

With my bad luck, I might have been on this ship for years without pay and been forced to listen to an alcoholic and an arrogant captain. I couldn't do anything about this matter, so I just must try to get the most benefits out of this trip. I decided to drown my disappointment in whiskey.

"Do you have that liquor left?" I asked the captain with a disappointed voice.

"Of course, we have. Let's drink the rest of it. You really are a good drinker!"

"Yep, that's right! We are already starting to get really drunk. This swaying of the ship does not bode well for tomorrow morning as I have a weak stomach, and I vomit easily."

"Don't worry about it today. For my side, you can vomit all day, as long as you don't mess up places. Yes, there is space for shit in the sea." The captain guided in a paternal style.

The next day went into a hangover lounging in the cabin of the ship. The crew did the rest of the work related to the departure. I, on the other hand, had managed to avoid all the work during my life up to that, like also now. As I got to know the crew better, I felt sorry for them as they had no hopes for normal family life. For me, this was my first Christmas away from home and alone in a strange environment. I felt miserable.

Chapter 4: Departure for an exploration

At last, the great arrived day when we could finally set off. We all started to be already really frustrated with the wait. My beard was unshaven, and I hadn't washed for a couple of weeks, so I guess I smelled shitty. I probably looked a lot older than my age. I had a little hangover, but I was in good enough condition to come to the deck to watch the departure. It felt amazing when the ship finally left the harbour. The salty scent of the sea got my mind excited. The sky was clear with a strong wind blowing us on a journey. Now then began that great journey that would change my life and the future of all mankind, as Professor Grant had prophesied. On that awkward morning, I really didn't expect this trip to make me a great and respected scientist. We headed towards the South Atlantic. Once we were within sight of the harbour, the wind picked up, and the ship began to sway in the waves. As a result, I immediately became seasick. I vomited in turn in the cabin and on the deck. My hangover only exacerbated my already miserable mood. The smell left by my vomiting in our cabin did not improve the captain's mood. The first night he slept on the warehouse floor. Since the others were already experienced seafarers, I was, of course, the only one who contracted seasickness. The crew laughed mercilessly at my expense.

It made me depressed. Didn't start honourable my career as an explorer. The artist Conrad made caricature cartoons of me, in which I wobbledon the deck vomiting. After watching them, I swore to myself to stop drinking booze. At first, I thought he, for malice, drew such pictures of me, but over time, after getting to know Conrad better, I found him to be a nice guy. He was a rather short and skinny man with bushy brown hair. He was artistically emotional by character and maybe a little simple in his mind, but I still liked him from the beginning. Conrad already had beautiful paintings of the nature of the South of England, which he excitedly presented to me. I've never understood anything about fine art, but I think those were beautiful paintings. That painting style may have been a bit too pale in colours, but those had their own calm, almost sleepy stagnant atmosphere. The first days went by, cleaning up my own messes and fighting with the cleaner. He was a bitter and nasty bastard who wanted to make me his own helper. I shouted at his face that I was a scientist and not a trivial cleaner. He was always complaining about me to the captain, who in turn advised me to be patient with the crew. The captain said in the evening in our cabin the name of the cleaner was Dawkins, Dick Dawkins. I laughed at the man's first name. That was a nickname for a man's genitals.

Within a few days, my body got used to the rocking of the ship, and the food stayed inside my stomach. FitzRoy had his nerves in shreds at first when things didn't go right by his mind. At worst, he was in the mornings inspecting the ship. If a sailor forgot to add "sir" while speaking to him, he wouldn't get proper teaching. I was useless because I couldn't work on a ship, so I focused on oriental meditation. The books and meditation I received from Grant slowly but surely began to shape my perceptions of the human race. I also got to know two officers tentatively. They were class-conscious, proud, traditional British gentlemen with their aristocratic customs. The purpose of the soldiers was to protect us from pirates and barbarians. The Wild Indians, plundered by CaptainFitzRoy on his first expedition, were kept most of the time in the hold of the ship behind locks. When I had nothing else to do, I tried to teach them to read. Based on the shape of their skulls, one could guess that they would never learn normal human habits. While the captain was free, we spent time in our cabin getting to know each other and discussing the different stages of our lives. I told him I was supposed to start studying geology at the University of Cambridge, but because of this expedition, I didn't enroll. He said I would be too old to study when I returned home. Anyway, I decided to tell him openly that I had never enjoyed studying at any school because the teachers were sadistically authoritarian.

For them, all the children were one and the same, an impersonal crowd. Teachers tried to defeat our personalities and standardize our behaviour to suit them. The captain said that's what it is everyone else has, and still, many succeed in their studies. You can't defend yourself by blaming teachers. I admitted he was partially right. I told the captain that, at best, I was an average student. I did not stand out intellectually from other students in any area of my studies. Discipline was severe. The teacher could beat up the map stick on students' fingers without any sensible reason. The school teaching had no positive effect on me. FitzRoy's experiences were very much the same, though he thinks there's nothing wrong with tough discipline as long as it's the same for everyone. Such a large flock of brats would not be able to be taught if they were not subject to severe discipline. The same was true of these rough sailors. The captain told of a previous voyage in which he had to regularly arrange public punishments on board. Otherwise, these simple sailors would interpret any kind of flexibility as a weakness. With compromises, he would lose all respect, and a rebellion could break out on the ship. FitzRoy's father was a harsh naval officer, so he was used to hard spanking already at home. For me, hard school discipline instead was a shock because I had been given a free upbringing.

"How were your university studies?"

"Not any better. I moved to Edinburgh to study medicine. My brother Erasmus had already studied chemistry there for several years. Edinburgh is a beautiful city, but the thought of studying medicine terrified me because I considered myself too young and, frankly, just too stupid for university. My father's will and money dictated more than my feelings in this matter. Now I only realize how happy I got to be when I even had the opportunity to study. My father paid for my studies, arranged my move, and was connected with the university. We lived in a small flat near the university, from which our father paid the rent. Erasmus was already engaged, so my brother's free time went mainly with his fiancée." I multiplied and watched to floor mouldings.

"What was that university studying really like?"

"It was a nightmare from the beginning. It was too free formed for me; I was not yet mature enough mentally to study on my own."

"What subjects caused you difficulties?"

"Latin language and mathematics. Nor was the study facilitated by the fact that the professors of the faculty were relentlessly demanding. The lectures were really boring, and I didn't understand anything about them. I only got through some of the courses with poor grades."

"Sounds sad. Did you meet Grant at the university?"

"Yes, he taught us human anatomy. I had a great time with those lectures because I liked his inspiring style of teaching. Grant is manipulative, strong, analytical, and practical in his character. Also, he is as intelligent as my father but much more impatient. He values the natural sciences above all else. He did not moralize anything and did not bother me with religious thoughts. He represents the new world of values of the university. On his advice, I joined an association called the Plinian Society, which had been established for scientific research."

"What kind of men participated in those events?"

"They were of upper-class background, proud, and narrow-minded men. I felt ashamed to explain to them why I didn't make it in my medical studies. There I became acquainted with other scholars who were openly atheists. They did not believe that any outside creator was needed for the birth of the Earth."

"An ideology that claims the earth was born by itself is absurd. How could the Earth be born of itself when this ship is not born of itself? Do you know how many different things need to be thoughtfully planned in order for a ship like this to sail the oceans?"

"I don't know, but Grant argued excitedly how everything might have been born by chance."

"He never told me anything so insane!"

"Listen to the end. According to Grant, individuals of different species have an inner need to evolve toward perfection. Hence their characteristics evolved as they attempted to adapt to a changing environment. As they multiplied, individuals will pass on these acquired traits to their offspring, who then will displace their less capable competitors."

"Do those species then change into other species over time? And where did those stem species come from then?"

"Grant didn't say that, and I have no idea."

"That's what I just said! It also makes sense of this, that nothing can appear from emptiness on its own without any outside help."

"In any case, it was far from a dull theoretical lecture. I did not pay any attention to the idea then because I did not understand it as revolutionary."

"Were these Grant philosophies related to your medical studies?"

"Not directly, but in Grant's lectures, I started to understand what I wanted from my life, and that fact brightened my mind. Grant freed me from the distressing religious sense of guilt. By the way, how have you become acquainted with Grant?"

"I acquainted with him in a lecture introducing the ancient British pagan religions." Captain said.

I was amazed at the answer, but I didn't dare ask about it anymore. The captain, in turn, asked me about my paternal relationship. I honestly told him what I thought of my father. That he remained a distant, indifferent, and cold man to me as a child, and I cannot say that I know him even yet as an adult man.

"What kind of man is he by character?"

"He is determined and serious. He does not tolerate gentle emotion, as he himself puts it. The father said I had inherited my mother's family's soft hag character. My father often spoke in a respectful tone about his own father's Erasmus Darwin's theory, which deals with people's constant struggle for the right to live. Ordinary people, on the other hand, considered my grandfather Erasmus to be an introverted maniac and alienated from reality. My father can't stand people who disagree with him. I don't remember him ever apologizing to anyone. I was afraid of my father. I can say quite sincerely that my father is the most intelligent person I have ever met. My brother later told me while we were studying in Edinburgh how disappointed our father was when I, as a child, showed no interest in studying. My father thought I would never achieve anything significant in my life. That's when I first realized I might never be able to earn his approval."

"It is useless to feel any guilt for that. Do you tell me more about your family history?"

"Maybe I could tell. Our parents were cousins to each other, as are my grandparents. That fact has always been greatly shamed for me. My childhood home is a big stone house in the peaceful, beautiful scenery of the countryside. At a time when hundreds of thousands of children in the British Isles were working six hours a day in the mines, we were playing in our fine white clothes in the backyard of our mansion."

"It's good that you had a safe childhood. No need to be ashamed if you are from a rich family. I have spent an upper-class childhood, though part of it has gone when sailing on the seas. Admittedly, that marriage to cousins in many generations is a dubious thing."

FitzRoy had lost his mother as a child like me. He was still a bachelor, and it didn't seem to bother him. The captain asked me about my mother. I honestly said my mother was the dearest person in my life so far, and I think I was the dearest child to her. She introduced me to the ancient British sagas in which the ancient pantheistic gods fought for the British kingdom against the conquerors. As a child, I lived with my whole soul on the heroes of those stories, thinking they were real.

"Wasn't your mother a Christian?"

"No, she wasn't. She wanted to create her own set of values. My mother wanted to shape her own worldview based on tolerance. I was often with her to the Unitarianism association in the philosophical meetings.

She did not believe in the Bible. To her, Jesus was only a morally good man, nothing else."

"How did she justify that belief? Did she have any historical evidence to supporther claims?"

"At least she never presented me with any evidence. Maybe she trusted more of her own feelings. For some reason, throughout history, women have always been more interested than men in all kinds of witchcraft and superstition, as was the case in our family. That might be one reason why I spent so much time with my mother."

"How did those beliefs manifest in her life?"

"In the autumn, she held spiritism sessions in our home with her female friends. They gathered in the guest room of our home. We children were not allowed to attend those events. I went many times, secretly behind the door, to listen to their sessions. At first, it was exciting to listen, but usually, the women's screams and the rumble of shattering dishes heard from the room soon turned my excitement into fear. I wanted to go see what happened there, but I didn't dare. I would have liked to help my mother. After these occult spiritism sessions, my mother was in a state of gloomy depression for many days."

"Why didn't your father intervene in your mother's witchcraft tricks?"

"I don't know. My mother died when I was still a child."

"What disease did she die of?"

"We never found out the cause of death. I remember the shocking events that preceded her death for the rest of my life. Our father tried with the servants to keep us from seeing our mother in her last moments. My mother died the night I woke up to her horrible cries in which she begged forgiveness from God. Her death was terrible."

"Did any of your siblings see your mother?"

"In Edinburgh, Erasmus once arrived at our apartment drunk after arguing with his betrothed. That's when he told me he had quickly seen our mother was dead. Our mother had been lying on her back in bed with her head turned to an unnatural position backwards. Her eyes were wide open. Before, such a gentle face now reflected only the horror of death. It was as if she had seen something supernaturally evil before she died."

"Damn! Was your mother buried in the blessed church land?"

"No, her urn was buried in the backyard of our home. Our children were broken by grief, especially me. I didn't see any outbursts of emotion from my father. I wondered for a long time, with the devotion of the little boy, why God let her die so young of an age. I felt depressed for many weeks. I want to remember about my mother only her smiling, loving character."

After I finished my speech, I decided to stop revealing family secrets.

Maybe I went too far already, not knowing the captain yet properly. I was surprised at how easily I could tell these things about my parents to an almost stranger man. Maybe this isolation on this ship made me open up. When I finished my speech, the captain bounced to stand, snarling in horror in a loud voice, claiming my mother was a witch. I felt offended by his comment. I think everyone had the right to practice their own religion in the way they saw fit. The captain acknowledged that right, but he also claimed that everyone also bears the responsibility for their choice, whether they realize it or not. We couldn't reach a consensus on the matter, so captain FitzRoy left our room in an agitated state of mind on the deck of the ship. After calming down, I followed him to the deck, where he steered the ship with a mate. I went to him, wanting to reconcile. He calmed down quickly and stated that it was not worth remembering the past too much. I moved to the edge of the ship to lookeast with my telescope. Far on the horizon was the coast of West Africa. I still remember that bubbling feeling of enthusiasm when our scout shouted that the Cape Verde Islands were in front of us. I could hardly wait for our ship to anchor port. Fortunately, we hadn't had to be quarantined, so I was able to immediately go into the woods with my research equipment. The captain warned me not to get lost, and the crew warned me about the cannibals. This would be my first real journey of discovery.

I had been waiting for this moment from the beginning. The sailors laughed at my walking style because I couldn't wave my hands at the right pace as I walked, so they hung against my body motionless. Anyway, I didn't care about these flaws but pulled the top hat into my head and headed for the woods. I soon realized in the woods that a top hat would have been worth leaving on the ship, as it was impractical for a digging job. In the forest, I made interesting discoveries about animals that had already died a long time ago. I found dozens of new insects and beetles. I killed the ones I caught, and I did attach them already to my extensive collection of insects. I felt great satisfaction as I pierced the bugs with needles as put them in the glass display case. I took everything possible from the forest with me. I also had a shotgun with me, just in case. I haven't met any other man who would have been as excited about a gun in the woods as I was. I enjoy the sounds of the shots and the sense of power that comes with the gun. Before I returned to the ship, I shot a few more useless animals just for fun. On the ship, I packed my smallest findings for Professor Grant to England. I also wrote a letter to him in the same package. In it, I briefly described my first research trip, my experiences, and my observations of the fauna and flora of tropical nature. I asked him to comment on the samples I posted. I also wanted clarification on what requirements he had from the natives.

What kind of samples does he want from them, and how do I take them? In general, I wanted to focus on what he was really aiming for on this exploration trip. Grant needed a lot of different material for his theory. I just didn't understand what he really needed such a theory for. I didn't get drunk once during the time we spent on the island. Didn't mind any liquor when there were meaningful things to do. During the time I spent on Cape Verde, my understanding of natural science grew more than in the three years I wasted in my studies. For the next few days, the skin on my hands was blistered, and my back was sore from digging. We continued our journey and set out to cross the Atlantic towards Brazil. Now the seaworthiness of our ship would only really be evaluated. Immediately the day after departure, we got a little storm to help us cross the ocean. The wind blew almost directly from east to west, with the help of which we rushed the sails round towards Brazil. Because I had a lot of idle time, I began to delve deeper into the findings I made. I tried to preserve the insects and plant leaves as well, so I cleared the storage space for rocks and animal bones. During the day, I just had nothing to do with the captain except when we were eating, as he had his hands full to keep us on schedule and on the right track. Until the middle of the Atlantic, the trip went fast, and I was in a hilarious mood. The ship just didn't sway, so I didn't get seasick.

After finishing my plant research in that regard, I got the idea to wash my clothes. I fetched water from the hold and also found a piece of old soap there. I dragged my laundry to the deck and told the cleaner Dawkins to start doing the laundry. He refused to do it and stated that he would only take orders only from the captain. I wondered what that damn cleaner really thought he was. Into hell, such a pointless cleaner! I didn't bother the captain with the minor thing but decided to manly wash my laundry myself. During that time, when I was playing with water and clothes, FitzRoy came to ask me what the hell I was doing. I replied to him that I was washing my clothes. To that, he asked in a sarcastic voice where I had gotten water. I stammered from the water reservoir in the hold. Upon hearing it, the captain exploded with anger and shouted his face was red: "That water is meant for drinking and cooking, not for the laundry of your shitty panties! Where do you imagine we get drinking water in the middle of the Atlantic if we run out of water? Food supplies had been carefully measured before leaving for the trip, and there was no water to waste. Did you think you drank seawater for the rest of the trip?"

Now I realized my stupidity. We really wouldn't get potable water anywhere before Brazil, and there would still be trips left for many more weeks. The feeling of fear made my stomach react.

In a panic, I started to mumble a prayer for help from the providence to make sure there was enough water. What did the crew think of my laundry? They would probably throw me overboard in their anger if the water ran out in the middle. Why didn't that damn cleaner warn me? This situation was entirely his fault. The captain barked at me and called me into a silly land crab. I tried to defend myself by blaming the cleaner for what happened. The captain told me to stop the accusations, or I could drink my own laundry water. In the end, he growled: "You must live on this ship with the same rules as the others. Dirty clothes, fleas, and cockroaches are a normal part of a sailor's life. This ship is not a beautysalon for hags."

After stopping his yelling, he set out in quick steps toward the hold to check the water situation. When he returned from there, he just walked past me without saying a word. Apparently, however, the situation was not entirely hopeless. To my shame, I went back to our cabin to read the books I had received from Grant. One incident showed well of the discipline maintained by the captain. It started out rather small but grew into an unnecessarily big thing. That boy was at sea for the first time. He had been too familiar with the captain during the voyage and sometimes forgot to say - "Yes, Sir Captain." FitzRoy wanted to make a warning example about him to other crew members so that discipline would not loosen.

The captain told four men to beat up the boy and then pulled him under the keel. FitzRoy invited us all onto the deck of the ship to watch the execution of the sentence. After a few hard blows, the bleeding but conscious boy was stripped of his shirt. He was then tied around from his waist with a rope, and the other end of the rope was twisted over the bow to the other side of the ship. Realizing the significance of his punishment, the boy started down on his knees and began to cry for mercy, but the captain remained in his decision. The men threw him overboard and began to pull him under the keel from the other side. I watched the execution of the punishment, holding my breath part of the time for excitement. The rest of us moved to the other side of the ship to see when the boy would rise to the surface. In less than a minute, the boy was pulled to the surface. The boy looked unconscious when he was lifted to the deck. For a moment, I thought he was already dead. Soon luckily, he came to his senses, and he took breathing, coughing, and vomiting seawater. Throughout the execution of the sentence, Commander-in-Chief FitzRoy stood calm in the middle of the ship with his hands relaxed in a gust of his chest while watching the events. When the boy returned to this awareness, the captain asked him if the boy had understood what he was being punished for. After the boy nodded humbly, the captain told him to go back to work.

After this punishment, everyone worked on the ship with respect and fear for the captain.

We were already approaching Brazil when the first dramatic event of the trip happened. We anchored our ship for the night near the shore, and soldiers guarded the deck through the night. We woke up in the night both with thecaptain to the rifle shots. We got up from the bed and ran to the deck of the ship. We saw soldiers on guard shooting one man who was coming over the edge of the ship. He dropped into the sea. Two robbers were already lying dead on the deck. "Alarm! Pirates on the ship!" Captain shouted. He pulled out his gun, firing at the man standing on the other side without hitting him. The man and his fellow criminals jumped into the sea where their boat was waiting for them. The situation was quickly over. There must have been at most a dozen pirates. They might have thought of us as a lightly armed merchant ship. They made a bad mistake. The soldiers were grabbed by dead pirates' limbs which they had shot and threw them into the sea. The whole crew was awake. Once the situation subsided, also our mood calmed down quickly. Soldiers and crew were already experienced sailors, so they knew that this might would have to happen anyway sooner or later. This was the first time in my life when I saw people shot dead. At the time, I didn't guess this wouldn't be the last time.

As we approached the coast, I found the first fleas on my body. Finding them was really just a matter of time because I had been wearing the same clothes almost all the time. After surviving the first shock, I set out to kill those as passage time. In the evenings, before going to bed, I had cockroach killing in our room. They were witty bugs. I decided to catch one of these alive for my research. I got one of them lured with a piece of meat into the glass jar. I managed to pierce it with a long needle. I watched excitedly as it raced, pierced by a needle. Its legs were extremely fast and developed. In that situation, I would not have guessed to spend the next years of my youth with fleas, lice, and cockroaches. The contrast to the home conditions was terrible.

Chapter 5: Slave Master

When it came to drinking water, we were lucky. It just so happened that there was enough water all the way to Brazil. I was probably the happiest man on board. We anchored at a port in the city called Salvador. Here I hoped to meet primitive wild people. At first, I just thought of resting from the stresses of the trip by exploring the city. I noticed on the streets that the local population consisted mostly of negroes. A waiter told at a restaurant that the city was the centre of the Portuguese slave trade. I returned to the ship in the evening, chatting with FitzRoy. In his own time, he had visited a large farm near the city. He was excited about what he had seen and praised livestock farming methods. The division of labour and management was excellently organised, in his opinion. He asked me to come tomorrow. We left early in the morning with the captain towards the farm. We arrived by horse wagon along a direct road to the manor yard. The road was shaded on both sides by large deciduous trees. We arrived in a large circular yard. Directly in front was a large mansion where the host and his family lived. The host of the house came to us and introduced himself in poor English. He said he was really flattered by our desire to get to know his farm. The host said he was a third-generation Brazilian. His grandfather had moved here from Portugal. He had a wife and three children.

We walked along the edge of a wide field and saw Negro men working there. He said that he owned hundreds of acres of land. The heaviest jobs were reserved for slaves. We continued from the field to a large building where the host said he kept cattle. The barn was dim, damp, and unpleasant in every way. There were indeed dozens of cows there. The host had a torch with him, and he walked ahead. The smell of manure was unbearable. I put a cloth in front of my face to protect against the stench. We walked to the back of a building with bars in front of the door like in prison. As we walked passing by it, there heard some painful moan. The host stopped in front of the door and shouted something in Portuguese. I asked him who was kept in that room. The host didn't answer, but after lighting another torch as well, he lifted both torches close to the room's door to show us what was there. Excited, I glanced, and my shock was indescribable. The small booth was crammed with starving, beaten, and bleeding Negro slaves. They were in chains. Some of them were struggling to get to their feet, but most of them layin the midst of hay and human faeces. Outraged by the shock, I shouted at the host, demanding an explanation for such ill-treatment. The captain came quickly between us, reassuring me. The farmer was surprised by my reaction. He said they had rebelled against him, and they had been locked up in a prison cell. He soon planned to release them and put them back to work.

I yelled out loud how miraculously anybody of them would be able to do any kind of work anymore. After all, they were in the hands of death. The farmer comforted me, saying he knew from experience the negro race is tough. He also wondered at my behaviour and said he wouldn't have looked like a barn if he had known my reaction. I asked the captain to go back to town with me. We immediately went to the horse wagon. I didn't say anything to this slave master, nor did I say goodbye to him. FitzRoy chatted with the host for a few minutes. I waited that time in the wagons. On the way to town, we said nothing. We went to a nearby restaurant and ordered a bottle of wine. We quickly drank the first glasses down our throats. The captain poured more wine into our glasses, opening the conversation.

"How were you so upset about what you saw?"

"How the hell were you not upset about what you saw?"

"Well, slavery has been throughout human history." The captain explained carelessly.

"And that justifies slavery? Shouldn't we as societies evolve? I cannot tolerate slavery, and I hate the forces that sustain it with all my heart!" I shouted at the captain and looked him angrily straight in the eye.

"Yes, you priests do speak beautifully, but tell me, how will societies stand up if slavery is forbidden? You should sometimes try to do some work, Mr. Darwin."

"People are not a trade commodity! Yes, the means will be invented. Societies are evolving. We invented new machines to replace slaves."

"And when will this paradise come true?" The captain asked cynically.

"I don't know, but I believe humanity is moving towards bright times."

"Waiting for it, cheers. While visiting that same farm yesterday, I discussed this matter with the farmer.

At my request, he brought many slaves to the scene. I asked them all with the host: "Do you want freedom?" They all shook their heads with big smiles."

"Captain, how can you be so stupid? What is the value of that answer when the host stands next to them with a gun in his hand? That answer had nothing to do with honesty! If slavery is once as nice as you just said, then why not become a slave yourself?"

The captain had furious, losing his temper completely. He threw half a bottle of wine on the floor and shouted completely non-printable words and insults toward my face. At the end of his tirade, he added:" Mr. Darwin! It is your job to keep me in a good mood, not challenge the dispute! If an unknown Negro slave is more important to you than my friendship, then we can no longer travel on the same ship!"

We both left the restaurant in different directions. As I walked from town to the harbour in the evening, I thought the captain might have already thrown all my stuff out of the ship. The gossip about our quarrel had already spread on the ship when I arrived. I met an officer, and he invited me to live in their cabin. Just as I had a conversation with the officer, a soldier came, conveying the captain's most humble apology for our dispute. He told the captain's request to return to his cabin. I accepted his apology and returned to the captain's cabin. We didn't talk to each other for many days because of this incident.

We raised the anchors and continued our journey south towards Rio De Janeiro. I had a great time on the ship, thinking about my next moves. In Rio, the weather was dizzyingly hot during the day. It haunted me because I wasn't used to such a distressing heat. On land, the crew headed to the nearest brothel. Apparently, because of that, they were in a liberated mood. They laughed among each other. I also got my share of their jokes. As they ran out of the harbour, they shouted, laughing at my face, "Doesn't the philosopher need a woman? Come with us so that you will forget the beetles!" I was like I didn't hear that. I was walking to the post office in a snobby style. To my surprise, I had received a letter, not from Grant, but from my former girlfriend, Fanny. I admitted that I was still interested in her.

Did she still feel the same about me too? I thought she had already completely forgotten about me after that last embarrassing episode. It felt really good to see her beautiful handwriting on the letter. She must have been smart enough to leave that Fred. I hurriedly walked to a nearby park where my fingers were shaking when I opened Fanny's letter.

My friend, Charles

How are you? I wrote to Catherine. She said you went on a research trip to South America. Be careful there with those wild humans. I was thinking of writing to you when I haven't heard anything from you in a long time. Too bad when our meeting last summer ended so miserably. I didn't want to offend you, but I had to tell you the truth. You're quite nice, but I don't love you. I'm getting married to Fred. He is a wealthy politician. I love Fred because he is so considerate. Let's stay friends and all the best to you.

Your everlasting friend, Fanny

After reading the letter, I crunched it into a small bundle and threw it on the ground, whether a silly letter. She wanted to hurt me thoroughly. "Let's stay friends." Why in the hell? I was really disappointed and angry. My chest cramped as a bitter piece rose into my throat. Fortunately, my gun was not included. I would probably have shot someone! I felt really anxious, lonely, and betrayed.

I walked to a nearby bench and sat down. Is this the feeling when you lose love? Why does God allow such a thing to happen to me? What for do I, as an adult man, need God? It would be made sense to go with the crew to the brothel, but what I could have done there? I had never even seen a naked woman in my life, let alone touched one. I decided to show it to Fanny and the whole world. I dedicate my life to studying nature and forget the philosophical bullshit talk about God. I decided not to respond to the letter andlet my future accomplishments speak for me. I got a lot more desire to succeed because of that silly letter. I returned to the ship and told my grief to James, who was one of the soldiers on the ship. He grabbed my arm, dragging me almost by force to his cabin. There he told me to sit in a chair. Then he sits opposite me. James began by comforting me in a friendly way, sharing his own experiences of female fraud. James thought it was pathetic to cry after some bitch. The world was full of them! He took the glasses from the cupboard, poured gin into them, and added some local juice. This is how the evening started going on in a familiar style. I emptied my cup with one sip. It tasted really invigoratingly good. I boldly asked James to pour the cup again back to full. We lightly tapped our cups together, wishing each other good luck in the upcoming women's hunts.

As the gin juice rose to our heads, James began to ask about Fanny. I told my sister Catherine to introduce me to Fanny after a riding trip to Wales. I explained in a wistful voice that Fanny was a typical British girl with round cheeks, large breasts, and wide hips. She had a big mouth and thick lips. It is these lustfully juicy traits that appeal to me. And most importantly, this shapely girl was from the same social class as me. I fell in love with Fanny at first glance. The more time I spent with Fanny, the more I fell in love with her. I desperately wanted to start dating Fanny.

"Tell me how you got her!" James asked in an impatient voice.

"It was one of those warm evenings of late summer when we had been riding all day again. That's when I finally got all my courage to introduce that matter to her. I asked Fanny to sit down on the riverbank. We sat under the deciduous tree curving towards the river, watching the sunset, and I realised my moment had come. I began my introduction by recounting how important it was to choose friends from the same social class to which you belonged. She quickly guessed what I was aiming for, starting to present the indifferent. I didn't give up, even though the mood became embarrassing. With fervour, I grabbed Fanny's hand and suggested directly that we start a relationship."

"What did she answer you?" James interrupted my narration in a boyish enthusiastic voice while sipping his glass blank.

"Apparently, Fanny was as surprised by my quick initiative as I was because her roundish cheeks were blushing. I looked straight into Fanny's eyes as she lay down her sight to the ground in embarrassment. Finally, after a time that seemed like an eternity, she quietly accepted my suggestion. Even now, my heart is warmed by the memory of her agreeing to my request. It was the best day of my life so far!"

"That's so typical of girls. In reality, they want to start a relationship right away, but they only pretend to be so difficult to achieve. They are fully aware of how humiliating that kind of blackmail is, yet they always act that way. How did it go? Did she feel comfortable with you?"

"I think we did well. With Fanny, I completely lost my sense of time, and I thought of nothing but her. Her wide smile was irresistible. Of Fanny, I was manly when I was hunting and shooting animals. I enjoyed immensely being able to teach her how to hold a gun. With Fanny, I felt alive." Drunk with a longing mind about Fanny, I told James my memory of my first love.

"You're incurable pathetic a romantic. In that lifestyle, women will be just stumbling blocks for you instead of a pleasure bringers. They will only hurt anddespise you if you eat from their hands."

James went on to philosophise, telling how he dominated women.

"So, how do you treat women?"

"I treat them like trash. I'm the boss of the woman. I determine how we live in a relationship."

"Have you had many girlfriends?" I asked enviously.

"I don't even remember how many!" James claimed, watching the walls. He drank his cup empty and then asked about my relationship pitfalls.

"At what point did you start to go bad?"

"It was that Cambridge time. From there, I sent Fanny a few clumsy letters. I only got an answer from her for one of them. Our relationship got the final bump when I once mailed her animal droppings."

"You're a hell of an idiot with women. Now send the animal's shit to a girlfriend." James said, rotating his head to look gloomy.

"After that, I didn't have any more letters from her."

"What a surprise. So, what did you do?"

"I visited her home. I tried with poor success to tell Fanny about the important research work involved, but of course, she didn't understand my scientific explanation.

Besides, she claimed I supposedly treated her like some kind of miner. I tried in every way to justify myself to Fanny by telling her about my inexperience in women's soul life. I find myself becoming sceptical about women at a young age."

"Never explain anything to women, especially about your inexperience in their relationship. Women are not interested in your explanations; they want to experience how you manage different life situations. And stop playing such a pathetic attention-grabbing martyr. That kind of whining just drives women away from you. Women are not interested in your difficulties; they want a successful and safe man to base their lives on."

"I guess you are right."

"When was the last time you saw her?"

"Last summer when I visited her home. I had already written to her in good time, and she was happy to meet me. I arrived for them in the evening, and Fanny was receiving with her mother. The mother-in-law's face had a familiar cool, contemptuous look. I didn't like Fanny's mom. The feeling had to be mutual. After eating lightly, I went with Fanny for a walk in the nearby woods. Fanny was happy and talkative. So, I asked her soon. Why are you so happy? Is it because of my visit? Fanny stopped and said with a smile:" Charles, I got engaged."

"What did you say? Why did you get engaged, and with whom? We had to get engaged!" "Because I love that man! You've never wanted to marry me or even hinted at one. Besides, this man cares about my feelings, and I have fun with him."

Fanny loaded her answer, facing my face. Her voice was gleeful. I tried to explain my studies and other obligations, but it didn't help. Fanny had made her decision with the favourable help of her mother. The man was reportedly someone Fred from the neighbourhood, and he was a good listener."

"Was that the only reason why she left you?"

"Probably not. I was reportedly more interested in beetles than in her. And she continued that I am phlegmatic and insecure in my character."

"That's what those women are like. It's a fact that if you don't chase that woman of your life, someone else will grab her, and it's usually the type you can't stand. How did that night end?" James analyses with an empty glass in his grapple.

"We quickly returned to Fanny's home. We both went to sleep without saying a word to each other. It was a long and sleepless night again. At night I wondered how disappointed I was for Fanny. She was to me a mere unloving traitor."

"Don't take it so hard. You're just ruining your youth because of someone hag."

"Yes, maybe it was my fault when I hadn't visited Fanny often enough. Probably I should have paid more attention to her feelings. It might also be that I wasn't interested enough in Fanny after all. In general, I don't get along very well with girls because I don't understand the logic of their thinking."

"Their logic males won't ever understand! Don't waste your time figuring it out. Charles, you must understand that a woman is not meant to be just a wife but also something else."

"Maybe you are right. I just don't know who I would like to share my life with." I complained to James.

"What did you do after rejection?"

"I sneaked back home from them during the rooster song. I did not say goodbye to anyone. I felt like an outsider and rejected everywhere. I certainly had different kinds of plans for that summer."

"What else did you do?"

"I didn't do anything fun. I tried to study at home with a private teacher to translate a few simple Bible phrases."

"Did you do nothing but study the translation of Bible sentences?" James asked in amazement.

"Of course, I practised math, but I lost my patience completely because my private teacher could not motivate me to study, and that's why I didn't learn math. I think the teacher was a complete fool." I replied, embarrassed.

The bitter fact, however, is that I don't have mathematical talent, but I didn't dare admit it to James.

"Wow, hell with you! Now we stop worrying and drink the rest of the liquors!"

Then he poured again. Who remembers how many times our cups filled in with gin-flavoured juice, and at some point, in the evening, we were falling asleep after the liquor ran out.

I woke up in the morning with a creepy hangover from the cabin floor. I slowly got up, looking around. I had a horrible headache, and my mouth was so dry. The room was really hot. James had already gone to perform his duties as a soldier. I greedily drank water from the jug on the table. Oh, how good that cool fresh water tasted. After drinking the pitcher empty, I climbed the stairs to the deck, where Captain FitzRoy ruled in his old familiar style. Seeing me on the deck, he waved his hand and wanted to talk to me. The captain said that he had replenished the ship's food stores and, at the same time, he had become acquainted with a merchant.

The supplies merchant was also an avid naturalist, so he knew near area very well. The captain had told him of my interest in nature. The merchant had promised to go with me on a short research trip to the local nature. I thanked the captain with great rejoice. He was a decent man, after all, I thought to myself. FitzRoy said he would go again tomorrow to get some more food, and at the same time, I could come along to get to know the merchant. As we walked into the merchant wholesale, I teased him about our last visit to the slave master.

"I hope this man wasn't the same group as that farm owner."

Captain replied in a serious voice that the man was only a merchant who kept his business with his wife, and in that work, he did not need slaves. The merchant's name was Derek. He was with his wife already in the yard of his shop, piling up goods ordered by the captain when we arrived. Derek introduced his wife, after which the captain introduced me. He seemed like a nice and honest man. I liked him right away. We decided right next week to explore the hinterland. Five other men would join us as guides, interpreters, and bearers of goods. We made a plan to travel along the coast to Rio Macao and from there on the same route back. The captain said he would repair the ship in Rio in the meantime. Before we left, I still received a letter from Grant.

Charles!

Thank you for your letter and samples. Those have been a great helpin developing the theory. You seem to have an interesting exploration trip. Too bad I couldn't take part in the trip myself. This work as a professor takes all my time from me. Your fossil finds deserve special mention. Those testify to the transformation of species into other species. Moreover, based on the way the mussels are attached, we can indeed conclude that the Earth is much older than assumed. It can be up to tens of millions of years old. Don't worry about it, even if you don't understand anything about bones and fossils. Just try to find more old reptile bones. Especially ones you don't recognise. They are the most important findings. We will then find out what you have found. When you meet the Wild Indians, try to get something from them. The best research material would, of course, be a skull. Try to get one. Dig even from some old grave. Good that you had read the books I gave you.

If you see Negroes and Indians being treated harshly, then remember you shouldn't be horrified by it. That is the law of nature! They have no future! It is an inevitable fact that most of them will perish. Only the strongest of them are allowed to remain slaves to serve whites. Be sure to take lots of notes. Draw what you can't describe. Don't think too much about the purpose of this trip. One day the whole of Britain, under the leadership of its king, will thank you for what you have done. Do as I have commanded, and we will take care of the rest.

Grant.

I felt a little surprised at the straightforwardness and brutality of Grant's letter. I was expecting more comments from him regarding my plant and animal findings. I also missed advice on the things on which I should focus. What struck me most was his claim about the age of the Earth. Does he mean that a few shrimps of shells prove the Earth to be tens of millions of years old? What does it matter what age the Earth is? I packed the goods for the expedition. I also took liquor and shiny fabrics for the Indians.

So, we went for a horse ride along the coast towards Rio Macao. I was in a good mood. I had to study nature properly again. Gradually, I began to get rid of Fanny. I wasn't going to bury myself in bitterness and self-pity. On the first trip, we passed many small villages where people lived in vicious poverty. They were not Indians but instead some kind of oblique-eyed, dark-skinned forest tribe. In appearance, they were pathetically ugly and short. They were incredibly dirty, stinking people, and their clothes were broken rags. In the city, we saw many times situations where naked slaves were publicly flogged as punishment for some trivial offence. They were usually tied naked from their wrists to thick logs. Over time, I began to get used to that sight. Inland, we met about indigenous people which I wanted to meet. We arrived in a village where we were kindly received. They wondered when I asked them for water to wash my face. These goblins thought washing was a waste of water. They held a big party in our honour, offering us their food, which was really spicy. For my part, I offered them alcohol and fabrics, which women, in particular, were excited about. Their only livelihood was rudimentary farming. They knew nature well and had their own herbs for diseases, though hardly any of them could even read. Fortunately, we had one man with us who understood their strange language.

After listening to their silly-sounding mumbling, I found that nothing could be reasonably discussed with them. Grant's theories of racial inequality began to seem real. I had always been inherently contemptuous of black races, but it had been somehow subconscious and innocent. It was just the usual prejudice without any scientific basis. Grant's books and the facts I saw opened my eyes to see the justified truth. I experienced a revival in this matter.

When we returned, we saw the execution of the death penalty. The accused was a thinny Negro slave who, according to what we heard, had stolen food from his master. We calmly watched about the start of the execution as the host and his assistants tied the struggling man's hands and put the rope around his neck. From the rope of the other end, they threw over a thick branch. The helpers held on to the slave as the master began to pull the hanging rope up. Slowly but surely, the convict's feet came off the ground. A hanged man waved his legs in horror frantically. That pathetic creature desperately tried to guzzle oxygen into his lungs. It looked like his eyeballs had almost bulged out of his head. Uselessly that poor creature tried to get his tied hands under the rope. Even if he had succeeded in that intention, it would only have slowed his inevitable suffocation.

The victim rose slowly and jerkily against the setting sun. After he had been raised hanging high enough, the master tied the rope head around the tree trunk. At the same time, the sight was terrible and sublime. Then he, together with their assistants, shouted insults at the hanged man. I was reminded of the Gospels, where people mocked the crucified Jesus. We quietly watched in scary at this slow execution. At last, after half an hour, the body stopped moving. In the end, the host shot the victim in the chest with his rifle. That shot echoed in my ears for a long time. I did not dare to say anything. With the help of an interpreter, Derek asked the host why he didn't shoot the victim right away, saving him from unnecessary pain. "Only soldiers deserve to be shot. Robbers and traitors are hanged." The host roared in response. Derek asked the master to lower the body and bury him, but the master thought it was better to leave the hanged for other slaves to see for a couple of days as a warning example. We warned the master of the danger of rebellion, but he said the Negroes had no chance of doing that because they were lazy and submissive to their fate. We had on continuing our journey in quiet signs. Grant's words came to my mind about how I shouldn't let these things affect my feelings. So, what about one hanged negro slave? I had received a rejection from a woman I loved.

We finally arrived back in Rio De Janeiro. I thanked Derek for his help and said goodbye to the other members of the group. As I walked into the harbour, I wondered how the nature of this country is truly richly diverse. The diversity of nature speaks in favour of the fact that there must still be great intelligence behind everything that exists. There has to be some root cause where it all comes from. Has everything in nature evolved more and more little by little, or was it all created at once? According to Professor Henslow, after creation, everything was ready, but due to the Fall, all plants and animals will slowly decay and sometimes become extinct in the future. According to him, species do not evolve but only adapt to different living conditions. I wrote my observations in my notebook and compared them to Grant's teachings. This will give me good material for my future book. In my letter to Grant, I wrote about my observations about the behaviour of the natives and their living conditions. The captain returned with his refurbished ship. Their journey had not gone smoothly either. Captain FitzRoy was absent. I asked him the cause of the grief, and it soon became clear. During the repair trip, three crew members contracted malaria. One of them was a boy who had been pulled under a ship keel. They had died within days. The boy's fate saddened me greatly.

I would rather have given that fate to that ship cleaner. The boy was an orphan and illiterate. It was only now that I realised I didn't even know his name. Did he realise at any point that he had even lived? Life was indeed unfair. My eyes began to open in the face of the harsh facts of life. I realised how easy and privileged my life had been. The captain was also sorry for the boy's fate, but he did not regret pulling the boy under the keel. We left Brazil behind, heading south. Our next destination was Montevideo, the capital city of Uruguay. We were accompanied on a long journey by a large herd of porpoises. Probably dozens of porpoises swam and bounced around our ship for a long distance. I followed them from the side of the ship for a long time and threw food scraps at them. They seemed much smarter than other fish. There was a strange grin on their faces all the time. It's like they smiled at me. The chicks swim next to their mothers, mimicking their movements. After I had watched for a while, they bouncing, I went to our cabin where the captain studied his maps. I wanted to get something else to think about instead of the malaria tragedy, so I challenged the captain to a chess game. FitzRoy accepted the challenge manly. He exclaimed loudly that he was the best chess player in the entire British Navy, so, beating a young boy like me would be just a mouthful for him.

I took those screams purely as the skipper's peculiar humour. I chose the white pieces so I could start the game. I always had the same plan I used when playing chess. Right from the start, I grouped the soldiers into a step-by-line lineup and between them with Bishops for attacks. FitzRoy, for hispart, started on The Queen in an attempt to attack me, leaving the King dangerously unprotected. Not long after, I had eaten the left side pieces completely. Losing his nerve and queen, the game was soon over. It was a surprisingly hard place for the skipper. I was startled by his aggressive swearing and told him the game was just a having fun. After a little time, he calmed down,took a glass of cognac, and sat down next to me.

"Where have you learned so well to play chess?"

"From my big brother Erasmus. He, on the other hand, learned it from our father, with whom he spent much time as a child."

"What kind of man is your brother?"

"He is talkative, intelligent, handsome, and successful in every way. As a child, I couldn't reach his level in anything. My brother already loved playing chess as a little boy. My sister didn't like that game at all, so he had to practice his skills against me."

"Did you ever win him?"

"I won him only once, and that too was due to his negligence. My brother is much more impatient by character than I am, and he couldn't stand my slow style of play without getting nervous. That time he inadvertently confused the king and queen. It allowed me to eat her queen. With a few moves, I took the king to the corner, and the game was over quickly."

"How did your brother react to your victory?"

"As a child, Erasmus was an even worse loser than you. He completely lost histemper, attacking me. He beat me up."

"Did you tell your father about it?"

"Yes, but our father did not care about my big brother's violent behaviour but only claimed it as an essential part of the growth process of young men. As a child, Erasmus was dearer to my father than I was."

"What kind of relationship do you have with your brother?"

"During our childhood, it was very divisive. Secretly in my thoughts, I envied and hated him, but I did not dare to show my feelings in public so as not to arouse aggravation. Today, our relationship is coolly neutral."

"How did you get along with your sister?" He asked, sipping a glass of cognac empty at the same time.

"She was already like our father in her character, and probably that's why she was our father's favourite.

Before starting my studies, Catherine tried her best to teach me to read, but with poor results. She didn't have enough patience to teach me, or I was just too lazy to learn. By character, Catherine is an extraordinarily ambitious, authoritarian, authoritative, and ruthless woman. She was the daddy's girl."
Skipper no longer asked anything but began to look at his nautical charts. For my part, I started reading a book I received from Grant.

In Montevideo, I immediately headed to the local post office. I had received a letter from Catherine. It was a typical letter written by a woman. She asked about my well-being and said he had given Fanny information about my trip. Catherine was getting married and seemed happy. Dad was reportedly happy with me when I dared to go on this trip. Well, something good from him. I wrote a letter to Catherine thanking her for the letter and asking for her help getting extra money from our father. During our stay in Montevideo, I made an exploration trip inland that stretched all the way to Los Minos. There we met mercenaries. As a side job, they herded cattle whenever they hadn't to fight. They were skilled riders and horse handlers. I was interested in the way they captured their cattle.

I watched as they rode beside the cow, after which they threw a rope around the cow's neck. That way, they made the cow fall, getting its legs tied. I asked them to teach this noble skill to me as well. One of them briefly told me about the technique, after which he let me try out what I learned in practice on his own horse. I jumped on the back of a horse and set off to ride at a brisk pace towards a lone cow. I swirled the rope nimbly above my head. The rope did not obey me. But instead, it dropped to the ground in front of me. At the same time, it wrapped around the horse's forelegs. In a panic, I instinctively pulled the rope, which tightened around the horse's legs. The horse fell forward, and I flew headfirst into the bushes. Everything went so fast that I didn't have time to realise anything at all. After surviving the aerial flight, I crawled to sit on the lawn. Thank God I only got a few bruises on my body and a couple of scratches on my face. The immense sense of shame was probably the biggest injury I received. The horse also survived without being injured. The cowherds were almost dying of laughter after seeing my aerial flight. They had never seen any rider lasso their own horse before. They were much more worried about their horse than me. Luckily, there was nothing wrong with that damn nag because otherwise, I would have been in really bad trouble.

The cow I was trying to get didn't react to my tricks in any way. It just kept eating grass. The mercenaries organised a party for us. We ate a good roast made of beef, drank raw rum, singing lewd songs, and best of all, we shot drunk racing with our rifles. I was so drunk that I half-accidentally shot a mercenary's dog after thinking it was a hare. It almost came to be a fierce fight, but luckily our interpreter calmed the situation. The cowherds were very animal-loving and temperamental men. For them, the dog was an important aid at work, while for us, the dogs were just a companion. I slept near the campfire with a tree trunk under my head and a sky as a blanket. I admired the lifestyle of the cow shepherds as it had genuine freedom and closeness to nature. In the morning, we gathered our stuff to leave back in Montevideo. During my expedition inland, the city police chief had asked our captain to help defeat the riot. FitzRoy had sent a couple of dozen soldiers to support the local police. The rioters were some stupid, poor rubbish mob in downtown Montevideo in breaking and stealing public property. I heard our soldiers treated them harshly, defeating the riot quickly. It would have been interesting to see their task. I had a lot of idle time, and most of it I spent lounging in our cabin room. As I stared at myself in the mirror of the cabin, I noticed my hair starting to get thinner out from the top of my head.

Not the biggest news in the world, but for me, it was a shock, as I hadn't even turned twenty-five yet, and I was becoming bald. The more hair thinned, the more other hair on my body growth thickened. I began to look like an ape.

Chapter 6: Gauchos

We hurriedly continued our journey along the Argentine coast towards Bahia Bianca. It was a newly established small town that seemed like a military base. This city is set to become a refuge for the Argentine population of Spanish descent against attacks by savages. From here, the Indians would no longer be able to rob cattle. The naval base to be built here is also intended to prevent Brazil from expanding here. We went to meet General Rojas, who ruled the country. We showed him our passport and the letter of recommendation we had received from the British Embassy in Buenos Aires. The general was visiting the city to check on the completion of the construction process. Rojas's other more secret mission was to control local Indian tribes that had attacked several army units in the past year, killing several soldiers. The actual task of the Rojas special department was to exterminate those Indian groups.

The general had bribed some Indian tribes to ally with the military. Rojas used the "break up and rule" method for the Indians invented by the ancient Romans. These Indian groups had been at war with each other even before the arrival of the Spaniards, so the allies with Rojas gladly helped the Argentines to kill their enemies.

Those tribes had wise chiefs, and thanks to that, they still had little hope for survival. Rojas had revolutionary thoughts, but he still seemed like a pleasant man. Instead, the major ordered by the general to escort us to the city was very sceptical of us. He considered us spies. We kindly tried to talk to him, but it was hopeless. He couldn't comprehend why someone was studying nature. He ordered his soldiers to follow us wherever we went. On the other hand, it was good, because that way we got the armed bodyguards with us for free. The local people did not want to call the Indians indigenous. In their view, those who establish, civilise, and build the state are its natives. Only they were entitled to the treasures of the land.

We left Buenos Aires behind as we rode along the dry savannah to the west. After finding the first bigger pond, we stayed there for the night. We always settled close to water to make cooking easier. When the others went to sleep, I chatted openly with Conrad by the campfire about everything possible at night dusk. We roasted steaks with hot reddish charcoal and, at the same time, drank local light beer. Conrad inquired with interest about my college studies. He had no chance to study just about anything because of his parent's poverty, and it seemed to be embarrassing him.

He had been in a school run by a Christian church for a few years, where he had learned to read and write. He had inherited artistic talent from his parents. They taught him to play the violin and paint. Thanks to those abilities, he had earned a little pocket money at a young age for his family. Conrad was genuinely interested in me, and he didn't seem at all envious, even though I told him about the wealth of our family. I comforted him by saying frankly that a university degree was greatly exaggerated. Most of the studies were completely futile rubbish. From the university, I got only bitter anger at all useless and dry theoretical book wisdom. I said in furies to Conrad.

"I guess there must be had even something useful there? What science did you study?" Conrad asked in surprise.

"Well, of course, there was something important. I had to graduate as a medical doctor." I answered with the same time and drank a big sip of beer. I wanted to escape this unpleasant topic of conversation to the soft hops that beer brings.

"Then you never graduated?" Conrad asked curiously while sipping his beer.

"I didn't graduate, but I can admit that I was envious of those reading larvae who read book after book into their heads. It didn't matter how they fared in the practical assignments, but for them, the main thing was passing the exams.

After the exam, the whole thing could be blissfully forgotten. Another thing that annoyed me was the completely uncritically practised at the university. Nothing was to be criticized, but everything had to be accepted as it was. For this reason, why questions were forbidden. It was a pointless and silly question for the professors. In their view, only a kid asks why questions. The professors wanted to give an omniscient picture of themselves. How canscience move forward if things are not questioned?" I preached to Conrad.

"I don't know. Maybe I haven't lost anything, even though I haven't studied at university."

"The third thing that annoyed me there was the public humiliation of the students. It was a consciously." I said angrily, looking at the embers.

"Did you feel humiliated?" Conrad asked cautiously.

I sipped more beer and said in a quiet voice I could tell, but this is then confidential. Conrad promised to keep my story to himself.

"I had to take an autopsy in the middle of my first studying year. I had managed to avoid them before, but now I had to go there to get through the course. Attendance was mandatory for all medical students, so there was no way I could avoid it.

By the time we went to the morgue, the mere clinical, sterile smell that floated in the hallway and the atmosphere of death made me thrill." I said in a quiet voice.

"What condition was that body in?"

"The deceased was an old alcoholic. The body was displayed when we entered the hall where the autopsy was performed. He had been stabbed to death. Seeing the face of the deceased with nudity made me feel weak and dizzy. Professor Monron first told us what he was going to teach us. I managed to stay behind the others when our teacher opened the skull of the deceased from the top. I was looking at other students at that time, whose eyes glowed with excitement when they stared at the brain of the victim shown by the teacher. After introducing us to the brains, the teacher opened the abdominal covers of the deceased. At that point, I mistakenly looked at autopsy. Almost immediately, I felt the blood escape from my head. My hands and feet became powerless. I felt very weak. I instinctively bowed down, breathing deeply several times, but it didn't make me feel better. I tried my hand on my forehead. I was startled to notice how cold sweat had moistened my face. It made me feel even more miserable. In a panic, I tried to think of nice things, but it didn't help.

As I stood up, my eyes got dark, and I fainted and fell on my back to the floor." I explained in shame.

"That was completely human. There is nothing to be ashamed of. The same would probably have happened to me. Don't be so harsh on yourself."

"Maybe, but that shouldn't happen to a medical student," I said, seriously biting my teeth.

"How did that situation end?"

"When I recovered from that, I noticed two fellow students holding my legs upright so blood would go to my head. Professor Monron, who had completed the autopsy, stood beside me, looking at me with a contemptuous look on his face along with his nose. The worst thing about that situation was when he used me as an example. The teacher explained in an audible voice how weak-nervous people can't stand seeing blood. Luckily, I didn't hear everything about that arrogant explanation he told me had happened. I wished to do was ask him to shut his mouth and leave me alone. I felt like a little girl and was immensely ashamed of myself. It was the last nail in the coffin of my medical studies. I realized I couldn't work as a doctor, and to be honest. I wouldn't have wanted that career. I went to medical school forced by my father, trying to earn his approval. I failed in both things." I told with a cry in the throat.

Conrad patted me on the shoulder, saying:" Then you should be ashamed if you had killed that man. Not, by the way."

I ponder Conrad's comforting comment. That's how it was. I hadn't been guilty of any crime. Why did I feel ashamed of the human reaction? I thanked Conrad for his friendly attitude, and we went to sleep.

We continued our journey to the vicinity of the city. From there, I decided to go on a research trip to a nearby area. I was already excited about it. I got in a lot of local Indian men. They could do the digging if we first found suitable research areas. One of them was a naturalist of Spanish descent named Diego. He knew a little English. By character, Diego was really serious, sassy, and nosy. However, he knew the local terrain well, so I listened to his explanations. On his advice, we ended up in an area called Punta Alta. We heard there was a low and soft ground. The locals had also found animal remains there. We excavated from several different locations. Some of them were canyon-type depressions. We found tremendous fossil and animal discoveries that were really well preserved. Some even had a coat of hair left. Our most amazing find was a landslide filled with carcasses of various animals.

There were dozens of carcasses in the same pile, both prey animals and predators. I was amazed to find that there were also different kinds of fish among the carcasses. How in the world had the fish gotten here inland? It was as if a large avalanche of mud had buried those animals. I just didn't get in my head where that kind of mudslide could have come from. Several of those carcasses had been large animals that had already become extinct. The questions began to throw to my mind. How did those animal carcasses end up here? Why weren't they had been already rotten? Or why had the scavengers not eaten them? What had caused all this and when? I had no idea about this. In the fish fossils, I was amazed that they had scales stored, and one big fish had a half-eaten small fish in its mouth. Judging by everything, those fish had suffocated in a sudden flood of mud. I discussed the matter with Diego with the help of an interpreter. In his view, this could not have been a normal, natural event because the animals got buried under the mud very quickly. My mind rebelled against such a supernatural explanation, but what natural event could have brought so much mud? How had that mud settled so quickly that the animals had not had time to escape? I must tell Diego some natural explanation for this event.

"How, then, can the horse carcasses in almost vertical positions be explained? Horses would not be able to be digging themselves into the ground, and why would they have done so? Why are carcasses of both horses and predators found in the same place? These animals don't move together. What do you think this means?" Diego asked.

"I have no idea. You seem to have a lot of questions, but do you also have the answers? What do you think this means?" I continued for Diego with a slightly annoyed voice.

He only muttered something about the great biblical flood. Then we found the canyon. We set out to walk along its bottom. I curiously examined the cliff's edge, concluding that in those visible seventy yards layers of land, we could see the history of millions of years ago. As I continued to explore the edge, my attention was drawn to the circular ridge that split the soil layers almost vertically from top to bottom. It was about two feet wide and more than fifty feet tall. Excited, I knocked the bulge with a pickaxe, noticing it hard like a rock. I hit it harder but didn't get a split piece of it. After looking at it more closely, I noticed it was a petrified tree trunk. I was shocked by the observation I made. Could it really be a tree? There were no trees anywhere here, just a grassy plateau.

And most shockingly, the tree trunk split vertically through all the different layers of the earth, which I imagined was the result of millions of years. How quickly does wood fossilize? Diego came down to me to the canyon.

"How far into the past can you see from this crack of the earth?"

"Millions of years from the past." I whimpered carelessly.

"What about the effect of the erosion that has taken place over millions of years and the skeletons or fossils of various animals?"

"Well, this is just a small sample of the whole area. After all, we saw a large number of dead animals yesterday." I replied a little indignantly.

"Those were all recognizable and couldn't be very old. What do you think about it? How could that tree trunk split these different soil layers vertically?"

"How should I know!"

"Is that petrified tree trunk also millions of years old?"

"Well, I don't know! To what are you really aiming for with those questions?"

"To do science! Each claim has an objection and either refutes or confirms the original claim." Diego shocked me.

What was that philosophical nonsense then?

What do you, a little shitty Indian, know about the science? I thought to myself. Before I had time to say anything to Diego, he came almost in front of my face, saying:" We need to explore all possible different options to find out the truth."

I didn't answer anything from this nosy little Indian; instead, I went to my tent to write down the day's events. I didn't like what I saw. This expedition raised more questions than gave answers. We decided to return to Bahia Blanca as we could replenish our stocks there. Arriving in Bahia, I told Diego I no longer needed his help. In fact, I couldn't stand his annoying counter-questions. I replenished my gear in the harbor and told FitzRoy that we were going on another exploration trip to the Sierra Ventana Mountains. He said he would sail back to Buenos Aires after receiving more goods so that we would meet there. I asked Conrad to join me as a company for this second trip. He could immortalize me in his paintings with the carcass of some extinct large animal. We went along the Rio Sause River towards the mountains. This time we got with us a big military unit. Our Argentine major said they would meet another military department south of the mountains and conduct a "cleansing operation" there to calm the area. The weather was great. The sun shone from the cloudless sky as the wind blew calmly behind us.

Here and there were deciduous clusters, but mostly the terrain was flat, lush grassy prairies. Along the way, we saw a termite pile more than ten feet tall. Seen from a distance, it looked like a broken tree trunk in the middle. It seemed incomprehensible to think about how termites had built such a nest. One would think that such a termite nest would decay rapidly as a result of decay, or at least rot inside, like a wooden English house. We stopped near it for a moment and watched the moving of termites. At first glance, it seemed as if they were rushing around at random, but despite all the hardships, each termite appeared to have some sort of task of its own, which they carefully accomplished. Some carried some building material in their mouths, others carried food to the nest, and the rest presumably brought the waste out of the nest. How did these creatures know how to organize work? How do they communicate? The initial journey went very calmly. We camped on a flat lawn along the river. On the first night, we relaxed by sipping our spirits drinks and eating well. As we ate, I asked the soldiers where the Indians really lived when we hadn't seen them yet. They just laughed and said they weren't interested in Indian tribe things. I thought in good faith that the Indians had moved out of this area. I slept the night like a log while the soldiers were in charge of guarding.

As the sun rose, we gathered our camp and continued our journey along the riverbank towards the mountains. Upon reaching the edge of the mountain, the major informed me that they would circle the mountain area from its south side. From there, we could then continue our journey together. It suited us well. We were allowed to be at peace when they didn't mess up what we were doing. We were heading to a narrow gorge towards the center of the mountains. The ascent was not very steep, so it did not cause any problems for the horses. The Indians carried some of the goods that could not be tied on the backs of horses. These domesticated Indians were strange in their ways. They bit the coca bush leaves almost all the time. It allowed them not to eat for long periods of time. Their empty, glazing eyes did not seem to have a soulful life. They seemed bittered and hostile. They were short, lean, and sinewy in physique. I didn't see them having a future. Our progress slowed down the higher we got. We were already estimated to be almost two miles above sea level. The temperature at these altitudes was already so cold that I looked at my best to take a thicker jacket over from my backpack. I watched in fascination around me the gorgeous mountain scenery with visibility several miles in every direction. At this altitude, sunrises and sunsets are certainly particularly spectacular.

From this perspective, man understands well his smallness. We noticed a large cave on the edge of a mountain slope. We decided to explore it, so we climbed along the edge of the cave with a few men. We went inside the cave. The exterior of the cave already contained remnants of sea lilies, petrified fish, corals, and sea urchins. I was really confused. How in the world could seaweed be so high? Curious, we continued deeper into the cave with torches to find more fossilized fish there. I took a few of them with us, after which we came out of the cave. I decided to explore the rocky edge of the mountainside. We were already close to the top, so we decided to get up all the way. At the top of the mountain, a surprise awaited us that we could not have guessed in our wildest dreams. We climbed to the flat top and saw a whale skeleton there! I watched that in shock and ecstatic. I estimated that skeleton was to be about fifty feet long. How the hell had this whale ended up here? That meant this mountain must have been under the sea sometime for a while! Others in the group understood a little bit about nature and were also amazed. We descended lower to the main group that had camped in the canyon. Moving in high and cold weather was very heavy. I felt hungry all the time. We decided to stay halfway up the mountain to rest. After that, we continued our journey to the south.

In the southern part of the mountain, we slowly began to descend towards the low grassy plain. Most of the mountain had gone unexplored, but I was still happy with our hike. The findings were really interesting, even though they were quite different from what I had expected. At the foot of the mountain, I looked closely with my binoculars to see signs of a military unit we were supposed to meet. We didn't stay to wait for them but went for a leisurely ride on our horses along to the plateau. As we rode, I also stared at the skyline with my binoculars and saw a large smoke statue a few miles away. I thought the military units were camping there. For some reason, I felt an uncomfortable feeling of doubt inside me and told others to camp here. I told them I would check it out and then return. I went for a ride fast towards the smoke column. When I got there, I realized that a cloud of smoke came from an Indian village burned to the ground. My doubts had been right. The Major's platoon had had time before us on the plateau to carry out its "cleansing operation." I saw the same soldiers walking in the village with whom we began an expedition. They had killed almost all the inhabitants of the village, including the children. The bodies had not been buried, and according to our Major, there were no plans to bury them. They should remain food for scavengers.

I calmed down my horse and landed on its back. I walked around the charred village ruins. The sight was scary. I watched the dead Indians. Most had been shot, but some had been killed with swords. The naked bodies of some had been disgraced by mutilation. I asked the major the reason for this mass murder. He said the residents of this village are involved in looting commercial caravans and protecting other robbers. At first, I doubted the explanation, but that was how it had to be. Those Indians who had been caught were interrogated. If they did not tell the hiding places of others, then they were brutally tortured. I walked aside to think about the books I had read. Could I possibly get more research material for Grant's theories from this case? I walked over to the major to tell us our location and asked him to keep me updated if they got anything out of the imprisoned Indians. He asked the reason for that suspiciously. I replied to him distractedly, stuttering my desire to be involved in witnessing their "cleansing operation." I rode back to my research team. I told them it was the same military platoon with which we started the trip. I didn't tell the truth, even Conrad what I saw, but I lied to them about the smoke caused by the army's cooking. I didn't assume anyone believed my explanation. We set up tents to stay overnight.

It was scary to try to sleep under the sky when there were hundreds of dead wild people nearby.

At night, an officer woke me up saying they got information when they tortured some wild Indian man about another smaller group. They were going to hunt down this group. He asked me to join him on a hunting trip. That request made me rise at lightning speed. I thought that boring shellfish research was now turning into a different kind of activity. Even though it was dark, I could still see in the torchlight how this sophisticated officer had his hands in clotted blood. I took my horse and followed him to the platoon shelter, where there were an estimated thirty men preparing for this operation. These serious-faced men seemed like a pretty mixed group. I guess they were all older than me. Only some had an army uniform, and the rest were apparently Gaucho mercenaries. They looked at me a little suspiciously as they cleaned their rifles. On the other side, long swords were sharpened, and equipment was packed. The lieutenant leading the group gave me some food. While eating bread, I walked nearby, and in my thoughts, I was almost hit wild Indian who was hanged by a tree. I feared that dead man so much that I loudly cursed his body. Tired because of sleep deprivation, I noticed that I had instinctively grabbed my weapon.

After a while, the lieutenant told us to get on the horses. So, we set out under his leadership to ride in the direction the Indian savage advised. And not for a while when we notice a noise raised by Indian tribe horses. We whipped our horses to the full gallop, reaching them soon. They were not prepared for our arrival. The Indians, with their goods, were apparently moving to another region. Upon noticing us, the savages were frightened and tried to escape by scattering in different directions, but it only weakened their ability to defend themselves against us. I rode behind the soldiers and felt the rage rise inside us like a thunderstorm. There was a lot of deadly anger in the atmosphere. I kept my gun in my hand the whole time, but I didn't shoot anyone. The soldiers spread out in a trained manner, and each of them set out to pursue their own group of Indians. From everything was seen that they had done this also before. The men who appeared to be in a leading position in the tribe were the first to be killed. It was the most effective way to paralyze the fighting ability of others. After that, the soldiers focused on killing the remaining men. They were pierced by swords. It aroused more insecurity and horror in women. Even the majority of the men were so horrified that they could not resist in any way. They just fled in fear and even abandoned their families.

If any of them were caught alive, then they fight tenaciously like wild animals, but as a group, they couldn't fight. I curiously followed a group that caught a young man who had been wounded from his side. When he was arrested, immediately this wild bite mercenary from his bare wrist, and he did not let go of the soldier's wrist, even though the soldiers dug an eye out of his head. Eventually, he, too, was killed. Next, women and children were attacked. Yes, I understood the killing of bandits, but these rapes and the killing of children went beyond my comprehension. I asked the leading officer why they were doing that. He thought it was better to kill the children as well because they are useless, and at the same time, we will eliminate every future resistance. Likewise, killing women was also important. It is the most effective way to ensure that Indians won't multiply anymore but that they actually die out. Besides, Indians multiply quickly like rats. We quickly completed our work. I wondered how easily everything had gone. If the Indians were some bandits, as the major claimed, I might think they should be prepared for our arrival. Condor eagles hovered above us, waiting for a moment when they could eat the dead Indians. I felt hungry. We went for a horse ride back in the direction of the morning sun towards our camp. We must have looked scary as we rode side by side against the blue skyline.

We didn't say anything during the return trip. The soldiers' clothes were in blood and dust. A few of them were slightly wounded, but the rest had only their clothes soiled. I didn't notice any feelings or remorse in them at all after the massacre we committed. I estimate that more than a hundred savages were killed. I didn't feel guilt or pity for what had happened because I hadn't hurt anyone. I just followed everything that happened from the side. What could I have done? This was a raw play, but it fits well with the new world order to be painted by Grant. Weaker and degenerated races must have been destroyed. I was in an important position to see how history was made. I realized this was a course of action decided at a high state level to seize lands from settlers and guarantee them peaceful conditions. Most likely, these Indians were innocent of the crimes with which they were charged. These South American countries were newly got independence, and these were, in many ways, in a very chaotic state. In these countries, a hard hand was needed to rule these people. On the way, we passed a destroyed Indian camp where the same major military group had performed a similar "cleansing operation" yesterday. The vultures were there for a festive meal. Our arrival made them fly away for a moment. They would return with the other scavengers after we left.

The major came up to me at the military camp and said he wanted to talk to me a little more at a distance. As we walked within earshot of the others, the major snatched me from the edge of my jacket, stopping me. He pulled me from my chest directly in front of him so that our faces almost touched each other. We looked at each other straight, eye to eye. He had a round puffy face adorned with black walrus moustaches. Dark big eye bags lined the tired blood-red eyes. He glared at me grimly from under his eyebrows, warning me sharply not to tell anyone what had happened, or else my butterfly collecting trip would experience a sad end. Fear made churn in my stomach. I pressed my gaze to the ground, saying my lips were sealed. The major loosened his hand from my chest. He glanced at me but said nothing but went to his own. I was surprised by the major's behaviour. Why would I have told anyone what I saw it? Did the major doubt the legitimacy of his actions, or what was he afraid of? After the major threats, I left for my group. They had prepared food. Conrad came to me asking with interest where I had been. I responded negligently, watching the skyline I had been riding endlessly around the prairie. He looked at me in amazement, contenting my explanation. I quickly ate my full stomach and went to sleep for a small nap.

I woke up to the major's loud shout when he hurriedly informed us that the military department would continue the journey immediately. They reportedly still had a lot of work to do. Finally, he inquired about our intentions. I told the major we would continue straight northeast towards Buenos Aires. He behaved as if we had met for the first time. There were not any signs in him in the last night massacre. I shook hands with the major, thanking him for all the help. He did the honour by raising his right hand to cap and leave the place. As we rode horses along the flat prairie, I thought of everything that had happened. We had been on this research trip for many weeks. What goals did I have for this trip? I didn't really know what I was looking for. My mind was confused by everything I saw. We left England almost two years ago. What had I seen? There was immense violence and injustice everywhere. I really took seriously thinking about my expectations for this whole trip. I thought this trip would have been more comfortable, and people would have been kinder to each other. Yes, Grant certainly warned about these things in his letters, but it was still somehow unexpected and distressing. The things I saw were wrong, but in a way, anything felt nothing at all. I had seen too many and too fast new, drastic events. I didn't have control of my life in any way. I suffered from mental nausea. I had like to weep.

The degree of deacon really had no use in the pitfalls of my life. I had not seen God anywhere in this world, and I had not read the Bible for a long time or prayed for anyone. Nor did I experience any call to evangelize these savage people. I would have liked to talk about my feelings to someone, but to whom would I have spoken? Who would have the answers to any of my questions? The more I researched, the less I knew. I wanted to drink liquor again.

I felt dead tired when we arrived in Buenos Aires. My mood didn't rise a drop when I saw the Major with his troops fighting near the city again. It was as if some curse was driving him and his troops, always on the same path with me. This time they had come to defeat the revolution attempt against General Rojas. Farm workers living in slavery-like conditions had started an uprising, demanding better living conditions for themselves. The city was almost in complete anarchy when we got there. The bodies lay here and there, and people robbed the shops. The windows of the houses had been broken, with some of the buildings were on fire. What benefit did these fools imagine they would gain from destroying public property? Who had encouraged these idiot-idealists to this insane attempt at rebellion?

Perhaps their living conditions were so miserable that they had nothing to lose. We didn't stay in the city center for longer but decided to go straight to the harbour. I was thinking in my mind that the captain and ship would be in port waiting for us. We had a stupid lieutenant with his troops to guide us to and protect our passage to the harbour. He lamented the confusion caused to us bythe coup attempt. I just said it wasn't his fault. The lieutenant said he would personally make sure that the perpetrators received the most severe punishment possible. I replied to him in this country. Everyone received "the most severe punishment possible," whatever the crime was. He did not comment on that. Rarely have I experienced such relief as seeing our ship in port. How that little, ugly ship felt so dear now. When I saw our captain on the deck of the ship distributing the orders, I felt immensely safe in my heart. I sent an Argentine lieutenant away and told the men to transfer our belongings to the ship. I boarded the ship to meet the captain. I was glad to see him again. Until a week ago, I wouldn't have thought one day I would be happy to see the skipper. He was in a good mood too. They had explored the coast, and FitzRoy had made nautical charts for the fleet. The captain said we could not fill our warehouses here, but we had to go back to Montevideo, so after loading my goods on board, we left immediately.

After settling into our cabin, I felt tired and feverish. I opened a skipper's gin bottle and took one sip from it to my cup. While tasting it, I decided to write briefly to Grant. I told him about our meagre scientific achievements and the fate of the Indians. After closing the letter, I gave it to the skipper. He promised to leave it with the rest letters in the post office in Montevideo. I thanked them and started drinking gin. Skipper advised me to eat and go to sleep instead of drinking gin. At his urging, I did so. I fell asleep immediately. At night, I saw a horrible nightmare about Indians murdered on the prairie. In a dream, I walked alone on the prairie. It was a dark winter night, and there was little snow on the ground. The moon shone from the cloudless starry sky. I wandered in cold weather along the open prairie. I found myself walking to a place where an Indian tribe had been murdered. Suddenly, the half-rotted corpses of the Indians began to rise from the ground. I set off to run away in horror. They followed me, shouting my name into the gloomy night. The hanged man in the tree shouted furiously that I would have to answer for my actions after I died. I screamed in horror at him that I was innocent. I didn't want anything evil for anyone. It felt like my feet were glued to the ground every step of the way. Eventually, I had to stop as the zombies besieged me.

They grabbed me and dragged me to their camp, where they tied me to their altar, intending to sacrifice me. Just as their Indian chief was hitting a dagger into my chest, the captain woke me up. I was all sweaty and frozen. I trembled as I had been on a high fever. Captain sought a doctor at the scene, finding me to have some disease. He gave me some medicine and told me to stay in bed. Under the influence of the drug, I fell into a deep sleep again. It felt like I had been in a free-fall some to a deep, dark bottomless gorge.

Chapter 7: Presentation of ideology in London

"Good afternoon, Robert, and welcome to the university. How are you?"

"Thanks, Edmond. Well, if the constant rain associated with the season is not considered, then I am fine. How about you?"

"I am fine too. A break from work did me good. Now I am full of burning enthusiasm for our ideology. By the way, I just got a package from your son Charles from his trip. It contained mainly fossilized bone fragments from unknown small animals and a letter of interesting findings. Have you received any letters from him?"

"No, I haven't, but his sister Catherine got a letter in the summer. That's when he seemed to have all things well. Had remained healthy, and the journey had gone smoothly."

"That's great, but if we went straight to the meeting room."

My father and Grant entered a room filled with cigar smoke, where gentlemen of different ages and dignitaries talked to each other while drinking tea and eating pastries. On the walls of the room were paintings of British men's powers of the past.

"Gentlemen, please, have seats. I will introduce you to Robert Darwin.

He is a medical doctor by profession and a generous supporter of our activities. His father, Erasmus Darwin, was a great naturalist and pioneer in studying human origin. As you know, at the moment, our research ship is sailing in the Atlantic, looking for routes for our fleet and mapping good bases. Also on board is Robert's ingenious son Charles. He is continuing his family's traditions, studying South America's wildlife. I got him on this trip at the last moment. He has already made really many unique discoveries about the fauna there. The journey has taken longer than expected, but I believe he will receive the compensation he deserves for his efforts. Here is my brief introduction. Next, each of us would briefly introduce ourselves to Robert. During the demonstration, we can enjoy the house's beverages and snacks. Henry, perhaps you could start when you are younger."

"Thank you, Edmond. My name is Henry Williams, and I just started as the new Head of the Department of the Ministry of Education."

"Nice to meet you. I hope you succeed in your work."

"Thank you, Henry. Please, would you continue Bernie next?" Grant suggested.

"That is fine. I am Bernie Harris, and I head the Department of Education. I have been there for over ten years.

Together with Henry, we plan and decide largely on what is taught in schools. I was pleased when Henry started on the Board of Education. Now we have our own man there instead of the old Forrester believer. This way, the textbooks can be gradually changed to match the time of the Enlightenment. It is a great pleasure to meet you, Mr. Darwin. I have read your father's writings, and they are really interesting."

"Next, we have Colonel George Smith from the ministry of defence. He is responsible for producing material that raises our army's fighting spirit. That material is used to train and motivate soldiers."

"It's an honor to meet you, Robert Darwin. We in the military are waiting with great interest for the fruits of this project."

"I believe that this will help the army in particular."

"Mark Rose represents our business life. His family has rapidly prospered in the coal and textile industries. Mark, please, could you tell us more?"

"Yes, indeed, we have been involved in the industrialization of Britain almost from the beginning. Over the years, we have noticed that the current market will not be enough for us. In the future, we will have to fight even harder for the market share we have made against companies in other countries. For that, we need new values and worldviews.

I look forward with great interest to the option you offer."

"Thanks, Mark. Then our soil specialist, please, Charles."

"My name is Charles Lyell. I specialize in soil research and, in particular, the age of the earth. I have already written a few books on this subject."

"Then, last but not least, my colleague from the university, James Walker. James, please, could you tell us a little about yourself?"

"Yes, with pleasure. I work here at the university as a professor of theology, but I have been an atheist for as long as I can remember. I want to destroy young people's faith in the God of the Bible rather than strengthen it. In fact, all my life, I have been much more interested in history and archeology than Christianity. My intention in the future is to study the region of the Middle East and look for evidence against the Bible there. I guess it will be easy."

"Thank you, James. Gentlemen, we can begin the meeting now that we have introduced each other. After that, we can go for a well-deserved dinner. As the invitation letter read, the subject of this meeting is the future of the British Empire. I will chair and give the floor at your request. If no one has anything against it, I will start with a brief speech of my own. I believe our nation is on the threshold of a new era.

The industrial revolution began in our country in earnest in the last century, and the results are slowly beginning to appear. We control the seas, being present on every continent. We are the world's leading kingdom. We are currently in the lead, but for how long? Who are our allies in the future, and who are our enemies? Is nationalism on the rise in Europe? The British need to be patriotic, but we need to curb nationalism everywhere else. France is still weak because of the revolution and the Napoleonic Wars. As you know, Britain has often fought against France, and the future is unlikely to change that. I see France only as a competitor, not as an ally. What about Central Europe? In what direction is it developing? Will the German-speaking regions merge into one state? If they unite, what would be the character of such a state? I think the Germans are an aggressive people. I would not count on them at all. Even though we only recently fought in North America, I still believe the United States of America will be our natural ally in the future. They are more useful to us as an independent nation. Their economy is developing rapidly because they utilize slave labor. How many times have I cursed our foolish politicians who forbade slavery in our colonies? What was the point of giving such a competitive advantage to others? I am convinced that competition will intensify between different nations.

We will fight for the best living space, colonies, and raw materials in the future. We must now take the decisions and measures that will ensure our leadership in the future as well. For this struggle, we need new values set as a nation. I argue that we will lose this struggle for survival if we adhere to Christian ethics. Edited of the Bible, we must say: We must now grab the sword so we do not perish. These new values must be based on scientific facts and already be taught to young kids at school. This is how we get a new, strong generation that is free from past beliefs. Beliefs that are not British and that only limit the development of the nation. Here is my brief introduction to the subject. Now, gentlemen, the word is free. Please, tell me your comments."

"Thank you for a good and concise introduction, Edmond. I agree with you, but what exactly is this new world of values you mentioned?"

"The new world of values must be based on the natural sciences and must overturn the biblical doctrine of creation. We will challenge the church. We have to because otherwise, Britain will become a merely pathetic charity organisation."

"I don't want to be sceptical, but how could that be possible? Where do we get the evidence for that?"

"As I said, Robert's son Charles is currently on a research trip.

He has sent me many fossils that no one has seen before. From them, it is quite clear that the earth is millions of years old. This is also evidenced by Lyell's books. Believe me, gentlemen, humanity is waiting for deliverance from the bondage of religion. This is going to be a lot easier than you can even guess. Now think about yourself! How many of you believe in the biblical account of creation? Well, how many of you believe in racial equality between different races? Yes, silly questions, our job is just to liberate people to think with their own brains."

"Does it affect morality if all people become atheists?"

"Who has said that atheism is the only option? That doesn't mean that we are pursuing a purely atheistic worldview, even if we eradicate the degenerative influences of Judeo-Christianity from our people. It would be foolish to deny all people's religious feelings. The French Revolution showed the consequences of a complete breakdown of religious authority. The result is anarchy. People retaliate for the injustices that they have experienced, and the nation plunges into civil war. People need to have some kind of deterrent in the back of their heads. Let it be a fear of hell, then. On the other hand, we can offer the people a British or at least European religious alternative to this current Judeo-Christianity. It must be a religion innovated on ancient British war heroes.

With such role models, we could raise our young men into warrior fighters who are proud of their race. In this way, they are ready to sacrifice their lives for the empire if necessary."

"Where do we find the ingredients for such a British religion? I find it difficult to believe people will be interested in that."

"Yes, they get excited because it is easier for them to identify with heroes than some Jewish bearded old men. Our God figures are masculine warriors and not pathetic cowards who turn the other cheek. They kill enemies or die on the front without begging for mercy. Ingredients for this British or, should I say, the pantheistic religion of Northern European is obtained from the ancient occult tales of the Germanic and Scandinavian nations. We will add to it some about British legends, and the rest comes by itself. The most important thing is to give the people an idea of what we are in reality!" Grant preached.

"What about this atheistic option? Can the primitive and stupid working-class population be liberated to an atheistic way of thinking? Do they understand how to behave responsibly? What if they start stealing and breaking the law? What about morals?"

"As for the stupid working-class population you mentioned, it is quite clear that they are not behaving responsibly.

That is why criminal law must be as severe as possible, with the death penalty and public execution for everyone all serious crimes. Did you have Bernie anything else?"

"Not this time."

"Thank you. Please, George."

"Yes, we in the army have long considered an alternative to the Christian worldview. It's a bad doctrine to motivate anyone to fight. Rather, it encourages people to pacifism. From our point of view, it would be best if we got into the ranks of the army, hardened young men for whom killing would have been in their blood since childhood. Christian upbringing erodes the innate spirit of fighting and killing. The military needs a youth who does not question our commandments but always obeys them unconditionally. Indeed, a new kind of value system needs to be created in which children are raised."

"It is true what you are talking about, George, but we cannot that yet be justified to Parliament by your arguments."

"If you allow me, I would like to continue."

"Sure, please."

"We have also made calculations at the army general headquarters of the costs incurred by the colonies, as they threaten to grow too high. We think there should be more financial profit from there. It is not our job to feed and educate those wild humans.

Does the business life representative have any suggestions for this?"

"Mark, can you tell us?"

"Now that slavery is forbidden to us. Then natural resources are the next destination. Utilizing them should be much more efficient. We must create an efficient transport network that brings us all the raw materials we need as cheaply as possible. In addition, labor must be cheap and easily accessible. The restrictive influence of society on business must be kept to a minimum. As a first step, the government should exempt companies from paying taxes."

"I am sorry for the interruption, Mark, but I would like to deal with our colonies and the policies they pursued as a matter of urgency. We already have a strong presence in India, and I see a lot of potential in that country. They are smarter than Africans. This suddenly brings to mind a few questions that need to be answered at some point in time. Should India be taken over completely? What natural resources can be found there? Is it possible to work with local people? How can we take advantage of Hindu superstition? How big can a country's population grow without becoming a threat to us? These are all questions for which some approach needs to be found. I do not take a position on the population or how it should be controlled, but I do believe that the majority of weak black races will, in one way or another, become extinct. It is not a moral issue but a fact based on the laws of nature. The strongest of them are allowed to survive to serve us in slavery-like conditions. In order for this situation to be realized, a new code of morality must be obtained for the nation. That means that absolute concepts of truth must be rejected. The people must be taught that human is the measure of everything, for man lays down laws, and so we also define morality. Morality must be proportionate to the situation at hand. We ourselves also define what truth is. When the truth is negative to us, we will deny it completely. When and if necessary, lies and truth are mixed together so that they both serve our purposes. The whole nation must be taught a relativistic way of thinking, for it will help us as a nation to adapt to the changes that come before us. The inevitable changes that will occur in the future are so rapid and drastic that we as a nation will not survive. These changes cannot be made if we adhere to Christian morality. We must also question the sanctity of human life. Secondly, we need to create criteria for who can be called human. What are the requirements for humanity? Does everyone have the right to get children? If not, who can reproduce? Races are unequal and scientific evidence is needed for that.

We need to justify these actions, and that justification can only be found in nature. How else can we justify the disappearance of entire nations from the face of the earth?"

"Edmond, that sounds very harsh. On what schedule can that happen, and how? Couldn't religion be used as a stick horse for state goals as it has been so far?"

"The fight for the right to live is fierce, Henry. We are not witnessing the outcome of our ideology, but the most important thing is that we are the first nation to embark on this necessary development. We need to incite wild people's conflicts among each other in their homelands. It causes famine and disease. Those take care of this extraordinary demographic problem by themselves. As for the use of religion in a war situation, George can tell better."

"Using Christianity to achieve military goals has never worked properly.

It's the same as trying to infuse iron and clay together. On the war fronts, I have seen how brutal the wild tribes can be. They are capable of that kind of Spartan cruelty, even to their own people, to which our pampered kids by our Sunday schools are incapable. On the war front, it is well noticed how Christianity paralyzes the will to fight.

I have seen many times in war situations where one should have fought to the last drop of blood, but the soldier, who is paralyzed by fear, has begun to pray. The result has always been the destruction of a soldier. Sometimes there have been situations where a believer on purpose accidentally shoots past an enemy. Such stupidity would not happen if we had some other kind of worldview. Before the Reformation, when people did not have the opportunity to read the Bible, it was easy to start wars and crusades. Nowadays, when almost every home has a Bible, and the majority of the people even can read, wars are difficult to justify by religion. The only option is to get rid of Christianity completely. Church buildings may be left on the grounds of architectural beauty, but new ones may not be built. Some churches can be converted into museums and concert halls. It will not be easy because religion is like a drug for weak human minds. As Edmond has just mentioned, we need a justification from science to defend ourposition as a superpower."

"This all sounds logical, but could that be so easy? What are the new values which will replace Christian values?"

"Of course, this won't happen overnight. The aim is gradual to infiltrate society so that in future generations, we will be able to teach these new values, mainly through the school system. So, what are those values?

Well, of course, they vary according to need and era, but as I said, in principle, all values must be relative. Of course, there must be some basic virtues that are taught to children, such as patriotism and respect for parents, etc., but we are free to take ideas from all possible doctrines that benefit us. Those ideas that do not serve our cause are left out. Let's keep this plan simple. Remember, we ourselves are the creators of this. We are free to use our imagination and learn from the mistakes of the past. This ideology is not based on fear of other races but on the right of the stronger. For me, this ideology is a life mission."

"How do we get politicians and the common people to our side?"

"We can easily get politicians on our side. They are promised so many benefits that they cannot refuse these changes. And as I have mentioned many times, the interest of the nation requires this change of attitude. We just have no other choices. As for the common people, their opinion is not needed. The majority of them are so stupid that they don't think about anything else but eating."

"True. What is the position of the royal house on these matters?"

"I haven't figured it out, but I think they are on our side.

At least they are generously involved in supporting our expeditions. I am not a supporter of the monarchy because they always have a conflict of interest with other monarchies. They are all related to each other, and in a war situation, it always negatively affects the kingdom. The best form of government is a nationalist dictatorship, which is what we must strive for in the future. Perhaps the monarchy will lose its popularity and collapse, but no more about that. Gentlemen, I apologize for the busy schedule, but time is running out. I soon have to be at the second meeting, and before that, I should still have time to eat something. Thank you all for this meeting. This gave me a lot of faith in a better future. Science is evolving, knowledge is increasing, and time is on our side. We will wait until Robert's son Charles returns from his journey. Then, we can begin to design this theory correctly with real action. The purpose of this meeting was only to get to know each other's and map out the situation. I am pleased with the day's meeting. I will keep in touch with all of you and tell you later when we will meet again. Does anyone have anything to comment on? If not, I'll end the meeting, so let's leave for a well-deserved dinner."

Chapter 8: Two missionaries

In less than a week, the fever was gone. I don't know why I was the only one who got it, but I think my exhaustion had something to do with it. We were already starting to be close to the Falkland Islands. Those islands had just rightly been conquered from Argentina by the British navy. During my fever, two missionaries had come to the ship from Montevideo. Their names were Paul and Timothy. They came to my room early evening to inquire about my well-being. These men were part of a larger Christian group that had been operating in South America for years. They were going to the Falkland Islands to establish a church for the British who would settle there. Paul seemed to be a leader. They were both simple men in simple clothes. Paul was rather short, bald, and Timothy a little taller and thick-haired. I felt humiliated as they said they had prayed for me. Why on earth do I, adult man, need their prayers, and what would be the benefits of them? Such fever is not to die. The more I talked to them, the more pathetic they seemed. They said they had taken on a life mission to evangelize these tribes. I think it was certainly doomed to fail. How in the world could these savages become Christians? I lay in bed looking contemptuously at these missionaries, wondering how miraculously people can become so naïve. They had not studied theology. There was a compassionate look in their eyes as I told them I had been studying theology for almost two years. In their view, God's work cannot be studied in man-founded schools, but God equips the people He chooses for His mission. I thought it sounded silly again. They reminded me that I had not studied any natural science, even though I was exploration trip. When Paul asked if I believed in God, I answered circularly, always on some level and in my own way believing in some higher power. I said I went to church sometimes, spent Christmas, and rested on Sundays. Like my mother, I wanted to shape the image of God to my liking. In his opinion, my answer was not Christianity but only customary religious culture. "So, what is Christianity?" I asked him.

Paul went on to say that as an honest man, I would probably find the truth in this matter if I wanted it unconditionally. I objected, saying that once we started discussing this, we would then go all the way to the bottom.

"All right then. To me, Christianity is that Jesus of Nazareth is the Messiah and Son of God promised by Old Testament prophecies. When the time was full, He was born from virgin to man in the world to die on the cross for our sins, but He did not remain a prisoner of death but rose from the dead. He still lives today and forever. He is the atonement of humankind's sins and judge of humanity. In Him, I trust in as my Saviour and as a Lord. In it is crystallized. Or, as the Apostle John wrote: *God has loved the world so much that He gave His only begotten Son, that who so ever believeth in him should not perish but have everlasting life.* The truth about Jesus is found only in the Bible, not in any of the books of philosophers. It is not my job to proselytize anyone. It is God's work. I'm just spreading the message of the Bible. Charles, did you know that God loves you more than anybody does? Do you want to turn away from your evil ways and repent? Do you believe that you are His own?" Paul asked, looking me straight in the eye.

"I do not know," I responded quietly with an uncertain voice and simultaneously pressed my gaze to the floor.

"Do you feel unconditionally loved and accepted as you are?" Paul asked in a sincere voice.

"I haven't thought about such things," I responded quickly, and at the same time, I felt a piece rise in my throat. How horrible heavy the words those were. *Unconditionally loved* and *accepted*. I got out of bed and asked them to leave. I shook Paul's hand to say goodbye, but as I looked him in the eyes, I could no longer hold back my tears and burst into a torrential cry.

I no longer cared about what others thought of me but openly wanted to be my own, weak myself. I grabbed Paul's hand with both hands and dropped to my knees at his feet. I stammered at him in a crying voice about loneliness, a constant feeling of inadequacy, failed studies, ended socializing, my mother's longing, poor relation with my father, my envy of my big brother, the Indian massacre, and the insignificance of my life. I don't remember how long I talked to them, but it felt really good. I felt cleansed internally while shedding tears and heavy loads fell from my shoulders. It felt like I had received complete acceptance of my existence from love itself. I wasn't ashamed of my behaviour, but it felt natural. Paul picked me up from the floor to my feet, looking into my eyes. He said in a serious voice that he respected me as a man. According to him, God expects only honesty from us to admit our own sinfulness.

"Charles, do you want to give your life to Jesus and follow Him?"

"I do not know. That question came too quickly. I would like to decide for myself my life. I don't to be ready to commit to anything yet." I explained in fear.

"It's the most important decision of your life. This was God's first call to you. The next time is much heavier. Usually, a person can only take up to two calls from God.

After that, the losses are then so great that man usually only becomes bitter toward God instead of being humbled." Paul said.

"What do you mean?"

"In His goodness, the Creator allows us difficulties to us, so we can stop to think about our short and so rapidly disappearing lives. God gives us the power to die to this world and our selfish character. Through suffering and loss, he shows us the disappearance of this life. Charles, what's holding you? What do you have to lose?" Paul asked in an enthusiastic voice.

"I do not know. I just can't believe it. What would my father think too? This is starting to get too heavy. I am still weak because of my fever and need rest. I think I will go to sleep. Good night, gentlemen, and thank you for this discussion." Having said that, I pulled myself out of Paul's hands and sat on the bed.

"Good night, Charles. We will arrive in the Falkland Islands tomorrow and stay there. We wish you all the best and the blessing of God." Paul said.

They went to their own cabin, and I thought about this conversation. What does it really mean to have a living faith and to believe in the God of the Bible?

What is the life of a Christian like? I was ashamed of my severity towards them. They weren't pathetic guys, as I had initially thought.

Chapter 9: Witchcraft

Our brave fleet protected our arrival in the Falkland Islands. I was still weak because of a fever, so I stayed on the ship. Paul and Timothy were already standing in the harbour with their belongings. I waved my hand from the deck to say goodbye to them and went to my cabin room. After the crew replenished our ammunition depot, we continued our journey towards Tierra del Fuego. It is located at the very bottom of South America, detached from the mainland. Our intention was to tour the entire American continent through Cape Horn. The weather was probably windy. The constant heavy rains made us uncomfortable. Our purpose was to study the southwestern archipelago for the military purposes of our fleet. We headed along the eastern edge of Tierra del Fuego Island to the south. I occasionally scouted the coast with my telescope. Suddenly, I saw large campfires and figures. They wave ragged cloaks. Some of them had fire torches in their hands. They were obviously local wild Indians. These bald-headed barbarians screamed wildly simultaneously and waved with their fire torches in the air. This was apparently their way of welcoming us. We decided to row to the beach and learn more about these barbarians.

As we rowed our boats in towards the beach, the skipper presented the bright fabrics he had taken with him, which he had reserved for the Indians. FitzRoy thought they would be happy with our "gifts." I, on the other hand, thought the wild people would only get mad by our trinkets, but the skipper swore this would always work. "How could they criticise any of our gifts when they had never seen anything of value?" He reasoned.

However, we did not count on their hospitality. Our soldiers had their weapons loaded and ready for action. When we got to the beach, we pulled the boats ashore. We walked gently to the land. They looked at us in fright, and we looked at them. The wild ones were surprisingly strong built. Their only garments were cloaks made of animal skin with which they had covered their middle bodies. The skin colour of these wilds was like bronze. The young men's upper back was painted white with a lightning-shaped pattern. They were all bald. It made them look abominable. The faces of these savages had defiant looks. I guess because they were trying to cover up their fears about us. The still life was tense on both sides. This group of savages reminded like of a herd of demons. The situation was only triggered when our captain walked slowly to their chief, giving him our gifts. He received them with a doubtful appearance.

The chief gave the colourful pieces of cloth to the men standing next to him. After the initial suspicion evaporated, they watched us excitedly. After that, they started to nod in our direction with a smile, and soon they were already starting to talk to each other. I have never heard such a strange language in my life. It was completely impossible to learn even one word about it. Do they know how to read and write? If they do, what kind of letters do they use? I listened more closely to their speech. It just sounded like a pig burping. I have not heard any European burp in such a harsh voice as these wild creatures. It was shocking to see how big the difference is between a wild and a civilized man. It is larger than between a domestic animal and a wild because man has a much wider range of different developmental possibilities. The oldest man in the group seemed to be their leader. He wore a ridiculously looking headdress made of bird feathers. In addition, strange patterns were tattooed on his face. Those made his face look comical. It was hard for me to hold back my laughter as I watched this toothless goblin who tried to be so important. That old man walked forward, knocking on his chest with his hand. Moving at the same time, he waved himself like a chicken. He came straight in front of me, swaying himself back and forth.

After finishing his performance, he slapped my back with the palm of his hand. Then he turned his back on me. Apparently, he was expecting me to do him the same way. At the skipper's urging, I slapped the old man on the back as firmly as I could. From the force of my blow, he almost fell to his knees. For a moment, he pulled oxygen into his lungs. Despite my blows, he seemed to be fine. We looked at each other in foolishness, and as if from a common decision, we all laughed. Our laughter relaxed the situation, which made the danger seem to be over. These wild beings relentlessly watched even our smallest movements. As soon as they noticed something in our behavior that was strange to them, they immediately began to imitate it. One of our officers, who was vain, was immediately the target of their mockery. His proud walking style seemed really whimsical when presented by the natives. In a way, these savages opened my eyes to discover the proud habits lurking in us. A couple of our sailors started teasing them. The sailors twisted their faces, grimacing at them as ugly as they could. One wild responded to the challenge with a more terrible grimace. His painted face only further accentuated the frightening grimace. As I watched the grimace of that painted devil, I noticed part of his teeth was missing. After the wild stopped grimacing, we offered them a small sip of diluted alcohol as a reward.

They drank their cups empty but apparently didn't like our drink. Our vain officer, who had been the target of the Indians' mocking, began to sing, intoxicated. The Indians were very amazed at the roar of the officer. Accompanied by a song, our soldiers began to dance with each other, and not for a time when some of these barbarians came along as third wheels. This wild thought the dance was a kind of fight, for, after his dance in it, he wanted to wrestle with our biggest sailor. He accepted the wild man's challenge. After his showing off, the Indian grabbed our man by the waist, lifting him up. The sailor got himself free, wrestling with this jungle creature. The savage tried to frighten us by grimacing scare him, but the sailor only laughed briskly at the Indian. He grabbed a savage man's hand, twisting it behind his back. The Indian dropped to his knees, screaming in pain in a blood-chilling way. Soon they, tired, stopped spinning in the sand and laughed at each other in all harmony. In this way, prejudices were dispelled on both sides. We did get along with the Indians when we understood to treat them like children. We returned in the evening with our boat back to the ship.

"Are you going to steal some savage also this time?" I asked the skipper.

He just grinned mysteriously, saying he would get me a wife from there.

I blushed from shame and yelled that I could never marry a wild Indian woman. In the cabin, he reassured me that he had not prepared for any extra passengers this time. The next day there was calmer as only a few wilds came to see us. Honestly, I wasn't really interested in plants anymore. I wanted to get to know the Indians. From them, I could get good research material for Grant. Our crew members had caught fish and shot a couple of llamas for a meal. The wilds came in amazement to watch our meal. They had never seen anyone use a fork and knife when eating. I gave one of them a piece of fried meat that little devil guzzled into his mouth at once like a dog.

As evening fell, the crew rowed back to the ship, but I wanted to go to the savages. After looking around me, I saw a statue of smoke rising a couple of hundred yards away and set out to walk towards it. There I noticed that the wild ones had ignited a large bonfire of fallen trees. I decided to stay to see what they had in mind. A young Indian woman sitting near the bonfire waved her hand at me, asking me to sit around the bonfire. Out of curiosity, I went to sit next to her. I had a couple of bottles of red wine included. The weather was already cool, but luckily the fire warmed up comfortably. It was dark. Only a full moon illuminated the cloudless sky.

The flames rose over ten feet high. Next to the bonfire was a five-foot-tall statue with an ugly grimace engraved on its face. It must have been their false god. There were a dozen people present, four of whom were women. All of them had white S-shaped flash images painted on their backs. The same old man I met yesterday came to me. He gestured to guide me to strip my upper body bare. After doing that, I felt like he painted lightning patterns on my back as well, after which he would pull a couple of streaks on my face. He seemed to be their wizard man. After that, he started touring the rest of us, who sat around a bonfire the whole repeating some mantra at the same time. He was assisted by a young woman who followed him. In his hand, he held a container of dark liquid. As I watched the others, I sipped my wine alone. They stared quietly at the fire with serious expressions on their faces. The old man stopped next to me. He pointed to my bottle of wine with his hands. I realized he wanted the bottle, so I gave it to him. It was my gift to them. The old man poured the contents of the bottle into his container, after which he drank from it, then he gave the container to his assistant and took the bird from a wooden cage. He raised a bird in front of him, whispering something like a spell. After the silence, the wizard quickly cut off the bird's neck with his knife. Blood splashed around as he waved the bird.

I also got a few splashes of blood drops on my body. After stopping waving the bird, he signaled us to stand up. The old man continued the ritual, shouting his spell in a high voice as the others joined him in his cry. Soon the old man's head began to sway like a rag doll. At the same time, his limbs moved unrestrainedly in every direction. How could such an old man move so quickly and flexibly? I stared into the old man's eyes, noticing only the whites of the eyes were visible. At the end of the dance, he pushed his tongue out of his mouth while letting a grim scream from his throat. Based on my mother's stories, I realized the old man was a witch who had sunk into a deep trance. At the end of the ritual, he threw the bird into the fire. After surviving the trance, the wizard man went with a knife in his hand to get around us. For the first woman, he stopped, making a small wound in the woman's palm with his knife. The woman did not resist. Then she also put her wounded hand on the old man's palm. In turn, the wizard made similar small wounds for all of us. Finally, we all touched the wounds of those sitting next to us. Then this witch took a container into which he had poured my wine and poured more dark liquid into it. After drinking it, he then gave it to the next one, so we all took turns drinking from it. I, too, sipped my mouth full and swallowed the liquid immediately.

As I gave the container forward, I tasted the aftertaste of the drink in my mouth. I noticed a bitter iron taste in it. A witch appeared behind the statue with an object in his hand. He walked close to the bonfire, raising his hand. At the same time, I realized he was holding a little girl child in his arms. I tried to look more carefully in the dark. To my shock, I found the child to be headless. The old man threw the child's body into flames. Now I understood why the drink tasted like iron. I still don't understand why I didn't vomit the drink out. Maybe I didn't want to offend the feelings of the Indians, or I assumed the drink's taste was due to something other than the child's blood. I only felt a strong connection to those wild men, the pantheistic-religious values. I felt completely calm. At no point did I fear they were violent towards me. After the ritual, we spent the evening by the campfire for a while longer. During that time, Indians danced and sang. For my part, I was drunk on my second bottle of wine while listening to their joy. At night, I returned to the shore in a little drunken hustle by rowed to the ship, and the wild Indians stayed to celebrate by the campfire. When I got aside to the ship, the guards helped me up to the ship. Seeing my painted face, they started laughing and mocking me as an Indian. I didn't care about their childish behaviour, but I went seriously into my cabin. FitzRoy was already in a deep sleep.

As I lay in bed, I thought about what had happened. After all, this really wasn't any innocent campfire play, as I had thought, but the worst possible witchcraft. Still, I didn't feel guilty at all. But rather, I felt strong. I didn't know about the potential consequences of the ritual anymore. I told the captain briefly about the campfire events. To some extent, the event apparently shocked them cause our captain decided to raise the anchors and continue the journey forward. I wiped myself clean of the paintings while trying to forget last night's events. The paint was very tightly attached to my skin.

We sailed towards the southernmost tip of Cape Horn. It went just as we guessed. The wind reached storm readings when we had only traveled for a short time, and the skyline turned almost black. The captain ordered the ship to be turned to a small bay in the south of the island. The temperature dropped rapidly near the freezing point. It was raining with the furious wind blowing around us. After anchoring in the cove of the bay, our ship was approached by the Indians from another tribe. They were on the move in a small canoe that seemed to be at the sinking point. They came to beg for food. I have never met such pathetic beings in my life. The savages of the east coast still wore llama skins as clothing, but these creatures from the south were naked.

There was even one woman with these men. She had a small baby in her arms whom she was breastfeeding. This baby was still alive after all, but for how long? The woman's ugly face had a discouraging look. They were really hungry and dirty looking. It seemed impossible to think of them as a part of humanity. I have often wondered if animals might realize their own existence. How much more reason could this same question have been asked of these savages? They did not have apartments, but they always moved elsewhere in search of food. Their behaviour can be compared to animals, for they could not learn from any experiences. Making a simple spear was probably the most demanding thing they could do. These poor things spend their nights side by side on an almost bare rock, intertwined with each other like animals. What might be the average age of these people? Judging by the diet, it could not be high, as it consisted mainly of mushrooms, tree roots, and some seafood. They started the party when some carcass of a whale, already in a rotting state, drifted ashore. I guess they are full of all kinds of diseases and parasites. At this stage of development, these Indians had already lived for who knows how long. It was clear evidence that in such a stimulus-poor environment, man could not develop rational action.

When I think about these savages, one wonders why they had ended up here at the southern tip of the island. What circumstances had forced this tribe to leave the good hunting grounds of the north for this barren land? Tierra del Fuego Indians are likely a vanishing tribe. Why would they live and have children?

After returning to Southern Argentina, Captain FitzRoy received a message from our embassy asking us to retrieve British civilians from the area. We set out in rowing boats along the bay, from where we reached the mouth of the river inland. Instead of rowing, I admired the magnificent cliffs, handsome woodlands, and clear blue water. As we noticed a high cliff point, we saw five savages on top of a cliff. They had thick wooden spears in their hands. They jumped like monkeys and screamed at the same time in a blood-curdling voice. We had to row to the beach because we hadn't eaten anything all day. Our landing made the wild men come to us. Their faces were rounder than those of the other tribe, and their eyes were slanted like Chinese. Judging by the shape of the skull, they couldn't be any smarter than their southern cousins. This tribe had painted red streaks on their faces. There were about twenty of them. Like clothing, they had, as usual, simple rags made of animal skin.

There were also a few children who were hiding behind. The men's hair had been cut from both sides of the head, and that hair fashion made them look silly. Some of them had the bow guns ready, but so did our soldiers with loaded rifles. We drew our attention to two men wearing British clothes. We tried gesturing to ask them about the clothes, but we didn't get an understandable answer from them. We thought the missionaries had given them their old clothes. Then they pointed their fingers to our stuff, demanding to have it for themselves. The greediest of them even pulled the buttons on our jackets to get even something with them. Some of them tried to appeal to our feelings of pity, but without success. Due to circumstances, we were forced to settle down for the night in the vicinity of these greedy savages. This seemed to be the strongest tribe on this island. Our surprise was quite large when we found out they had more men at night. There must have been hundreds of them, and they had come all the way to our tents. Now even the slightest kindness of these wild men was gone. A few of them came before us with their bow guns. We had no choice but to shoot warning shots at nearby trees. We thought for a while that we would have to shoot the wild man's feet closest to us. Like animals, they were completely incapable of judging our strength. The most brazen of them even throw us with rocks.

Fortunately, those stones passed, for otherwise, there would have been a massacre. The captain fired a couple of warning shots past the head of one of the Indians to scare this fool further. The barbarian stopped at that place, startled to touch their own head. The escape did not seem to be part of their behavior. It was difficult for me to take the position of these beings to understand their stupid behavior. FitzRoy ordered the sailors to begin dismantling our tents like the rest of the soldiers guarding the Barbarians. The savages realized we were leaving as they quietly began to retreat. After getting our stuff in the boat, we slowly set off rowing along the river towards the hinterland and soon arrived at a village. We got to the beach and walked into the woods, where the Christian mission station supposed to be. We arrived in the yard of a building on low ground. No one was visible in the front yard. We shouted in the yard and knocked on the door. We didn't hear any signs of life, so we decided to go inside the house. There was a ghostly atmosphere. Everything was messed up. The food had not been eaten, and the documents were on the floor as if the occupants of the house had suddenly left. A horrified scream from a soldier in the backyard of a building interrupted our search. He shouted for us to come to the backyard. Excited, we ran through the rooms to the back door of the building.

From the window, I saw at a glance how the missionaries had happened. The sight was shocking. The man I noticed first was tied to a tree, and three arrows had been shot in his chest. His head hung down. I rushed out and saw another man lying on the ground with an ax beaten into the head. Both bodies were naked. Due to the rotting state, they smelled awful. Now we realized where the wild had gotten the British clothes. We were in a state of rage. Those murderous criminal devils should be punished. After burying the bodies, we returned to our boats, where we told others what had happened and evacuated the rest of the British from another village. We got back in the direction where we came from and arrived at the place where we had spent the night in the company of the wild Indians. The military department rowed to the beach under our captain's command. I also came with them. The others were left in the boat tens of yards from the shore while another department protected them. We advanced vindictively towards the forest. We found the same natives collecting mushrooms. The same group included those men who wore missionary clothing. These fools didn't even realize they had committed the worst of the crimes. The officer who led the unit once fired into the air while the soldiers besieged that mob. We said nothing, but the soldiers arrested the men we assumed were behind the crime.

A few savages tried to help them, but our soldiers struck them in the teeth with rifles. They stayed lay on the ground. The women screamed in horror. We dragged the two suspects with us to the beach and took off their British clothes. The officer who headed the department then read the charges to them, finding them guilty of robbery and murder. They were sentenced to death due to the shooting. The convicts were dragged to the cliff's edge, where the sentence was immediately enforced. The shots echoed handsomely, hitting the targets intended for them, executing justice. We threw dead wild men's bodies from a cliff into the sea, from where the tide would take their cursed bodies farther into the ocean for shark food. We quickly returned to our boats. The task was accomplished, albeit slightly different than we initially planned. With our citizens, we went by rowing back to the ship. We accommodated our compatriots in the hold of the ship. They will stay in Chile. Before that, they should be able to cope for a few days in slightly worse conditions. I went to my cabin room and thought about what we had done. We had taken a right into our own hands again, but on the other, what options did we have? Professor Grant was right. One could write a book about these experiences.

Our captain had raised anchors and sailed towards Chile. The ship flowed slowly along a narrow canal shaped by nature towards the Pacific Ocean. I felt like nothing out of the ordinary had happened yesterday. No feelings of guilt, but my well-being was excellent. I was very rested, and it was relieving to be safe on board again from those filthy trolls. Best of all, I got to sleep in the right bed. After eating quickly, I went to the deck. The sun shone from the cloudless sky, and I admired the majestically stunning scenery. The mountains rose to higher than a mile with white, sharp peaks. Some of them rose almost from the seashore. From shore to halfway up, the mountainside is bordered by a gloomy dense forest, and the peak was forever covered by ice. There were lavish waterfalls that plunged with great noise through the woods into the sea. Conrad painted stunning little paintings of those landscapes. We left the British missionaries we rescued in the small town of Punta Arenas. This time I didn't succumb to any kind of religious conversations with them. It felt good to get rid of them and be on my own with a familiar group, even though most of the crew treated me like some kind of weird philosopher. They considered me a mere entertainer of the skipper. It was only with the painter Conrad that I got along with. The atmosphere on the ship soon began to take on a similar too when we crossed the Atlantic.

I quarrelled with the captain regularly, and he commanded the crew in his familiar abrupt style. I was again reading books that I had received from Grant when our captain suddenly rushed to our room with two soldiers. He came next to my bed and told me to get up. I got out of bed in amazement. Before I had time to ask or say anything, he loaded a mad accusation into my face. "You have incited crew a revolt against me on the ship."

"What!" I exclaimed in shock.

"Yes, you heard right, Darwin. I will arrest you on suspicion of rebellion against the captain. Soldiers! Capture that man and lock him in the booth in the hallway."

"Good skipper, you can't be serious? Can I defend myself after all? Who is blaming me, and on what grounds?"

"We'll tell it to you." FitzRoy roared.

So, the soldiers grabbed me and dragged me to the booth. They threw me on the floor of the dark room, locking the door behind them. I pounded my fists on the door, demanding the captain release me, but to no avail. I heard the sound of their footsteps fading. I fell down to the floor of the room, talking to myself. Unbelievable, skipper is completely gone mad. Everyone else is also in danger here. Know even if he gets to sink the whole ship. I slept on my back on the floor. In the early evening, I woke up when I heard keys noise at the door lock.

They were apparently coming to have released me. Captain FitzRoy slammed the door open as the soldiers stood behind him. I got up slowly.

"Well, Darwin, let's go to the deck to listen to the charges."

I answered nothing but glared at him angrily. The soldiers tied my hands behind my back. The captain walked in front of us as the soldiers pushed me forward. With my heart pounding with horror, all sorts of questions revolved around my mind. What was the real motive of the captain? For what was he aiming? What was he going to do to me? Would he pull me too under the keel? I was really afraid, after all, that I had seen how ruthless a man he could be since the beginning trip. We were far from Britain and out of reach of justice. We climbed the stairs up to the deck. I was so horrified when I walked onto the deck. The ship was anchored with the entire crew standing in line on deck. They stood with serious faces in their position. I was trapped in fear as Commander Captain FitzRoy led me in front of the crew. He opened the ropes from my wrists, came next to me, and said to me with a smile: "Happy birthday, Charlie."

I had my mouth open in amazement. The crew burst out laughing under the skipper's leadership. I was completely surprised.

"How in the world did you remember my birthday when I had already forgotten it myself?"

"I'm not as nasty a man as you think! Now let's celebrate!" Skipper shouted between his laughter.

The crew split in two, and behind them, a table was revealed, covered with a wide variety of delicacies.

"You, Charles, should be sitting at the head of the table once you're a day hero!"

"Thank you for the glory. Please, could you sit next to me?"

"Of course. Sailors and soldiers! Let's start eating."

"Cheers, Charles. I guess you're really scared of my pranks, aren't you?"

"Yes."

"I didn't even know that you were scared about me that much. But now we eat, drink, and have fun. I told the crew in the morning that is enough, as long as we are ready to continue the journey at noon tomorrow."

We drank beers, after which we ate fish soup as an appetizer. After we started eating the main course, I noticed I was left alone at the end of the table again. The captain chatted with the officers, and the sailors were in their own gangs. Some of them had to leave immediately after eating to take care of their work. I saw Conrad wobble on the deck with a cup of wine in his hand, so I quickly hinted to him to come to sit next to me.

He said with a slight stammer he would stay in Australia. Conrad wanted to settle there in his to start a family. He was clearly older than me. Conrad thanked me for the travel company before going to bed. Also, the majority of the crew had gone to sleep. As the evening faded and my head filled with alcohol, I surely did not want to go to my cabin room yet. As the vodka rose to my head, the perverted desires from my dark mind came to the surface. When I drank, I often began to want in my mind to shoot with my rifle. So far, I hadn't hurt anyone with this sick obsession. I wasn't going to shoot alone in frustration, but instead, I asked a couple of sailors to come with me. We retrieved from the warehouse my rifle and a handful of cartridges. Everything would probably have gone pretty well if I hadn't got the idea to wake Dawkins. The old gaffer was sleeping on his hard, small bed, short dreams that the skipper let for him as I tore him up from the narrow and hard bed. His annoying creaking voice immediately made me furious. I told him to shut his mouth and quietly go up the deck. I dragged him from the neck with his underwear to the deck of the ship. There were no more people there than me and those couple of crew members. I told Dawkins to stand on the edge and hold the watermelon above his head. I loaded my rifle and aimed the melon in the middle. I sarcastically told him not to jump if he wanted to live.

Dawkins stood against the dark sea, shaking in his nightgown. Probably his tremor was due more to the cold than to the horror. I shot from about ten feet distance to the middle of the melon. The melon exploded into pieces when a bullet hit it. There were pieces of watermelon on the top of Dawkins' head. The sailors looked at each other in confusion as the shot echoed mightily from the nearby mountains. The sound of a shot probably traveled along the water for miles. Fascinated by the hit, I handed him an empty bottle of wine and told him to place the bottle above his head. As I was loading the rifle, Captain FitzRoy rushed to the deck.

"What the hell, you Darwin, are shooting here! Are you going to kill my crew? Give that rifle right here and go to sleep!"

"Well, but skipper, this is just innocent play. I'm not shooting anyone here now, just one melon." I roared in a tired, drunk voice.

I glanced at the captain and realized he was so furious that I thought it would be best to give my rifle to him immediately. The sailors ran scared to their cabins. Apparently, the captain thought they were also victims of my whims. Fortunately, the others did not come to the deck. I went after the skipper in my shame to our cabin to sleep. Due to the risen hops, I didn't get any sleep because the bed felt to spin in a round under me.

I had to get up a little to ensure I didn't vomit on my bed. When I woke up after a poorly slept night, I was in the grip of a terrible moral hangover. I felt ashamed of my last night's stupidity. I remembered memories of study times when I drifted into gangs of marginalized men. With them, I wasted the money I got from my father, sipping alcohol late into the night. We played cards, and after intoxicating ourselves, we started singing raucous songs. After the liquors ran out, we headed drunk to the night city streets in search of people who we could beat up. Usually, we met some older people which we humiliated. That sense of power when I was able to disgrace someone who was more authoritative than myself brought me great satisfaction. Just like I would have done it to my father. It was, in my opinion, the only way to dispel the feelings of bitterness that had been caused by failed me in my studies. I dropped back from my memories to this moment as the captain came into our cabin. I apologized to him, regretting the recent events. He surprisedly took my apology, ordering me to apologize to the cleaner, who had done nothing to deserve such a treatment. I went to express my apologies to him as well. Dawkins' face had a mischievous grin as I had to humble himself in front of him. He said nothing to me, only nodded uphill proudly.

The crew had lifted the anchors, and we had already, for a while, made the journey towards the Pacific Ocean. We turned our course right north, continuing along Chile's rugged coastline. I fell ill again with nausea when our ship started swaying on the sea. There was hellish to lay on the bed and vomit into a bucket. My stomach was messed up, my head was spinning, and I couldn't eat just about anything.   Again, I lost weight. Due to the headache, my eyes were so sore I couldn't even read. I lay on the bed facing the wall. I quietly wished in my mind a merciful death to free me from this pathetic state of being. The pouring rain drummed on the deck of the ship. Nothing special happened except for the suddenly imminent death of a sailor. Skipper said our doctor wrapped the body in cloths, after which a couple of crew members dumped him from the stretcher into the sea. It had been an inconsolable decision of a barren life. No wife, no children, no relatives, and no farewell fanfares.

Chapter 10: Israfil

We approached the island of Chiloe, which is the second-largest island in Chile. I would have liked to see it, but we passed it because we had to replenish our stocks. This year we intended to cross the Pacific Ocean. As we sailed north, the weather warmed. In the city of Valparaiso, the temperature was already pleasantly warm. Calm sea, cloudless, sunny skies, dry, calm winds, and marvellous mountain sights welcomed us to this Chilean coastal town. My stomach also rejoiced in the calming of the sea. In the city port, our ship would be repaired. In the meantime, I would have time to write letters and make a field trip. I immediately set out to explore the city. This city was built on a hillside. I walked quickly towards the city center. I felt awesome. The storms of winter and meeting with the wild Indians of Tierra del Fuego were just a distant, awful memory. How good it felt to have solid ground under my feet. I jumped in relief along the streets, having been a full land crab all my life and proud of it. There really is nothing glamorous in sailor life. First, I hoped to go to the city post office, where an old moustache clerk man informed me that I had received two letters. In a state of excitement, I wondered from whom those might be. Those were from Henslow and Grant.

I had been waiting for a letter from Henslow in particular. I wanted to know how he was doing. I missed him. His honest and calm character made a lasting impression on me during my studies. I don't understand why I hadn't written to him before. I guess I tried to be too loyal to Grant. With great interest, I opened Henslow's letter.

Dear Charles

I decided to write to you when I haven't heard anything from you since you left. I got your travel plan from your father. How are you? Have you been healthy? What have you learned during your trip? Have you made any scientific discoveries? My family has gone well. My son has been walking for over a year now, and he's already talking some. I still teach at university and enjoy my work. In my spare time, I have spent time with the Lord. I have grown a lot spiritually. Charles, how is your Faith Life going? It would be nice to meet you when you get back home. We pray for you and wish you all the best.

Sincerely, John

I had been touched by Henslow's humane letter. He seemed happy with his family. After reading his letter, all this futile wandering in the savannahs seemed utterly insignificant. What interesting did his level of intelligence professor see in me? Why hadn't I written to him before? How could I have been so vainly proud? Well, now I would have a good reason to correct that mistake. I returned to the ship and immediately started working in my room. I wrote him a long letter thanking him for all the support. I also told him a little bit about beautifying the main events of our trip, and I promised to bring him some fossil finds as well. In that burst of joyful enthusiasm, I almost forgot Grant's letter altogether. Opening his letter was a little harder because I knew it had obligations to me.

> *Charles!*
>
> *Thank you for your samples. Those will be of great benefit to us. In the future, be sure to lock the boxes containing animal remains better, as now one box has been slightly open, and the samples had already rotted. Your report on the Indians was awesome. As I read it, I realized we were on the right track. Don't embellish the events, but tell all the details, no matter how brutal. I hope you learn from those events.*

Both letters were manly short and concise. Grant's letter was typical of him. Grant is a practical and ruthless man. Had he himself seen the massacre? I was surprised to read that he told others about my trip. What things does he say? What exactly is he aiming for with my help? It's sometimes so hard to find out about him. In everyday life, he is terribly outspoken, but on the other hand, so mysterious about his goals. I should be grateful that a genius like him writes to me. Whatever plans he has for me, it must be something valuable and important. I also wrote to him, though this time, I did not send any samples. I decided to go on a more comprehensive trip to the mountains, so I got myself a guide and one assistant. This time I just wanted to put some air in my thoughts. I planned to tour the Andes Mountains as a passage of time. Initially, we headed straight north along the coast. After reaching the first mountain range, I continued my journey alone to the top of the mountain.

In the evening, I camped halfway up the mountain and set up my tent for the night.

At night, I woke up to an incredibly bright light that shone from outside the tent. I pulled the boots to my feet, and I crawled out of the tent. On the outside, I saw an infinitely beautiful feminine creature in front of me. In it, she hovered in the air in a narrow crotch position with long blond hair. Thick curly hair fluttered freely around her body, and her hands were invitingly outstretched towards me. She looked at me with her charming eyes, smiling enchantingly. Her eyelashes were thick, and her eyes were dark in colour. It formed an arousing contrast with her yellowish hair. Her beautiful lips made me aroused. She was absolutely incredibly beautiful. I was so enchanted that I couldn't say anything. She was wearing a skin-tight black leather suit. It further accentuated the sexy shapes of her feminine body. She introduced herself as Israfil and said tonight that she would consecrate me to an important mission. I was amazed as she spoke, for I could not hear the speech with my ears, but her velvety soft voice was heard inside my head. Israfil asked me to come with her to the top of the mountain where she would say her message. I was as if hypnotized and gladly agreed to her request. I would have followed Israfil, even to hell, if she had asked for it.

Israfil grabbed me by the hands and so together, we flew in the air towards the top of the mountain. All that way, I stared at her in enchantment. When we reached the top of the mountain, an angel lowered me to the ground, after which she spoke to me. At first, Israfil said she was happy that I took part in a witchcraft ritual organized by the Indians, then she said she had visited my mother already while she was still alive. My mother had asked her to consecrate me to carry out this great mission that would affect all of humanity. This task would bring much-needed freedom to all. Israfil told me with a serious face to continue the journey to the end, which my family had started, whatever it would cost. She promised it would be worth all the effort in the end. I didn't care to ask anything about this task because I felt such an unnatural admiration for that enchanting nymph. I don't even remember half of what she promised me because I was so ecstatic about her soft feminine voice. Her confident, feminine smile completely confused me. Whatever Israfil told me to do, I would have done it unconditionally. Soon, far too soon, we flew across the dark night starry sky back to my tent. After lowering me to the ground, she looked into my eyes, saying now she was leaving me. I fell to my knees on the ground in front of her and prayed for her to stay, but Israfil said with a gentle smile it was impossible.

Then I asked her to take me with her. The nymph replied that I could not follow her alive, but after I died, I would get to the same place where she was with my mother. I asked her to kill me so that I could join their company, for I no longer had any desire to be left alone in this ugly world. Israfil smiled tenderly and scolded me, saying I had to be obedient to her until the end because that was the only way I could accomplish my important task. Finally, she promised to come to strengthen me when difficulties arose. Having said that, she said goodbye to me while slowly getting up in the air. In farewell, Israfil handed me a plane kiss, after which she just disappeared into a dark emptiness. I cried longingly after her, asking when I would meet her again, but my cry echoed into the dark starry sky against the mountainside. Without receiving an answer, I burst into hysterical crying. I felt completely orphaned. I was inconsolable and sadly entered my tent and fell asleep immediately.

I woke up when my guide shook me off my feet. I got up and looked around me. There was bright sunshine outside. I thought I had a dream at night, but I was startled to notice the dirty boots on my feet. Did I had I been out at night talking to an angelic being? I did not dare to mention my experience in a word to my guides. After assembling my tent, we descended the mountain.

At the same time, I desperately tried to forget my last night's sight, but I just couldn't. Honestly, I didn't even want to forget what I was experiencing. The more I remembered what happened, the more I missed it. Now I feel I have an important role to play in this life. My life had a purpose anyway. I tried to think cool about what I logically experienced, but this time it just didn't work. What other secrets had my mother taken with her to the grave? How had this creature become acquainted with my mother? I just wanted to join Israfil, forgetting everything else. After we walked down the slope, we found another of my guides at the foot of the mountain, where he was by the campfire eating. We sat with him and ate ourselves to satiety. After breakfast, we went for a horse ride towards Santiago. My nightly meeting with the nymph popped into my mind again. I felt great boyish joy as I remembered her. I didn't get her beautiful sexy red lips out of my mind. I felt a deep sexual passion for Israfil. She was so charmingly beautiful, far more beautiful than any other woman I had ever seen. Actually, I couldn't have imagined such an arousingly beautiful woman even in my wildest dreams. With her, I felt completely free and independent of everything. With Israfil, life would be passionately exciting and worth living. Without her, everything seemed so frustratingly boring. In my mind, I am missing her.

Even I tried to focus on riding. As while we were riding, I drank diluted whiskey from my bottle, thinking again and again in my mind of the enchanting Israfil. I didn't think at all whether that beautiful creature was morally good or evil. I just concluded that such a beautiful creature could not be evil. Besides, she said she knew my mother, so she had to be morally good. I also thought about the purpose of other things in my life. Did any of the events ultimately have any purpose? Without receiving an answer, I decided in frustration to forget all sorts of philosophical nonsense. According to another guide, there was an old Indian ruin village nearby, so we rode our horses there. My stomach had been loose due to drinking for some time, and as we approached the ruins, I felt unwell. I saw a big block of rock just over a hundred yards away, so I decided to go behind it for my needs. I ran there, and at the last moment, I had time to lower my pants to the ground before it came into my pants. I closed my eyes and, with a sigh of great relief. At the same time, one of the Indian guides came behind the stone. Seeing me shitting there squatting down, he was terribly upset. I snatched my pants up and asked him, in my poor Spanish, why he had that reaction. He said the stone was a holy place for the Indians, commemorating the dead warriors. I apologized for what had happened, saying I had no idea.

For the rest of the trip, this Indian held silent because of what had happened. We rode our horses to the west, continuing along the seashore towards the town of Valparaiso, which was our terminus. This trip was a complete fiasco for nature research but very relaxing for my mind. Because of its revelation, nothing would be as it used to be. Upon arrival, I said goodbye to my guides and paid them a small compensation for their ailments. In the harbour, I saw the captain on the deck of the ship talking loudly with Lieutenant Forsythe. I boarded the ship and went to them, but they ignored me. Our captain seemed somehow absent and completely exhausted. I stayed to listen to their conversation to the side.

"Sir. Captain FitzRoy. You must continue as captain of the ship!" Demanded a lieutenant.

"I can't take a day anymore. Try Lieutenant to realize that I must relinquish my duties as captain of the ship, or I don't have time to do my other duties. I haven't slept properly for many weeks. I am already completely confused by these nautical charts that I have to make for the fleet. If I have to continue as captain of the ship, I will commit suicide!" Cried the captain desperately.

"Stop such childish martyr preaching." The lieutenant shouted contemptuously.

"I urge you, Lieutenant, to assume the duties of captain of this ship and to sail immediately back to England via Cap Horn!"

"I'm not going to do that. Under no circumstances will I sail back through Cap Horn. I don't put the ship and crew anymore in such danger!" Shouted Lieutenant Forsythe.

I tried to interrupt their quarrel to say my own suggestion, but like from one mouth, they told me to keep my mouth shut.

"Returning to England without completing the mission would be a betrayal of financiers and a terrible personal disgrace to me. The task must be completed regardless of the price, even if it takes 10 years! Captain FitzRoy, I suggest you sail back to the Chiloe Islands. We anchor the ship there for a while, and you get to rest all the time. Is this arrangement right for you?" Forsythe asked.

"All right, but I want full discharge from the captain's duties for that time."

"You will have it."

That is exactly what I would have suggested to them. Fortunately, the captain seemed to accept the lieutenant's will. I looked mercifully after FitzRoy as he dragged himself down to our cabin room. Only now did I realize what a heavy workload he had been working under all the time.

At the same time as I was collecting butterflies and sipping gin in the cabin, he was making a massive number of maps for the fleet. He had in charge of the ship, the cargo, and the crew, and on top of that, he still had to steer the ship in time to the right destination. The financiers' expectations of the expedition timetable were unreasonable. The schedule they set for this trip was too tight. The skipper has had to be under really hard stress all the time. Our excursions with the Indian mass shooting probably didn't make him feel easier. There were too many duties for one man. I would probably have collapsed in a week under such responsibility. The skipper had been in that situation for years! I had never heard him complain about his workload. On the way back, FitzRoy lay in the cabin on his bed and snuggled quietly into himself. I urged him to sleep, but he did not respond to my chat. It was scary to be in the same cabin at night with an armed man who seemed to have lost his sanity. I solemnly promised in my mind not to tell anyone about this embarrassing event as long as he would live. The atmosphere on the ship was frighteningly quiet in the days that followed. Everyone was on their toes. No one raised their voices or looked for dispute. All of us seemed to be careful not to cause any stress to FitzRoy. It was an odd situation. Afterwards, I wondered how my life would have gone if we had turned back to England.

What would I have done with my life? Would I have written a book about our expedition or tried to study something else? Would I have gotten enough research material from here for Grant or gone back to these seas and researched the areas that would have gone unexplored? I can't give a definite answer. I probably wouldn't have returned because this exploratory trip had been so strenuous. The surest answer is probably that I would have lived the rest of my life as I do now, that is, with my father's money, spending the life of a baron in a rural mansion.

The main port on the island of Chiloe already had two large catching vessels. After we had anchoring next to them, I went to visit the ship. The deck of the ship was full of big harpoons. The crew told me they were whalers off the east coast of the United States. I asked to speak with the ship's captain, and they kindly directed me to their captain. He said they had been on a whale-hunting trip for more than a year and a half. I asked him for permission to join on the next trip, which the captain agreed to. Excited, I went back to our ship and carefully opened the door of our cabin. FitzRoy snored on his bed in a dim room with his face facing the wall. I sneaked cautiously next to the bed to tell him about my plan. He lay on other worlds without shaving.

I asked him to come along to get his desire for life back, but he just grunted something in response and waved his hand at me to walk away. I left our cabin room quietly. I told the lieutenant my plan, who was now in charge, to be sure. He didn't even glance at me when he announced that he had nothing against my intentions. He must have been relieved in his mind when he got rid of me. I slept the night before the whaling trip brilliantly and was excited about the upcoming trip. I quickly boarded the catching ship. The weather was cloudy but dry. It was, according to them, the best weather for whaling, then the sun did not dazzle the sea surface, making it easier to look around. Watchmen climbed the masts. I didn't suppose they expected me to be of any use on the ship, though they knew that beforehand. After all, I said I came to them only to get to know their interesting and manly work. I was talking on the way with a harpoon man. This really strong-looking man said he had only recently begun whaling but had still had time to kill more than forty whales. Each time was reportedly quite unique because the whales reacted differently to the hunters. Some of the whales fought back. Others were just trying to escape in fear. It also mattered if they had a cub with them. According to the harpoon man, it would basically be very easy for a whale to overthrow a rowing boat and kill them all with its huge flukes.

I asked him not to scare me with stuff like that and told him playfully I would bring them good luck. We sailed west towards deep seas. There we would find the sea monsters we were looking for. After our meal, the observer shouted, "Whale on starboard!" To which the captain answered: "Let's lower the boats into the water!" The crew exploded into action the second the captain gave his orders. Harpoons, ropes, and all items needed to catch were quickly picked up and loaded onto three rowing boats. Nine men went to each boat. The men using the harpoon went to the bow of the boats, and the rest of the crew got to rowing the boats. I got on the last boat. We stayed behind the other boats to observe the situation. At the captain's command, we dispersed to try to encircle the whale. The scout did not recognize the whale, but the crew hoped it would be a sperm whale because they would get the best price from it. Whale fat was used primarily as fuel oil in lamps. The crew would have a chance to eat whale meat. Maybe after this trip, I would get to taste the whale soup. The captain's boat set out to row towards the whale. The captain frantically roared his instructions to the men who were rowing towards the whale. As I listened farther from the other boat to his shouting, I thought the captains of all the ships were similar in character.

At the same time, the whale escaped from them, diving into the depths before the boat got a hundred yards closer. We followed the development of the situation a short distance away. The second boat was about fifty yards from the captain's boat. The captain told all the boats to stop rowing and lift the oars up. Came deadly silence. The boats floated motionless in the unnaturally calm sea. We looked at each other, and no one whispered even a single word. The situation was exciting. What would be the next move, and who would do it? Captain or whale? They knew the whale would rise to the surface at regular intervals to breathe, which would be a good opportunity to strike a harpoon into a whale, but would it rise near us or hundreds of yards away? Just as I had begun painting the skyline with my thoughts, the sea level exploded in front of us. A whale rose to the surface with crushing power, colliding with the bottom of another rowing boat. The force of the collision threw the boat several yards in height. The men flew into the up like rag dolls. They shouted in horror, knowing full well they could die. The boat disintegrated into pieces, spreading like wood chips around the sea surface. A whale hit on the surface of the water, burying one man under it. Pressing his huge head into the dives, it slapped the surface of the sea with its frightening flukes, killing the harpoon man I had met on the way.

The rest of the men started swimming in horror towards the captain's boat. The captain's boat rowed quickly towards them, throwing harpoons after the whale, but it was far too far away. The whale was too fast. It all happened so fast that I only jumped in a panic to my feet. I was almost to knock down our boat, but luckily a harsh sailor pulled me by the sleeve to sit. He told me to calm down. For a moment, we already imagined that we had survived the accident with only two dead crew members until one of those caught in the water noticed the fins of sharks moving on the surface of the water. He panicked and desperately swam straight to our boat. One of those predatory fish reacts to his swimming. Immediately the shark attacked the man. He was just reaching for our boat when a shark in front of our eyes grabbed that poor man's feet. We tried to expel the shark further away, but we had no way to help that man. Helpless and stiffing by horror, we watched the painful expressions of a man struggling to die a few yards away. There was such much horror and fear in the man's gaze that I could never forget it. The scariest thing here was our complete helplessness. I wish I had a rifle with me. Shocked, we watched as the sharks caught two more men as their prey yet. The men screamed in pain when the shark bit their lower bodies into a bloody pulp. The sea surface was quickly stained with dark, bubbling blood.

The water bubbled around the men as the sharks shook their prey vigorously. Such a furious shaking must have exacerbated the bite injuries, probably as a means for sharks to hasten the victim's death. Soon sharks were already pulling lifeless men underwater to dine in peace. At the same time, we set off rowing fiercely towards the rest of the men and got one of them lifted into our boat. Two men got aboard the captain's boat. In this situation, afraid was the smaller problem compared to the fate of the dead men. The sperm whale disappeared into the depths of the sea, and good so. However, we couldn't have killed it in this situation. We quickly got back on the ship, where the crew waiting eagerly asked where we had left the catch. After telling them the nasty events, they went back to their chores quietly. On this hunting trip, I was taught really tangible how dangerous the job of whaling was. Now I understood very well why it was paid so well. Even if the pay was good, I don't think this job is what I would have wanted to do. We set sail before the night towards the harbour. The ship had a mirthless atmosphere. I watched the dark starry sky from the deck as I thought about the shark attack. Although the situation was gruesome, in the name of honesty, I can say that afterwards, I experienced it at the same time very passionately exciting.

It was awful when those men died in such a cruel way, but I couldn't mourn them because I didn't even know their names. In the harbour, I was looking for the other ship that went hunting with us at the same time, but it hadn't returned yet. Had they had better hunting luck? Thinking about it, I walked over to the sailor, who also said he was expecting another ship to arrive from his fishing trip. This young American man introduced himself as Hermann Melville. He had the look of a young man exuding calm deep wisdom. Hermann said he left the United States for whaling years ago. He was going to write a novel about his adventures at sea. We were standing on the shore when another catching ship finally arrived slowly into the harbour. On its other edge hung a dead whale. Hermann said it was a medium-sized humpback whale. Questions about transporting a whale came to my mind, and I decided to ask them.

"When a whale is killed, doesn't it sink to the seabed?"

"It won't sink into anything. It floats on its side like a bottle cap." Hermann replied calmly.

"That was new to me. How do you get that whale attached to a ship?"

"It is case-specific, but usually, it is tied with a chain to the edge of the ship from the fins, flukes, or jaw. Smaller whales are lifted onto the ship immediately for chopping.

Transporting a whale is not the hardest part but finding and killing it. The biggest job in transporting is how to keep sharks away from the catch during the incoming trip." He explained proudly.

We saw how the carcass of a whale was hauled ashore with the help of horses. I followed excitedly as it began to be chopped with giant saw-like knives. A thick layer of fat was exposed under the skin, and then the internal organs became visible. Part of the carcass was thrown back into the sea. I admired the catch team's achievement on the site. I told Hermann of my great respect for them. It was really great to hunt such a giant sea monster. I wondered how far humanity would reach. As science advances, we have a great future ahead of us and can forever take advantage of nature's endless riches. As I pondered these thoughts, I also felt immense envy for future generations. How interesting and easy their life becomes. We gathered the whole fishing crew at a local sailor's diner to eat. At first, we held a quiet moment of remembrance in memory of the men who died at sea. The food was a soup made from a whale. With the soup, we sipped clear tequila liquor. I didn't particularly like whale meat, but tequila was a pleasant new acquaintance. After waking up at noon from the floor of the canteen, I navigated in a spooky hangover towards our ship.

There, the going had been similar for part of the group. Once the ship was serviced, the crew had time to lazing, and you will notice it. Captain FitzRoy was still lying on his bed without shaving his face in our cabin, indifferently depressed. The biggest surprise for me was that at the same time, I had been on a whale hunt and drank. Also, at the same time, our ship's surgeon McCormack had made awesome scientific discoveries in the local wildlife. He openly told me of his findings. I felt jealous of him at first, but I asked him to show his findings to me, so we went to his cabin room to learn more about them. McCormack promised to go with me again tomorrow to explore the nature of Chiloe Island, as long as I only survived the hangover first. He said he would be happy to give me his discoveries and notes for free. In order not to seem like a pathetic fool, I demand that I could be paid a small sum from my father's funds. Fortunately, he agreed. I rested in the cabin to feel better. The next day McCormack and I set off on a horse ride. I was infinitely excited to get to know the animals on the island. We planned to make a short trip to the interior of the island, so we only brought with us all the essentials and some food. We initially rode along the seafront. We saw owls and finches in the trees. They really looked bigger here than in England. I was thinking in my mind about why I didn't bring a gun.

I couldn't even imagine this as a better opportunity to get research material on virgin nature. McCormack had big butterfly nets with that he caught a few finches. He studied the beaks of the finches in more detail, noticing that they were clearly different. Some of the finches were also clearly larger than those he had met before. McCormack came to the conclusion that different birds had adapted under different conditions. However, they had remained the same species. I didn't understand what it meant, but it was awesome for a long time again to explore the treasures of nature. We continued along the beach. We arrived at a steady stunning sandy beach that was almost full of giant turtles slowly walking themselves toward the sea. I walked next to one and knocked with a stick against the shield. Immediately, the turtle pulled its limbs and head inside the shield into its shelter, and it no longer responded, no matter how I beat its shield with a stick. I left the scene to follow the turtle further. After a while, it came to life, continuing its journey slowly, dragging towards the waves of the sea. I didn't dare put my thoughts into words as I thought about the durability of the turtle shield. Would it have taken a shot from my shotgun? Maybe it was good I didn't bring a gun. My travel companion would hardly have enjoyed my experiment. We rode back inland. During that time, we discussed my hunting hobby.

"So, you are an avid huntsman? Have you been hunting for a long time?"

"Yes. I got my first shotgun when I was sixteen, and since then, I have been hunting whenever it was possible. There, all the nasty responsibilities and problems will be totally forgotten. There is no better hobby than hunting. In the woods, you can feel like a truly free man. Hunting is completely different from some silly lecture in some dusty lecture hall."

"It probably depends a bit on what you study and how you succeed," McCormack replied sarcastically.

"Since childhood, I have had an immense desire to shoot everything that can move. As soon as I heard a little rattle from the bush, I headed my shotgun right away in that direction and emptied the barrels into the bushes. Many times, I was excited to shoot the same bird as my companion, and once I almost accidentally shot my brother. The ammunitions I usually wasted twice as much as other hunters. It's really nerve reassuring when you get to shoot towards the birds. Fresh outdoor air and suitably warm weather make my mind relax." I told McCormack excitedly.

"Do you do anything else but hunting?"

"I also collect beetles. I look for them everywhere. The best places are often the toilets, where many species nest in the vicinity."

He did not comment on that in any way. Instead, he wondered how different animals could move to such a distant island. McCormack was an extraordinarily intelligent and friendly man. He quickly realized the things that occur in nature. Afterwards, I got the best conclusions and animal data from him, which I submitted to Grant. I wasn't going to tell that to Grant cause the matter was completely indifferent to McCormack. I paid him later, as I had promised. When we returned to the ship, we had pleasantly surprise. Our captain had recovered to healthy, with which he had regained his desire for life. FitzRoy was busy on deck in his familiar style. From everything, that rest had done him good. We left the island of Chiloe behind us in good spirits as we sailed north towards the town of Valdivia. Heavy rain escorted us off as we sailed along the Chilean coast. Fortunately, I did not become seasick cause the biggest storms would still be ahead. We celebrated the turn of the year in, with the skipper leading as vigorously we fired fireworks from the deck of the ship into the sky. Maybe it was stupid. Someone might have thought we were in a maritime emergency. However, we were far from the beach, so we didn't expect anyone to see our fireworks. I was relieved to note things had returned to normal. As we sailed closer to the coast, we witnessed an awesome play.

We got to see the fireworks properly arranged by nature itself, as the local volcano erupted without warning. At first, it was for a few hours like a smoldering campfire. Little by little, its brightness grew as it grew until it exploded with furious force. Lava and the bright ash of red plunged for miles high into the dark night. The eruption stood out well against the dark sky. I looked more closely at the mountain with a telescope. Molten lava flowed down the slope into the valley, igniting everything burning in its path. I stared enchanted at this play well to the morning. I wondered feverishly what forces made it unleash so drastically at irregular intervals. When I woke up in the afternoon, the volcano had calmed down. We continued our journey along the coast. I would have liked to have taken a closer look at the volcano, but our surgeon McCormack said it was dangerous because of possible aftermaths or rupture. In that situation, toxic gases would also come out of the mountain with the hot ashes. My trip could have ended rudely. I didn't even think about such gas eruptions. I told him that I had smelled skipper's farts in the same room for years, so I would endure anything. McCormack acknowledged my comment with a hard laugh.

After we arrived in the harbour, the sun proclaimed us welcome in its glory. I was left alone to explore the local nature. At the same time, the rest of the men went to town. I walked to a flat open area that grew only short of grass, sat down on the ground, and looked at the beautiful scenery. I slowly turned on my back. I felt tired. I thought I would fall asleep for a while. After relaxing, I closed my eyes, listening to the hum of the wind and the sounds of nature. I was overwhelmed by a relaxed feeling of well-being. I felt like I was doing the right things in my life. I dreamed of lecturing myself at various science events around England. People would respect and admire me. I would have been worshiped. I would get money, awards, and fame. At last, my relatives would have to admit my greatness. I would show them. While when I was lying on the lawn, I couldn't have guessed how quickly the plans could change. I felt light how the ground rocked a little beneath me, then again. Soon the swinging turned into a wild vibration. It took a while before I realised I was in the middle of an earthquake. I tried to stand up, looking around me at what was happening, but the sway of the ground knocked me back to the ground. It felt like I had been on a ship in a severe storm. In less than a couple of minutes, the quake was over. After I survived the worst, the question of the fate of the skipper and crew came to mind.

Would they have survived? I set off to run towards the city. There, the sight was earth-shattering. The houses built of wood had been torn to pieces. There were pieces of planks thrown from the houses around the streets, and there were fires here and there. I did not see dead people in the ruins of the buildings. Instead, the streets were full of people fleeing in horror. Some of those poor's wandered in shock, repeating the names of their loved ones. I soon found our captain and crew in the city's central square, where people had gathered. They had been outside during the quake, surviving without any scratch. We did not have hospital supplies with us, and without language skills, we could not help anyone. We decided to go back to the ship to continue our journey. However, we would not get supplements here. We continued north. During the trip, I pondered the earthquake we experienced. The ground you assume to be stable will vibrate like the surface of the water. I felt pity for these humans who had to start all their lives all over again. Who would compensate for the financial losses they experience? As we approached the coastal city of Concepcion, we were faced with a catastrophically depressing sight. The entire coast was covered with all sorts of rubbish for miles. There was furniture, trees, sacks of stuff, tables, and pieces of houses in the ocean. It was as if the coast had washed into the sea.

It looked like a shipwrecked ship was here. We had to leave our ship outside the harbour. On the beach, our first attention was the ubiquitous chaos. We could not have come at a worse time because there was a shortage of everything. At first glance, I saw that this city had suffered even worse than Valdivia. I asked the captain for permission to go by horse to explore Concepcion. He had nothing against it as long as I came back within a day. They stayed in the vicinity of the ship. In the meantime, the crew would try to get some replenishment for the ship's food stores. I said I would return by evening and went for a ride by a horse towards Concepcion. Along the way, I was confronted with a familiar sight. People who had lost all their possessions. As an inconsolable herd, they walked with glazed gazes in their eyes towards the harbour in search of food. Some of them had rushed themselves to temporary accommodation by the roadside. Noticing I was riding towards them, they sadly held out their hands, begging pathetically asking for help. I hardened myself by riding fast pace past them. For a moment, I already regretted leaving for the city alone without a gun. After all, there could be going on complete anarchy and looting. I reminded myself again that we were not now in the British Isles, where everything was so punctual. However, I decided to go to the city center. It was closer than I could imagine.

Upon arrival, I could not comprehend how the city had survived with such a small loss of life. Most of the houses had collapsed on their sides to the seaside. At the same time, the sight was creepy and interesting. I had never seen any such complete destruction of buildings before. I rode from end to end of the town and returned to the ship via the harbour. How did such a short and seeming series of events wreak such massive havoc? Here, too, the edges of the roads were full of all kinds of rubbish. I decided to ask somebody from the port for a reason for that. After several unnecessary questions, I found a man who had tolerable skills in English. He said a big wave hit the city a few hours after the quake. When it retreated back to sea, it had taken away all movable property. Just when they thought the situation was over, another similar wave of tsunami wave had struck again, finishing the devastation. These massive waves were apparently caused by the fact that the center of the earthquake had been deep in the seabed. That giant wave explained that destruction everywhere. I just couldn't fit in my head how an earthquake on the seabed could cause a big wave that would plunge to the ground, burying everything underneath. What would happen to the British Isles if a similar wave struck there? One can only imagine how quickly a new era of civilization would decline after such a tragedy.

I went back to the ship and told the shocking facts I saw. We wouldn't get any foods from here either, so we had to start reducing our consumption. Our captain had met British officials at the port. They had advised him to proceed directly to Peru, as due to the earthquake, the Chilean government had taken control of food. They would not be sold to foreigners, so the skipper decided to continue our journey further north. Apparently, the devastation of the earthquake had not reached as far as Peru. I jumped on the ship satisfied. I had no interest in staying here in the middle of a shortage. Although the immediate continuation of the voyage to Peru meant strict regulation of the ship's foodstuffs, I still wanted to think about it from a positive point of view. At least the climate would warm up as we approach the tropic of Capricorn. The food was scarce, and it was very one-sided. It was heavy for the crew because they had to do the same tasks as before, but with half the amount of food. The atmosphere on the ship was really tense. It was almost a miracle that no fights broke out among the crew. Skipper promised to reimburse the crew for their efforts princely. His use of language towards the crew was considerably more restrained this time than before. He could not afford to annoy men in vain. For my part, I tried in every way to stay out of the way of others and be as invisible as it was possible.

When we arrived at the port of Lima, we were all nervous and had lost weight. Along the way, I had written a letter to my sister asking her to send more money to Sydney, which would be our next destination. In Lima, I went to look for a local post office. As a city, Lima was awful. It was in a dilapidated condition, although the effects of the earthquake had not reached this far. People were poor and apathetic. I quickly returned to the ship. Our captain had visited the British Embassy to inquire about social conditions. With their help, he was able to arrange food supplements for us. The skipper had promised the crew a few days of paid leave. They wasted their money and leisure time at local brothels where the ugly Indian women sold their services. I instead focused mainly on Oriental meditation.

Chapter 11: Galapagos Islands

When the ship was fully loaded, we were able to set off for Australia. The captain estimated the trip to take three months. I wondered again how I would spend that time in a rocking ship in the middle of an empty ocean. Our first sea sign was the Galapagos Islands. If the winds were favourable, we would be there soon. During this trip, I focused on eating. I wanted to get the lost pounds back. As I stood on the deck, I heard the mate shout when he saw the island with his telescope. At the skipper's command, we headed for there. As we approached the island, I dug up my telescope. I felt hugely disappointed as I looked at the island, as these islands seemed really barren. This was black-gray wind-blown unfruitful land so far as I could see. These were the complete opposite of the lush paradise islands we had visited before. We anchor the ship to the cove of the largest island. Unexcited, I set out to explore the nature of the island. Nature looked gloomy, and the weather was horribly hot. I was walking around the island, and I didn't see a single living being during that time. My impression of this Galapagos Island was that it was unapproachable. These islands consist mainly of ancient lava. The landscape was very one-sided. On my behalf, we could continue our journey immediately.

These islands were already on the captain's nautical charts, so he had no interest in staying here either. The location of these islands was also geopolitically indifferent to the fleet, as there were no strategically important sites nearby. My friend Conrad recorded the hostile faces of these islands in his paintings. He would have liked to paint me a picture with the island in the background, but I refused because I didn't want to identify with such barren landscapes. We continued our journey immediately towards the Tahiti islands of trade wind bulged our sails. That's how we got to catch up on the schedule.

Chapter 12: "Cities need to be slummed"

"Gentlemen! I welcome you to our meeting tonight. It is very pleasing to note that so many of you have been able to attend a meeting on the future of our great nation. My name is Edmond Grant, and I am working as a professor at the University of London. I am really excited about this topic, and I think this will be of great benefit to all of you as well. My friend Mark Rose asked me to tell you in which direction we want our country to develop in the coming decades. We are both involved in a task force appointed by the Royal House to map out the threats and opportunities for the future of the British Empire. We have been researching various social policy options for our nation for some time now, and we believe that the right direction is already beginning to emerge. I'm not going to go into the details more here. Instead, I'll focus on tonight's main line. To begin with, I would like to talk briefly about a young man who is doing pioneering work for our revolutionary ideology. He is the ingenious Charles Darwin. The name probably doesn't tell you anything yet, but he's just on a research trip in South America, and they've made unprecedented scientific discoveries there. The fossil discoveries they make will completely change our perception of the birth and evolution of life.

These facts will also fundamentally change the values of our country. Scientific discoveries open a whole new page in the birth stages of humanity. On the basis of them, we can prove that human races were born simultaneously on different continents, and since time immemorial, they have competed with each other for living space. We will return to this interesting topic later when he returns to England. Now I go straight to our topic this time around, where I deal with the social structures of our country's population. I will also deal briefly with the direction in which these structures should be developed. I have been using all my free time and energy to develop our ideology. After my introduction, we can continue with a general discussion. Before we can put things right outside the borders of our country, we must first put our own nest in order. I roughly divide the social problems of our country into two groups of people. The first group includes those who are not intelligent but are able to support themselves. The second group consists of those who are only a useless burden to the state. We can use the first group for heavy and simple work, so they are well suited for industrial works. The development of the heavy industry will cause a growing need for labor in the near future, so as a result, people will move from rural to urban to working.

The devil knows what kind of mob will flow from there to here, but one thing is certain. They are only slightly above the animals from their intellectual level. In London, this decay direction is already visible. Due to the explosively growing crime, the city's costs are threatening to get out of hand, which is an unsustainable trend. Areas must be set aside in the cities of our country to accommodate these groups of people, and poor living conditions must be provided for those areas. These future workers and poor's areas must be slummed from the outset. Only the most basic needs for their survival are provided on behalf of society. They must not be encouraged to take care of their cleanliness, but vice versa. The streets in these poor residents' residential areas must be narrow, and no drainage must be built. The whole family must be able to live in one room, in which case they will not have time or energy to cause problems for society. Anyway, they are not our biggest concern. The worst problem is the other group. A population that produces nothing but only incurs costs by its very existence. They include the mentally ill, the disabled, the lazy, the drunk, the criminals, and the unemployed. These parasites are unwilling or unable to adapt to the responsibilities of a new future society. Simply put, they consume more of society's resources than they produce.

Our society is completely indifferent to the thousands who are unable to support even themselves, yet at the same time, these ungrateful arrogances are demanding more rights from the state. The cost of living for this ballast group is actually coming up to us. We need youth with a hardened heart, for only such a generation will survive in the coming battle between nations. The current course of action does not give the strong what naturally belongs to them. They will get only with obligations and taxes. Rights have not been distributed sustainably, only the weak are favored—only the degenerate benefit from social care. Our legislation promotes the growth of the weak and oppresses the strong. The Christian doctrine of equality for all people is a fundamental mistake. The Christian churches are the main culprit for the current trend, for by helping this human rubbish group, they have only weakened our nation. They are cruel to healthy and strong people. Mankind can only progress toward perfection through a stronger right manifested in battles. That is, only the fittest people are allowed to survive. Our children must be taught that life is a constant struggle for the right to live. Survival is not a matter of course. It must be earned. The struggle is the law of nature and the mechanism of development!

Since the offspring inherit the traits acquired by man during his lifetime, it would be foolish to allow the weak-talented to multiply. They need to be sterilized. All forms of gratuitous subsidies provided by society must be abolished. They only distort the structure of society by allowing the non-viable to survive and thus prevent the inherent phasing out. My idea is to transfer the struggle which happens in nature for the right to exist into our society. It means a permanent change in social structures. How will Britain then change? So that we do not build our future on mere conjecture, now is the time to do something about it. I will give the floor all of you. Now everyone can speak freely. Has anyone questions or suggestions?"

"Thanks for the introduction, Edmond. I have a couple of critical questions for you. Why should we voluntarily provide poor living conditions for any section of the population? Isn't that an unnecessary risk to society peace?"

"Because they would not multiply too much. Secondly, this must be done precisely because of society peace—the next question."

"What will happen to the productivity of factories if the working population lives in poor conditions? Aren't you afraid of running out of labor?"

"That's not a problem. There will be no shortage of labor, rather the exact opposite. They are already now breeding like rats!"

"What if there are political movements that seek to equalize different sections of society?"

"I don't think that's possible. That is against all prevailing laws of nature. Our society will never tolerate such movements."

"I think this whole topic is completely outrageous!"

"Who are you?"

"My name is William Booth. I am involved in charity work. I think your thoughts are sadistically ill. On what sciences, evidence or social order are your arguments based on?"

"Who invited you here? You don't have to be here! You can leave here immediately. In any case, we will achieve our goal, either with you or without you. There is no need for gentle fools here. Get out of here!"

"I'm leaving gladly. Goodbye."

"Were there any others? Good, let's move on. There is another thing to keep in mind, and that is food. Who has enough of it, and for how long? In his book, economist Thomas Malthus writes about population growth in a geometric series. It can be expressed in numbers as follows: 2, 4, 8, 16, and so on. That is, the population thus doubles, while food production increases in an arithmetic series, like in numbers 1, 2, 3, 4, 5, and so on.

This inherently results in a battle for food that the stronger wins. We can also call this development a natural selection. What is the population of our country that the state can feed? 20, 30, or 50 million? I am not going to present any of the figures here because it is not the number of people that matters but their quality. Our task is to define what kind and what level of people live in our country. So, what are the metrics by which people are measured? Probably racial purebreds, health, intelligence, productivity, and other things that benefit the community."

"Edmond! Sorry for the interruption, but you should get involved in politics. There could be a lot of support for your ideas."

"Why would I join in that kind of pathetic clowning? In that case, these progressive ideas would be the merchandise of just one political movement. Now they are available to everyone. People are inherently so envious of each other that they can't admit a good idea for good if it's invented by someone else. There is no reason to limit this ideology to the use of a single political movement. Let's talk about back our subject. In addition to all this, we must also be able to be questioning the sanctity of human life because only then will we be able to justify these necessary actions.

Christians have lied to us for centuries about the uniqueness, irreplaceability, and holiness of human life. Nature tells us something completely different. Human life is not sacred, and the lives of different people are not as valuable. There are more valuable people, less valuable people, and completely worthless beings. Man's achievements show them worth. People are born unequal, live unequally, and die unequally! Given these facts, it would be madness to let everyone multiply. Society must clearly define in law who is allowed to reproduce and what are the criteria for reproduction. Another thing that comes to our attention is the education of children. Should education for all children be guaranteed in the future? I don't think so."

"Why not? I think it is better that we have literate people."

"It is even better if a certain part of the population is born into poverty and ignorance. From them, we get brisk workers in our factories and sacrificing soldiers in our army. What about if everyone is in the leading position and starting to imagine being unique? Someone must do some dirty work. Does anyone have any questions to add to our topic? If not, we are slowly starting to conclude for tonight.

Finally, the most important thing I want to say is that each of us has a responsibility to shape the soil of human minds in favor of our ideology wherever we influence. We need to be present at every level of society to influence decision-makers. I am giving all of you a memo at this meeting which you are free to use. I thank you all for participating, and I wish you a good workday tomorrow."

I was watching apathetically bored from the edge of the ship into the distant horizon when we were sailing on the Pacific Ocean. We were surrounded only by a mere foamy blue sea for the unseen. In it, as I swayed against the edge, memories of my childhood jumped to my mind when I moved a lot in the woods. This ocean landscape was completely different from that of the forest landscape. The forest is full of life, but what about the sea? In the heart of nature, I really feel alive. In the forest, I felt like I was part of some big supernatural entity. As I have explored nature, I have experienced the happiest and most instructive moments in my life. Nature is unforgivable there. Every living being must earn the right to its life. As a child, I was shocked when I first saw a predator catching its prey for food. Back then, I still didn't realize those events were an integral part of the life cycle.

I started to get bored when there was nothing meaningful things to do. I had already read Grant's books many times. The savages we brought with us had been handed over, so they were no longer entertaining me. With them, I felt smart. The good thing about this was that I wasn't sick with seasickness this time. Best of all, we sailed in a good tailwind all the way. I spent my time on the deck in a few clothes as a result of sunlight burning my face and neck. My skin colour turned red and came off pieces at night. I got some skin cream fat from our doctor that I was rubbing on my sore skin. It only caused intense itching at night, so I couldn't sleep well. I figured we would soon bypass the Tahiti Islands if we maintained our course. I looked with my telescope at the distant horizon, finding a small island there. As we got closer to it, its lush vegetation enchanted me. We lowered the anchors in a nearby bay cove and paddled to the shore. Immediately we were greeted by the children of the natives, and they were followed by their parents. They were sincerely happy and kind. Their faces were softly round. As for clothes, they had some rags or skirts. The women's breasts were covered, unlike the other wild ones we had met before. None of them had tattoos on their bodies. They were the complete opposite of the wild tribes of South America. The men guided us to the apartment of missionary Williams.

Williams came to meet us in the yard of his apartment, inviting us into his modest house. He arranged a friendly welcome for us at his home, offering a refreshing juice made from fruit. I had an interesting conversation with him. I asked Williams if the native people had always been equally friendly. He stated that not at all. William said he came here more than thirty years ago and learned the language of the native people. At that time, this island was like a home for demonic spirits. They lived naked, and they publicly engaged in all sorts of sexual distortions, homosexuality, pedophilia, and incest. They solved their problems violently. In war or famine times, they ate each other. Shocked, I listened to his narration. Williams told his case sincerely, looking gently straight into my eyes all the time. I continued our discussion by asking if he was not afraid of death while living alone here. He said he was prepared for martyrdom. I think that kind of talk was silly idealism. As if to prove his recent comment, he said he was in danger of death many times, but as if by a miracle, he had been saved. Williams saw it as God's protection. He said he had preached to them from the Bible the law and the gospel for so long that gradually some of them became believing Christians. He taught them to read and acted as a self-taught doctor whenever he could. Over the years, he patiently civilized them.

My opinion was he wasted his life on an island like this. Williams disagreed sharply. In his view, the same gospel he had heard at an early age also belonged to these tribes. According to Williams, only the Bible provided man with moral guidance for life. That is how we British had lived like animals before Christianity was brought to us. For my part, I told him of my own faith in man's inherent human goodness, reason, and morality. He laughed sarcastically, saying that he himself believed in human goodness in younghood until he realized he did not see that goodness anywhere. Even though we disagreed on some things, I still greatly appreciated this honest man.

On the day of departure, we went to wash ourselves in a small pond, and at the same time, we also washed some of our clothes. Tahitian children were playing on the beach. They came to us and sang us some local songs. We didn't understand a word about it, but we all were glad. As we left the island, they came to say goodbye to us under Pastor Williams. Older native people recited poems written to us in dialect English. So, we headed and relaxed towards New Zealand. A gust of strong wind made it difficult for us to anchor in the port of Auckland, but we still got there safely. I met a local priest at the city bank.

His name was John Spong, and he was already a third-generation priest in his family. As a man, he seemed willing to compromise, fearful, and weak-minded. At last, I met a man who was mentally below me. I felt contempt for him right from the start. This Spong was of the opposite character compared then Williams. He promised to leave as a guide for us as we explored the nearby village where he lived. My shock was immense when we got to the village. Clearly, Spong's humanist philosophy had not borne good fruit. These natives were called Aboriginal, and they looked awfully ugly. Their facial features were almost like those of monkeys. I realized these ape-men might be one of the missing links between man and monkey-like Grant had told. By their conduct, yes, they would have deserved that honor. The male population of the village seemed to be drunk on self-made booze during that time we spent in the village. And it wasn't the worst matter in their history. Before the arrival of Brits, these too had been cannibals. Spong said the first missionary ended up in the mouths of these ancestors. We toured the village, exploring the homes of the natives. These were in shockingly poor condition. We talked to an old man while Spong was our interpreter. He had a nose with really ugly, big nostrils. His round face looked very annoying. This almost toothless old man told us about a time when there were no Europeans here yet.

He showed us the pagan statues of the gods of nature of his own people, to whom they had even sacrificed their own children during periods of loss. Famine times, they had killed the old women and eaten them. It was reportedly wiser to kill the elderly than dogs. The dogs were able to help with the hunt, but the old women were of no use to anyone. The buttocks were considered by this Aboriginal elder to be the most delicious part of the human body. I didn't bother to tell all his stories in more detail because they were so sick. The most annoying thing about him was that viciously loud laughter with which he spiced up his disgusting stuff. I liked the idea shoot that sick bastard, and I shared my opinion with the skipper. He said with a smile that he thought the same. Spong was clearly ashamed of this situation. According to him, the situation was better in another village. I was disappointed with what I saw. Williams 'claim of man's inherent charm to evil seemed, at least in part, true. Before we left, we went to a church led by Spong to listen to his speech. The church was almost empty. I had eaten well, so I fell asleep on the bench during his childish speech. Afterwards, I wondered how someone could talk in such a boring way on a topic that could have gotten a lot more out of it. If Professor Henslow had met this Pastor Spong, he would probably have considered Spong only as a liberal bread priest in office.

At the end of the ceremony, we said goodbye to Spong and set sail for our ship. We hurriedly continued our journey towards Sydney, Australia. I was relieved to leave the pier. When the harbour disappeared onto the horizon, I went to the cabin and uncorked the drink again in honor of our departure.

In Australia, artist Conrad decided to stay in Sydney. I helped him carry the goods to the nearest inn, where he rented a small cozy room for a couple of days. There, Conrad offered me a whiskey as a farewell gift during our conversation. He wanted to know about my future plans. I replied in surprise that I had no definite plans beyond this trip. He asked about my university studies again. For some reason, it was like an obsession for him. I decided to answer with the truth. I think he deserved it, and anyway, it didn't matter what he thought of me. I spoke openly about a letter I received from my father telling me to come home as soon as possible.

"Was the letter related to your medical studies?" Conrad asked.

"Yes, I guessed from the content of the letter that my father had received clarity about my poor academic success. I still remember that feeling of fear from my father's upcoming reaction. I waited with fear to meet him. My father was not at the station.

I met him until I arrived home. I looked him in the eye as we shook hands. My father was like ice. During the meal, we discussed my brother's successful studies. We then went to his office to discuss."

"What did he want to talk about?"

"About my totally failed medical studies. He told me to sit on the bench of his study. He himself sat behind his desk diagonally towards me with his arms crossing on his large chest. My father stared at me with a critical gaze for a long time without saying a word. I sat in a chair watching along the walls. I thought he would be driving me out of his house. My father started by asking, "Well, my son, how have your medical studies gone?" There was a pity look in his eyes. I realized I was in a trap, so I shared a few reasons why my studies didn't succeed."

"How did he react to your explanations?"

"My father interrupted my defense, saying sharply that he did not want to hear excuses, and continuing in the same breath with an equally determined voice, he said that he had been in correspondence with some professor. I remember that feeling very well. When my heart was pounding, I tried to guess what they had written about me.

"What had they decided for you?"

"Like lightning from a bright sky, my father suggested that I finish my studies in medicine."

"What did you answer him?"

"Nothing, because I felt like somebody had beat on my head with a tree. I was ashamed of myself for not being to succeed, but at the same time, I was also relieved that I no longer had to continue my studies."

"How did he comment on your silence?"

"Not in any way. I guess he was extremely disappointed, but my dad knew how to hide his feelings for me. His earnest wish had always been that I would have continued in his profession as a physician." I said, looking at the bottom of the empty whiskey glass.

"How did your conversation continue?"

"Before I dared to ask my father anything, he had already informed me into Christ College Cambridge to study theology. It doesn't even be part of the prestigious University of Cambridge but a separate Christian boarding school."

"Why did your father want you to study theology?" Conrad asked in amazement.

"He wanted me to become a deacon of the Anglican Church because he thought that was the best way to make sure I didn't become a layabout. The most outrageous thing about the whole thing was that at that time, I was discovering my true calling as a naturalist, and that is why my father's order to start studying as a deacon seemed so frustrating!"

"Have you ever believed in God?"

"As a young man, I still believed in my own way, but I did not experience any call to the position of deacon." I answered succinctly.

"Did you tell your father?"

"Of course, I said many times, but he always replied angrily that it takes no faith in God. It is just a post like any other state official. According to my father, I could be in a small village as a respected church worker to practice charity and help the poor. It would reportedly be an honourable work, and in that position, too, I could study the nature created by the Creator. This is how my father justified his decision. Can you imagine? Think how boring life would be like that! Now I can laugh about it." I looked at Conrad, who couldn't be without laughing. After laughing his time, he continued.

"Apparently, your father doesn't believe in God?"

"Not at all! He considers himself a humanist free thinker. Now you know how I had to study to deacon in Cambridge."

Conrad put his glass on the table and looked at me with a pity look on his face. Before he had time to ask anything, I told him I didn't need anyone's pity. I'm going to make it in this life without a college degree. Conrad said he believed it, but still, he continued his curiosities.

"Tell me what your life was like in Cambridge?"

"At first, I thought my life would become even more boring with the studies of a deacon, but the truth was everything else. In Cambridge, I found completely new sides of myself that I didn't even know existed. That's when my social life began. I threw myself into it with full sips. I wanted more stimulation to grow apart from my patronizing father. Free time in the evenings was the only moment when I felt alive."

"What did you do in the evenings?"

"I went to the pub almost every night, and there I met new people with whom I learned to smoke. I felt manly as I smoked with my new pipe. Light English beer and tobacco are the best combinations I can imagine."

"How did you finance your life? Did you work while studying?"

"I did not want to use my free time to work like other students, although they had no choice. I financed my expenses with money given by my father, which I wasted in a few months. I wrote a letter to my father begging him to ask for more money." I said with a laugh.

"What did he answer? Did he send money for you?" Conrad asked with an astonished look on his face.

"Yes, he sent, albeit with a letter of condemnation. My father wrote that he was appalled by my lifestyle. He couldn't comprehend how I dared to waste hundreds of pounds of money in about a short time."

"If you were once there on the going all the time, how did you cope with the teachers?"

"Not at all the better than in Edinburgh. The principal sent letters of complaint to my father regarding my behavior at school. In those letters, he complained that I often disturbed the lessons. According to complaints from the dormitory, I frightened people by shooting crows flying past my apartment window with a drunken shotgun in the evenings. Their gossiping testified to me that most of the teachers were mere devils in society. It is a pathetic job." I said in a contemptuous voice.

"Well, did you shoot crows there?"

"Every now and then, but it shouldn't have bothered anyone."

"Did you graduate from there as a deacon?"

"Yes, but I could hardly have gotten through it without Professor Henslow's help. Although I read that final exam in earnest, I still received only avoidable grades in other subjects, except for a history of Christianity that was commendable. Despite the intense reading, my average was the second worst in the final exam." I stated succinctly.

I decided to change the topic of discussion to Conrad's own plans for the future. He was going to support himself by painting and doing all sorts of dumbbell chores.

I did not comment on his plans in any way, but we shook hands and wished each other good luck, and I said goodbye to him. I walked out of the inn to the bank to inquire about my possible father had sent about money order. My heart pounded almost in my throat when I was thinking about my sister's benevolence. Would she have told my father about my need for money, succeeding in making soften his heart? When the clerk came with a small package, I felt really relieved. I hurried around the bustling corner to open the package. I excitedly tore the package open. I took the banknotes in my hand to count the money. It had almost four hundred pounds. I rejoiced in my mind as I counted the money. With this money, I will survive for a long time. I quickly wrote a letter to Catherine, thanking her from the bottom of my heart for the help I had received from her. I promised a thousand times to reimburse her for all her efforts on my behalf as I arrived back home. I left with a light mind to explore Sydney in more detail. I was pleasantly surprised by the cleanliness of the city. There were a lot of new, fine houses in the city center, built in the Britanian style. It made me feel at home. I had thought Australians were people of inferior social background, as the majority of the population consisted of the descendants of former prisoners.

In fact, these people were easy to approach because they lacked the vanity that again plagues us aristocratic Englishmen. It seemed that the Australians were probably good fellows to the drinking party. After six beers, I returned to the ship in the evening, where the skipper told me of his plans to paint the ship. In the meantime, I would have the opportunity to take a little hunting trip inland. With the money my father received, I hired two Christian-converted Aboriginal servants to take care of my belongings during the trip. For the same price, I also got a horse for myself and donkeys for my servants. I was far wise when I initially paid only half of the agreed amount. The rest maybe I will pay when we get back. So, we went on horseback towards the hinterland. The terrain was very rugged, almost desert type, and almost woodless. I had long felt a passionate desire to get hunting. I felt an immense need to shoot some animals. Throughout my life, I have received great satisfaction from handling weapons. It has that feeling of power and freedom that no other thing can produce for me. We rode for about ten miles and spent the night on a farm run by former penitentiary prisoners. They told me here live ostriches, which are tall but flightless birds. I really wanted to see one and would love to shoot one at least. As we rode on the prairie, we saw the first ostriches.

These got scared of us, running away at such a rapid pace that I couldn't catch them with my horse, no matter how I beat it with my whip. For a moment, I thought I had got a weak old horse, but my servant explained that the ostriches were faster than the horses. My plan was to get close to the ostrich with my horse, so I could shoot by shotgun to its little head. After this plan failed, I had to resort to a contingency plan where I thought of sneaking close to the ostrich. I took a gun, and we slowly rode closer to an ostrich. I told to servants to be waiting for a little further distance. I quietly moved closer to the ostrich. I slowly got up to the half-knee position and took the ostrich in my sights. Before I had time to aim precisely at it, I realized the ostrich had noticed me. It started running towards me at a wild pace. I loaded my gun in panic, aiming quickly from my hip, but I shot past. I didn't have time to reload, so I threw my shotgun to my back and started running towards my horse. The ostrich reached me just as I was approaching my horse and kicked me with a hard force directly to my ass. I flew to my face next to the horse. My butt hurt so terribly. I was ashamed and furious. Despite the pain, I got up to reload my gun. I aimed at the ostrich again with trembling hands, but again I shot past. I cursed my bad luck in my mind. I glanced at my servants and found them laughing at me.

I pointed my gun at them and warned furiously not to laugh at me. I wondered for myself what went wrong in a recent situation. A second shotgun should have been given to that other aboriginal monkeyface for safety. Why didn't that hell ostrich escape from me? I swore in my mind not to return to the ship until I had shot at least one ostrich. Wise from the damage, this time, I gave my shotgun to one of the servants. This black wild brazenly claimed to be a good shooter. Not long after, we already saw another ostrich. I was less than a hundred yards away from it. I was still sitting on the horse's back, yet in my immense lust for revenge, I decided to shoot it right away, but again I shot past. I started to doubt the functionality of my shotgun. Managing my bad luck, the aboriginal standing next to me was shot by a shotgun, emptying both barrels and hitting the ostrich's thick middle body. The ostrich dropped dead to its side. I was envious of the aboriginal after he shot the ostrich. I grabbed my shotgun from his hand and threw it on my back. I walked over to my horse, thinking of my bad luck. Hell, how on earth could I be a failure in hunting? We wouldn't have time to hunt longer today as the evening began to get dark. We had to make a big bonfire and camp before night. Aboriginals should make the bird a tasty roast. I was angry with myself when I didn't take the liquor with me. Now it would have been of use.

I could have drowned my frustration with heavy hops. We ate quietly in the darkness of the evening and went to sleep after that. With a stomach full of good ostrich meat, I began to calm down. I calmed myself to sleep by saying I got the one ostrich that I wanted to shoot. In the morning, we continued forward inland and soon arrived in a small, ruined desert village. It had been inhabited by Aboriginals. Only the foundations remained of the huts in which they had lived. My servants did not know the reason why the village was deserted. As we walked into the open area, the Aboriginals stopped and bowed their heads. I asked the reason for such behavior. They said this area is a cemetery. At the same time, I got a great idea. From here, I would get bones for Grant and the theory he developed. I picked up a shovel from the horse's back and immediately started digging the ground as the wild stared in amazement at my digging. After digging dry land for four feet, I found the first well-preserved bones. It had the whole skeleton. I took the skull bone and tibia into my sack. I would clean those in England properly with water. I didn't feel there was anything wrong with this. I was a scientist studying nature, and human bones are an integral part of it. This is how I got my revenge for these wild ones. They thought they could laugh at my face because of my bad hunting luck. One of them dared to call me a grave robber.

I silenced him quickly, glaring angrily. I was a little disappointed when there were no treasures in the grave. Apparently, these poor creatures could not afford to decorate their deceased. After finishing my examination of the tomb, I decided to turn back to the coast. I was pleased to note that the objectives of this expedition had been met. We went for a horse ride towards the coast. The Aboriginals with their donkeys came after me, keeping their distance from me. I told them I was paying them to obey me unconditionally and not to question my policies. I promised them to treat the remains of the corpses with respect and to hold a beautiful Christian funeral for them in England. Bullshit, my grandfather Erasmus Darwin, too, as a young man, had dug a fresh Tasmanian corpse out of the ground and put it on display in a school embalmed. Now I had achieved at the same level as him as a scientist. I had never seen a real human skull before. How much does such an aboriginal skull differ from the skull of a normal European person? You would think there are clear differences in it because there is such a huge difference between a white and wild man in intelligence alone. This was a rather good trip, after all. Gradually, I began to get over the humiliation that that damn ostrich caused me. In Sydney, I paid a fraction of my promised salary to the servants, after which I sent them with my threats on their away.

In the harbour, I saw our ship, which was already almost completely painted. The end result looked handsome. I went to report to the skipper, which was in full swing in renovation work. FitzRoy treated his ship like his own son. Skipper was shaken as I introduced him to the Aboriginal skull. He said it would bring me bad luck. I did not comment on his opinion but laughed at his superstition. I thought it would have been best if I had gotten a freshly dead body in my hands. Then it could have been filled like an animal and put in a glass display case in England. Before leaving the mainland of Australia behind for good, we briefly visited the small island of Tasmania below.

Chapter 13: The last Tasmanian

The island of Tasmania seemed boring, a dead place. I hoped we wouldn't stay here long. In the evening we went with the group to the beach to eat. We lit a bonfire from trees drifting to the beach while the sun simultaneously sank quickly to its lands. As we sat all around, we were joined by a few Aboriginals who entertained us with their pagan dance. I wasn't interested in their rituals. I focused on sipping wine in a gentle breeze. Fire clearly meant something supernatural to them. Here was another big difference between the wild and the normal human. A few of our drunken sailors joined in their dance in it while singing lewd their songs. As I watched that, memories of Tierra del Fuego came to my mind. I had almost forgotten that scary night. In the ascending hops, I excitedly shared my memory of that evening with the skipper. This time he listened intently. He considered my participation in that witchcraft ritual a really bad thing. I tried to beautify what had happened, but FitzRoy remained in his position. After we argued for a while, the skipper took an object from his pocket, exposing it to size against the flames.

"Do you know what this is?" He growled in his rough voice.

"Not a clue," I answered indifferently.

"This is the Order of the British Navy awarded to me by the King. Our Wilhelm IV! King of the Sailors!" Skipper roared with the power of hops.

I listened for a while to the skipper's ventilation, which aroused my interest in this object.

"Show me a little more detail. When did you get this, and on what merits?"

"It was awarded to me on the merits of this expedition and handed over in Australia while you were there on an ostrich hunting trip. The governor himself attached it to my chest." Skipper said proudly.

"Congratulations!" I said enviously.

I was sure I had earned at least a similar medal for my achievements on this trip.

"Thanks, Charlie. Although this does not mean anything, but this makes the man's mind so proud." Skipper said flatly.

After talking the whole evening, we went to the ship to sleep after midnight. In our cabin room, I asked the skipper to go with me tomorrow for a little trip inland. He muttered something as a sign of consent. When skipper survived the worst hangover, we went on a horse ride. I felt great because I drank only a few cups of wine yesterday. I took my shovel, rifle, and sack with me. I did not tell the skipper that I intended to dig more bones of the Tasmanians who died from the graves, as he might begin to moralize my research work. Should I have gone alone? I don't know. I just wanted to include someone higher than myself so that I would get legitimacy for my industry. For security reasons alone, it always makes more sense to move in these wildlife areas with a group of more armed men than alone. Besides, it was much more comfortable to move with a compatriot than with an aboriginal. I was completely hooked on the idea of these skulls of dead wild people. I wanted to know what Grant would say about those. We rode directly to the village cemetery. As the evening was already getting dark, I started digging at the first mound. A skipper asked what for I had a reason to dig as if he hadn't figured it out. I told him in a cynical voice, doing scientific work for Professor Grant, who in turn represents the royal house, so we are in the fatherland business. We need research material for our work to obtain evidence to support our theories and be credible in other researchers' eyes. We intended to put a bone in the throat of critics. I asked the skipper to take care of the horses and keep a watch so no one could surprise us. I was excited to strike the shovel into the soft sandy ground. After digging for a while, I found the first bones. They were small in size, apparently child's bones. Well, it didn't matter. The main thing is that the material was found. For what disease was this damn cursed creature dead too?

After I threw the bones in my sack, I went to dig the adjacent grave. In it, as I dug open another grave, I humorously thought of one career of my future options as a funeral contractor's job if my scientific career didn't take success. I continued to dig carefully so I wouldn't just accidentally break the bones. I shoveled the pit deeper and occasionally wiped the sweat off my face. I threw the shovel to the ground and decided to rest a bit. My sweaty shirt was glued to my back. This was a heavy chore for a man like me who refused physical labor work. I took a deep breath and continued digging. The howl of coyotes and the occasional scream of birds accompanied my toil. Soon my shovel hit something, and I threw the shovel to the edge of the grave. I cleaned the bottom of a pit with my hands and noticed there was some dark cloth in it. It was a sack with a body, I guess. I took the knife from my belt to cut open the sack with it. Then I tear the edges wide apart. The cloth bag contained the body of a big adult man, which was almost completely rotten. I watched the upper body in the twilight. The skull was still attached to the body with a few pieces of meat. I grabbed my shovel from the grave edge and tapped with a sharp edge across the cervical vertebra. I took the skull, cleared the soil, and got up from the grave. I lifted the skull to the upper level of my eyes and watched its empty eye sockets against the darkening horizon.

After admiring it, I gently put it in the sack. Was this the skull of a European man? It will be found out in time in England. Now we would have enough research material for Grant. After shoveling the soil back into the empty graves, I shouted to the skipper that we would head back to the beach. We would get there before dark. The skipper was gloomily quiet during our arrival. He thought I had acted wrong. Skipper said he understood our scientific work but disturbing the dead would not be any good. I asked his opinion on how he could justify slavery if he once did not tolerate the examination of dead bones. Skipper thought the slave could affect their own life. The dead instead did not. I was disagree cause it doesn't matter what happens to the bones of the dead— only life matters. We could not reach a consensus on the matter, so I let him keep his superstitious opinions. As I rode the horse, I chuckled out loud to myself. I was excited. I was rejoicing in my mind. I did it again and didn't feel any regrets. I was sure that the scientific world would appreciate the sacrifices I made. As we arrived at the harbour, I saw myself in my fantasies as a respected scientist studying the origins of humanity. It felt really tempting to think of all the splendour in it. At last, I would get my revenge on my enemies. The sweetest revenge felt when I thought of Fanny. I had almost forgotten her already.

In the future, it would be humiliating for Fanny to realize that her politician husband is a mere loser compared to me.

From Tasmania, we continued our journey west along the south coast of Australia. Soon we would be sailing on the Indian Ocean. I decided not to mail these bones to England, as they would not have arrived any sooner. Moreover, it would have been embarrassing to tell the contents of the package in the mail. Time passed slowly on board as the days were completely boring. Skipper suggested I could work. I could reportedly do some simple work for the crew. However, I was not enthusiastic about it because I would not be paid any compensation for it. Frustrated with boredom, I used to spend my time in the cabin, lazing around or walking snobby way on the deck back and forth. I woke up at night with a nightmarish realization of how my life flowed insignificantly past without being able to influence it in any way. I lay on the bed, looking into the dark emptiness, realizing I was twenty-five and had not gotten any decent degrees yet let alone my own family. Where had I wasted my youth? What will happen if my father no longer gives me money after this trip? Who will help me then? Will I meet that Israfil nymph again? My head was full of all sorts of absurd questions and fears.

Was I going crazy? I took a deep breath, trying to fund myself. I thought logically that I had a much better chance of succeeding in this life than most British men did. Still, I hadn't even managed to get myself a tolerable girlfriend. The more I thought about these things, the more I panicked. It felt like the walls of the ship had fallen on me. I immediately wanted to get off this hellish ship. I had been a prisoner here for many years! I need to reap some benefits from this futile journey! Grant is forced to compose a book about my illogical, insanely shabby diary entries! I no longer longed for even worldly glory, but I would be grateful for it already, as long as I maintained the remnants of my mental health. As I pondered these cold facts of my life, I was once again overwhelmed by an immense craving for boozing alcohol. I wanted to escape my inability to the deceptively warm charm of rising hops brought by alcohol. I set out to through my stuff in a dark room. I walked next to the captain's bed and knocked on his back.

"Wake up, skipper! When do we get home?"

"What?" He asked in a sleepy, grumpy voice.

"When do we arrive in England?" I yelled at him.

"What is the emergency you have?"

"I want out of this ship. I feel like I'm going crazy here."

"Does your conscience accuse you?"

"It's not, but my life will be wasted here." I replied with a sigh.

"We will be in our home port in less than a year. Even then, only if there won't be any problems. You are confused about your grave robbery expeditions and therefore receive a justifiable punishment from God. Shut up and go to your bed or tell the soldiers to lock you in the closet again!" He roared.

Depressed, I went to my bed to lie down, thinking about my future in fear. For the first time in my life, I was afraid of it. The confidence I experienced on the island of Tasmania was gone. I was thinking about the life of my relatives at home. Spring was now at its most beautiful in England. I didn't fall asleep while listening to the skipper's snoring, so I got out of bed and started by candlelight, writing my events in Tasmania in my notebook. As I wrote, my mind calmed down. I still wrote as the skipper got up. I apologized to him for my nightly stupidity. I tried pretending to laugh, to turn it into a comedy, explaining that I really didn't understand what was going on with me. Skipper didn't laugh at my explanation, but instead he looked at me calmly straight into my eyes, to ask if everything was truly fine. I replied, pretending, laughing, that everything was truly fine now. However, for the sake of certainty, he advised going to the doctor's office.

When he left our room, he told me to reduce my drinking. Liquor, he says, confuses even the head of a healthy man. I yelled after him that I hadn't drunk myself too drunk for many days. He no longer answered but closed the door. I sat on my bed and decided to start meditating again. When I finished it, I got on deck to watch the seemingly endless bluish sea around us. From where had so much water come to the earth? Without getting an answer to my question, I continued walking towards the stern of the ship. At the same time, with a sideways eye, I saw the cleaner Dawkins carrying buckets of faeces to empty them. I walked over to the skipper without looking at Dawkins. The skipper would be a valuable enough person whom to talk to. We advanced in a strong tailwind and were ahead of our schedule. He thought we were approaching Cocos Islands. FitzRoy decided to get around one of these islands. I protested to him, saying I wanted to go to Africa quickly. Skipper did not respond to my childish requests anymore but, in turn, looked at the islands with his telescope. He told me in a comforting tone how beautiful the nature of the islands was. His narration still piqued my interest, so I asked him to borrow a telescope for a little while for me. The beaches were covered in white sand, and the coconut palms swayed lightly in the gentle breeze. As I watched that beautiful view, I felt my mind calm down.

How good it felt to see the land after so many weeks of staring at the sea. As I watched the island, I began to consider its birth. How old were these islands? How were these born in the middle of the ocean? Was it caused by an earthquake? If there were animals, how had they come there? I felt like I ended up tired of all this research. My mood swung back and forth between enthusiasm and melancholic depression. I just wanted to get home quickly. As we left the islands behind, I also realized the fact that there really is no romantic in working on the sea. It is only hard and ungrateful work.

We sailed thousands of miles in the Indian Ocean towards the islands of Madagascar. Until then, there would again be only the ocean in my sight. I sank back into the hold to kill time by sipping my liquors. There, I wondered what I had achieved on this trip. What else could I find? Would these my findings be of any use? Would anyone be interested in these? Was this trip of any use to me at all? What would I do next? How can I move out of my childhood home? Does Grant need me anymore after this trip? Frustrated with my uncertain future, I continued tasting gin. However, in the triumphant intoxication of ascending hops, I found that I had grown from a boy to a man during this time. I had seen all sorts of things.

It cultivates character when you see the mass slaughter of hundreds of people happening before your eyes. I was no longer a bona fide fool. Instead, I began to understand how this world works. All I have to develop plans for myself with a view to my future. We passed the island of Madagascar, continuing towards the tip of South Africa. The crew was afraid in advance of the storm that would await us there. Captain comforted them by saying that, at worst, there would be no storm here compared to Cape Horn. Once it has been cleared, we will survive here as well. I could no longer meditate in the cabin, but I tried to spend most of the time on the deck of the ship in the fresh weather, keeping company with the skipper and first officer cause that's why he had asked me for this trip. Now I could already laugh in my mind at Grant's plot to get me on this ship. He probably knew exactly the difficulties of this trip all the time, which is why he dropped out on this trip. Apparently, I had been the dumbest of all his candidates and the only one who agreed to be part of this unpaid trip. All in all, I had no other tolerable options in my life than to go on this exploration trip. While watching on the deck of it, I didn't realize at all that my idleness was causing deep irritation in the crew. Every now and then, I heard embarrassing comments from the crew about my usefulness.

I didn't pay attention to them until, through some unfortunate coincidences, I got into a fight with the cleaner Dawkins. On the other hand, it was only a matter of time because we both hated each other so much. The dispute ultimately began with a ridiculously small matter, but due to circumstances, it grew unreasonably large. It started when I used my microscope to look at a dead fish on the top deck of a ship. I was sitting in a chair, and I had lifted another chair as a table for my microscope. I was overwhelmed by a deep passionate interest in studying the structure of fish cartilage. At the same time, behind my back, Dawkins was cleaning the deck of the ship. He was scrubbed on the floor with fanatical rage and his back towards me. I was just researching the inside of the fish when Dawkins collided with his back on my back. In the same second, I hit my eye on the edge of the microscope, pushing it to the floor. The largest eyepiece in the microscope shattered as it dropped on the deck, and I, for my part, fell on my face on the deck. I still don't know today whether it was pure damage or a protest against my laziness, but I lost my temper completely. I got up in my rage and glanced behind me. I saw how Dawkins slowly turned around with a surprised look on his face. I immediately kicked him in the leg. As he held his leg, I pushed him to his shoulder. The old man faltered a little, and I kicked him straight to his ass.

Then I poured his mop bucket. I shouted at Dawkins, telling him to go to hell with his mop to disrupt my work. It was a bad mistake because, at the same time, a terrible strong crew member who was his old friend from the previous trip came to the scene. This blond Viking did not say a word but hit me straight in the face with his big fist. It was such a hard straight punch that I flew from the force of the blow to my back on the floor and hit my head to the floor. He lifted me up from my clothes like a glove while angrily looking into my eyes with her little ice blue eyes. Those eyes were unnaturally deep beneath the gloomy corners. He stared straight, mercilessly deep into my soul with those lifeless eyes. He had waved me like a rag doll, he said viciously between his teeth. "Never again challenge a dispute with the crew of this ship." His angular face was filled with pent-up anger, bitterness, and the brutality which had resulted from a hard life. I hadn't feared as much in my whole life. I thought he was going to kill me in that place. I immediately realized that now it was worth believing what this big man said. I had no assume to rely on my acquaintance with the captain, for I knew he would always stand by his crew. I muttered from the frontiers of consciousness that I would never again interfere with their work. He then dropped me on the floor and left the scene. I lay on my back on the deck of the ship. I saw stars in my eyes, and I felt dizzy.

The blood tasted in my mouth. I got up, half to sit. I spat blood on the deck, and I instinctively touched my teeth with my tongue. These felted to be in place. My wandering gaze found Dawkins on the deck. There was a nasty mischievous grin on his face. In my shame, I took my microscope from the floor with trembling hands and went quietly into the cabin room to lick my wounds. The left half of my face was completely numb. Fortunately, none of the teeth detached from the force of the stroke. Luckily his fist hit my chin so low that I didn't get a black eye. That would have been embarrassing. Presenting the baron would have been a difficult eye in black. Among all that, I totally forgot the cane of fish there on the deck of the ship. I let it be there and decided, instead of taking a big cup of gin again. In it, while drinking, the skipper came into the cabin. He had heard of this of our little melee on the deck of the ship and blamed me for my conduct towards the crew. In slightly boozy hops, I told him of my own version of events, saying in a dramatic voice that I had been subjected to barbaric assault. Skipper said he heard a different version of events. I had reportedly started the fight by kicking the cleaner. In a way, it was true, but he had pushed me at first, causing my microscope to be gone broke.

"I don't want to argue about it anymore. However, the crew is paid, so they are above you on the scale.

You are just a companion whose job is to keep me in a good mood and not cause annoyance. You may be better off stopping the booze with it when it doesn't seem right for you at all. Keep yourself fit and think about your future. You still have a life to live after this journey. Pull yourself together, man!"

"I'm full to the brim of this ship, and I want to get home soon!" I shouted in a crying voice after him.

"You will get home, but you will never have anything to do in my ship under my command." He said calmly at the door. Having said that, he left back on the deck. I stayed in the cabin room, a piece in my throat. I felt humiliated. After we rounded the Cape of Good Hope, we arrived in Cape Town. There I wrote letters to Grant, Henslow, and Catherine. I briefly told Grant about the latest events. I also said he was right when he told me about the differences between the races. On this trip, I gained a lot of evidence for those things. I thanked him for quoting his books and promised to return them as soon as possible. I ended my letter by promising to come to visit him right away, as long as I first went home to meet my family. I wrote a letter of thanks to Henslow for all the spiritual support I felt I had received from him over the years. I apologized for not writing to him more often, but I would love to meet him after getting my life back on track. I wished all the best to his family.

In the end, I added my comment that I would never do Christian work. I wrote many thanks to Catherine for the invaluable help she had given me. Without her, I probably wouldn't have gotten as much money from my father as I got. I found myself writing letters in order of priority. Despite everything that happened, I valued Professor Grant the most of all people. Whatever his motives were in my, however, he helped me the most in my life. I went to town to take the letters to the post office. This city was one of the outpost fortresses of the British Global Empire. I wanted to meet local people to get clarity on their moods. I set off to walk slowly towards the city center. The local population, I hear, consisted mostly of African Negroes. With the migration, the British, Dutch, and Germans also moved there. Europeans had civilized and built this country. I talked to a few white men about the social situation in this country. One of them said that slavery was abolished some time ago. The Negroes had been guaranteed full civil rights, but this had not improved their social status, as they were unable to live the systematic life required to go to work. I told them I had come to the same conclusion. I was no longer emotionally worried about slavery. I had matured intellectually to understand the fact that slavery had its merits in society. Perhaps the Negroes were destined for slavery.

In slavery, at least, they didn't have to take responsibility for their own lives. I took a rickshaw ride to the outskirts of town. I saw a large white building that was fenced with a high iron fence. I asked the driver to stop. I got off the ride and asked him to wait for my return. I had no idea to ask him what this building was, but I went straight-headed to walk towards it. In front of the building was a large gate that was a little open. I decided to go in. In the courtyard, I saw two men who had a heated debate with each other. They wore similar bright orange clothes. Their conversation seemed interesting, so I decided to join their company.

"No creator is needed for the birth of the world! Everything is born out of explosive chaos! And life on Earth has come from space by alien beings. They have brought the necessary raw materials to the Earth." He had round glasses and a bushy grayish beard.

"No, everything has been born of Krishna Janmashtami. He has laid a great egg from which the ancestors of all living beings were born." Challenged by a young Indian man.

"That was the worst bullshit I've ever heard! Roaring bald, bearded man. Where had that hen's egg come from, and what about all the living things inside that hen's egg? Where are the evidence?"

"Can you ask the same question yourself? How could all life have arisen from chaos by itself?"

I listened in my time to this heated debate that didn't seem to lead to anything at all. Just as I gathered my courage to participate in the discussion, we were joined by eight men. They all wore white uniforms and wooden batons with their belts. Seeing these men, the chatters were in silence immediately. The men in white jackets grabbed them by the hands, starting to drag them one by one into the building. I looked at that action and found that it was better for me to walk towards the outer gate. One of these men in white jackets asked me my name and the reason for my visit. After introducing myself to him, I just said I had passed this place by chance. I wasn't specifically looking for anyone, and I didn't come to see anyone. The guard stared at me and told me to leave the yard immediately. To be sure, he escorted me to the gate. I asked the guard at the outer gate about the purpose of the building. The man looked at me like some idiot, saying this is a mental hospital. Having said that, he turned away, locked the gate, and walked inside the building. I was left stunned with my mouth open to look after him. Mental hospital! Had I listened to the insane people debate without noticing they were insane? Fortunately, my rickshaw driver had been waiting for me. I asked the driver to run the most direct way to the port.

Sitting there on a carriage ride, I wondered about the recent situation. Now it was already starting to amuse me. I laughed to myself in my mind. Maybe it's quite healthy at times to take things a little looser and learn to laugh at yourself as well. I said to myself that I don't have to always be so snobby. On the ship, the skipper asked me nervously where I had been. I told him over my shoulder that I was hanging around in the city. Instead, he told me good news, as we would continue our journey immediately to England. That was definitely good news! After several delays, we would finally be able to go home! This interval would be the longest leg of the entire trip. We would only stop once to replenish our stocks in Portugal and avoid barbaric savages. I spent our last stage primarily in my room exploring my collection of finds. There weren't many of them anymore, as I had mailed most of them to Grant in London. The ones I would take to my destination consisted of a few fossilized remains of animals that were probably already extinct. I had put the insects I found in a glass display case. The most interesting were the bones of the Tasmanians I dug. In particular, I measured an adult man's skull and tried to compare it to my own head in front of a mirror. I asked with fun the skipper if this Tasmanian wild had had a big enough nose to be in the captain's mind, a strong man in character.

He had told me at the beginning of our trip that he could determine a man's character based on his nose. Skipper remembered the reason for my allusion but did not comment on my humorous question in any way. He only said that I had lost my sanity because of the liquor. I reportedly should have let the dead be at peace. Those bones, he thought, should have been given to the pastor, who would have buried them in the blessed church cemetery. I didn't care about his comments but continued to examine the bones while writing down notes of my conclusions. On that side, I concluded that it is probably wise to try to stay within tolerable relations with the commander-in-chief during this voyage. FitzRoy has influence, and maybe if someone wants to interview him about this trip too, then it would be important to get a positive assessment of me. I would endure the hardships of this final journey biting my teeth like a man. When I get back to England, there will be new challenges ahead of me. I looked forward to meeting Grant with great anticipation. Hopefully, he can offer me some work on his "future science." I was a little worried about my future. I couldn't, and I wouldn't necessarily want to spin in the corners of my home as my father's nuisance indefinitely. How was my family? At least my siblings are already married. I had read that from Catherine's letters.

On top of all that, my brother had probably already in a prestigious job. I felt panicked as I realized my competitive situation against my better big brother. It was a race where I couldn't make it on my own. I moved my thoughts to our father. How can he? He must have continued to heal patients as before. Even though we didn't get along with each other, I still respected him. Because of the money my father borrowed, I was in great debt to him for the rest of my life. It was kind of paradoxical, however, that I didn't feel any feelings of love for my father. It had been years since my mother died, but I still missed her immensely. Especially after the revelation of that Israfil, I experienced a deep bond with her.

"Young men, welcome. My name is Edmond Grant, and I work as a professor of medicine here at the University of London. Please follow me. We go to the basement, where I store rare animal and plant finds. Please, wait until I find the key. Now I open the door, and you can see with your own eyes what I meant. All of you come after me and spread out around the table. It's a little dark here, but I think you understand what it's all about. These discoveries are made by my friend Charles Darwin. He is currently on an exploration trip, during which time they have made several significant scientific discoveries.

Probably, they will return to England soon. We could each take one of these dishes with us. Let's go to the upper floor class to take a closer look at these. It is brighter and more comfortable there. You two, take those glass showcases with insect collections, and you can take that box from that corner. It has the bones of already extinct animals. Take the remaining three big glass jars. Please, transport those glass jars with extreme care. From here, go up the stairs and then right. I'll follow you after I lock this door. The classroom is there on the first floor, just off the first door on the right. Just go inside. The door is open. Put these dishes on this big table. So, let's open this first box. Here you see the skull of an ancient herbivore. As a herbivore, it is identified by these flat teeth. I believe this to be the ancestor of current horse breeds. This species must have become extinct millions of years ago."

"Sorry for the interruption, Professor Grant. On what basis do you think it was the ancestor of horses, and based on what evidence did it die millions of years ago? Please, could you give any more precise definition of time?"

"Good questions, young man. I don't know exactly how old this is, but I think it's incredibly old because the bone material seems petrified.

Second, the shape of the skull indicates that this animal was very closely related to Equidae."

"Why should it be millions of years old?"

"Well, of course, it doesn't have to be so old, but it makes sense to think that such fossils don't form in a hundred years, but it takes a much longer time. Besides, there are no indications of such animals in history. Second, all scientific evidence suggests that the Earth is much older than assumed. The best examples are the geological discoveries of the soil made by Professor Lyell." Grant claimed.

"What are those findings?"

"I can't tell about them because there are only a fraction of the samples. In addition, they still require a lot of further research."

"Professor, could I ask what you aim for with your research?"

"Isn't that quite clear now? I am trying to find a more valid explanation for the birth of the Earth than what the Bible tells us. This study of ours is firmly based on the natural sciences and is, therefore, more valid than any model of religious explanation. There are too many unexplained things in the story of the Bible. I believe life is much more complicated than we can even imagine. It is because of that complexity that I think life has taken millions of years to develop."

Grant explained indignantly.

"How do you think the churches will react to your research?"

"We've been thinking about their possible reactions. At first, we intend to gradually prepare the ground for this. As soon as secular rulers favoured this idea, we could present our ideology to a wider audience. I am not alone with these opinions. I know a lot of people think about these same things. I am also quite sure that many of the priests of the Church do not believe in the Bible. Perhaps they, too, will agree to update their doctrine to the level of today's requirements. Time is on our side. There is also a psychological side to this. Most people knowingly or unknowingly expect liberation from the religious patronage of the Church. Whatever ideology gives them this justification, they will gladly accept it. The people do not need to understand anything about this ideology. But, lest we waste the whole evening on mere chatter, let us examine these insects quickly. Take a look at these butterflies. Aren't they great? There are no such things in Europe. These are probably some brand-new species. This proves that nature is becoming more diverse all the time. More and more new species are emerging at a tremendous rate. Everything has perhaps started to evolve from amazingly simple species. What all new and amazing are we still finding? Yes, time is running out.

The evening is already getting along, and I, unfortunately, must move on. Thank you to all of you who came to the scene. Did anyone still have any questions?"

"Professor, unfortunately, I disagree with you. I find these evidence far too weak to support your theory. Now we saw a few jaws, a couple of fossilized mussels, and a collection of insects prove absolutely nothing yet. Second, on what evidence-based is your claim on constantly born new species? Rather, do those excavations not prove that the species is extinct? Why have those already extinct species been larger than the current species?"

"Young man! Do you dare to doubt the scientific abilities of my group?"

"This is not about that but about the need for stronger evidence to support such a theory. Yes, I have great respect for your scientific work, but I think all theories should be approached critically. I just wanted to express my dissent."

"Well, thanks for that. The matter became clear. As I said, our work is still at the beginning, but it is continuing at a rapid pace. If there was nothing else, then this time, we will end here. Leave these samples here. I'll take them back to the basement tomorrow. Lectures will begin next week. Now young gentlemen, goodbye and have a nice weekend."

Chapter 14: Homecoming

I kindly tried to ask the captain about his future plans, but I didn't get a clear answer. He had no wife or family. All in all, he was in no hurry about those things. Skipper and his crew had no passions in their lives other than working at sea. I started packing my stuff. I carefully recovered my last discoveries, especially the bones of the Tasmanians. The spirits had already been drunk some time ago, but for that purpose, they had been included. With all its difficulties and illnesses, this journey was a tremendous ordeal for my body. I am six feet and one inch tall, but after weighing myself, I weighed under 130 pounds. My character also changed drastically during this five-year trip. Probably my psyche got sick during this time. I still remember the moment like yesterday when I heard the sailor roar enthusiastically, "Land is visible!" He had seen the southwest corner of England. We would be at the port in the evening. What a sense of relief, I finally got home! Soon this suffering would be forever over! After surviving the strongest emotions flow, I walked to the bow of the ship and looked at the land with my telescope. Seeing the British coast, my mind became sensitive. I felt weak and small alongside everything that had happened. A few tears rolled down my cheek. The events of this trip filled my mind.

When I set out on this journey, at the time, I was still somewhat traditional Christian, but during this journey, I was enlightened, so I was now sceptical of the Bible. When I embarked on this journey, I was just a boy. How could I have been critical of anything? A boy of that age could not be required to think scientifically. Then I did not understand anything about scientific matters. Life was so light, without a serious foundation. Now that omission from the deacon's consecration no longer annoyed me at all. Grant was right about that, too. What would I have done with that futile piece of paper when under no circumstances would I continue that path? Such a deacon's work is for women of tender minds. Thus, towards the end of the journey, I wanted to focus on reminiscing about the good aspects of this expedition. I realized how much I had seen revolutionary things like new animal and plant species. I also acknowledged the irreversible difference between human races. As I recalled, I went to get all my stuff ready for the deck, so I could leave immediately after anchoring in my home port. I stood with my luggage at the ship's bow, staring at the skyline. In the afternoon, I had already separated the coast with the naked eye. I stood at the bow of the ship in the drizzle, staring slowly at the approaching harbour. In a few more hours, I'd arrived. I planned in my mind what I would do in the next few days.

As we approached the harbour, I felt a tingle of excitement in the bottom of my stomach, and my heart pounded violently. Our pace slowed as the skipper told us to lower one of the big sails. I lifted my backpack well in advance and moved my suitcases to the centre of the ship, where I would be the first to leave the ship. I had no intention of staying to say goodbye to the crew, for I had had enough of their barbaric company. I angrily looked at Dawkins as he stood on the deck of the ship. How frustrating it is to do that kind of work all your life. He had no hope for better. He must have envied me. After dark in the evening, we arrived at Falmouth Harbour. Sails and anchors were lowered. As soon as the gangway was put in, I jumped along it to the ground without saying goodbye to anyone. How awesome it was to walk homeland for a long time again. I had arrived back in England. Finally, these years of humiliation would be forever over. Now I just wanted to get home to Shrewsbury quickly. I walked in the pouring rain with my belongings to the nearest inn with a big backpack on my back and bags in my hands. I might have been an amusing sight with all my stuff. When I arrived, I was totally wet, dirty, hungry, and dead tired. I asked the man at the front desk to get something to eat. After overcoming the initial shock, the innkeeper suggested to me in a cautious voice that I first wash myself.

I reportedly smelled quite intolerable. That was probably true, but I just wasn't aware of it myself, for I had been the dining table of parasites for so many years. The receptionist directed me to the back room of the inn, which had a separate bathroom. In this case, I could use it for free. He brought hot water and a piece of soap. I took off my dirty clothes, which were more rags than clothes. After doing that, I quickly went to the bath. When I was lazing in it, it felt amazing to be almost home already. After bathing, I threw most of my clothes in the rubbish because they were so full of bedbugs and fleas. I quickly ate a dry loaf of bread and went to a narrow, hard bed to sleep. I fell asleep after midnight. I only woke up very rested at noon when the innkeeper hurried me away. I left the inn hungry with my belongings. Now I had to get a ride home. After quickly eating a cup of disgusting-tasting vegetable soup, I found a man offering a ride north. Due to the crampedness, the ride was really uncomfortable. I was worried all the way about my samples. In addition to me, an older couple was in the carriage. It was hard for them to understand why I had wasted the best five years of my life on some unpaid sailing trip. That annoying woman thought I should have been married already, and on top of all that, I reportedly looked pathetic with a suitcase in my armpit.

Sure, I would have preferred to hold a young woman in my armpit, but things in life don't always go the way I want. I didn't bother to waste my strength telling that simple-minded woman the reason for my trip. Her behaviour showed well the fact that the woman is intellectually staggeringly below the man. A woman is not meant to be a man's conversation partner but bringer of pleasure. Fortunately, they soon leave off the ride. We arrived in Shrewsbury. For a small extra charge, the horseman agreed to drive me all the way to my home. It was early evening when I arrived in the yard. My hands shook with excitement. I had finally arrived back home. There was no one in the yard and only dim lighting inside. In that twilight, I looked at our yard. Everything seemed smaller than when I left. I opened the front door and stepped inside. There was a tasty smell of meat food floating from the kitchen. I counted my suitcase on the floor and asked if anyone was there. Catherine came into the hallway after hearing my voice.

"Is that you, Charles? Oh my God! You're back home!" Catherine exclaimed happily.

She looked at me with her eyes wide open with her hands in front of her mouth. When she realized it was me, she rushed to my neck, hugging me warmly.

"It's so wonderful to see you for a long time. We were so worried about you. We have missed you very much.

How are you? At least you have lost weight! Are you hungry?"

"Thanks for asking. I'm fine, and I'm really hungry. Have you already eaten?" I asked with my stomach screaming.

"Not yet. Let me look at you more closely. That beard isn't right for you then at all. Shave it away." Catherine said with her eyebrows playfully wrinkled.

"Well, maybe." I promised with a smile.

"Wait, I'll get Dad here. Dad, come down! Charles is back home!" She yelled excitedly.

"Catherine don't bother Dad yet. I have time to meet him later." I tried to stop her from yelling at Dad, but at the same time, the upstairs door slowly opened, snarling, and dad came out of his study. He walked down the stairs with restrained dignity. He was bald and overweight. Our father walked awkwardly slowly in front of me. We shook hands formally, just as if we had last met a week ago.

"How are you?" He asked.

"Fine, thanks." I replied nervously.

"Were the expectations of the trip met?"

"I think so. I mailed samples to Professor Grant. Personally, I am pleased with the results. Thank you for all your support." I stammered in response.

When I mentioned Grant's name, my father's gaze looked a little troubled.

I would have liked to ask many questions for father about the many secrets that were had in our family, but I didn't dare because I was still so financially dependent on him.

"You look skinny. Shall we go to eat?" My father responded, quickly changing the subject.

"Yes, please." I moaned in relief.

Nothing seemed to change in my relationship with my father. He still felt to me like a stranger. Our father left for another moment in another room. The service staff came to greet me, and some of them opened bottles of champagne and wine in honour of my return. How relieving it was to sit in a chair in our dining room, aware that I would soon be allowed to eat good homemade food instead of its monotonous ship food. Everything would have been perfect if Mom had been with us. The maid poured me a glass full of red wine, after which she served a delicious bird roast. I immediately started eating. Due to a terrible hunger, I ate like a barbarian. Catherine looked aside my piglet with a sideways eye, kindly asking if I had forgotten the table manners during my long absence. After apologizing, I said I hadn't eaten properly for many months, and now I was going to fix that deficiency. The servants drank wine alongside their work at a rapid pace, and some of them were already getting intoxicated. They said they would celebrate my return all night after doing their job first.

That night our home had a liberated atmosphere. After being satisfied with my greatest hunger, I wanted to know what had happened during my absence.

"Where is Erasmus?" I inquired from Catherine with a mouth full of food.

"He's an assistant doctor in London."

"As a medical assistant? Shouldn't he have become a chemist?" I asked in a slightly gleeful voice.

"Yes, apparently, he also works as a midwife or assists in childbirth. I don't know exactly; most likely, he will focus on chemistry in the future. Charles, he's a changed man. Erasmus is no longer as arrogant as he was when he was younger. You must meet him." She said as if apologizing for our brother.

"I see. What about your husband? What is his business?"

"His name is Kevin Langton. Like I wrote you, we got married last year. Kevin is a lawyer in a law firm in London."

"Well, that's good. There must be plenty of work. I thought of traveling to London soon to meet Professor Grant. At the same time, I could meet them as well." I said confidently.

"I'm already going back to London soon. I came here by chance to help Dad. By the way, we had an absolutely wonderful wedding! There were a lot of guests, and we got absolutely wonderful gifts.

Kevin and I traveled for a honeymoon to Paris. There were so romantic. If you only had were at our wedding. There were a lot of beautiful bridesmaids. There would have been one for you too. Are you still in touch with Fanny?" Catherine asked in a flirtatious voice.

When she mentioned Fanny, I pulled a piece of meat in the wrong throat and coughed the food out of my mouth on the plate.

"I didn't know Fanny was still that close to your heart." Catherine giggled.

"You know just as well as I do that woman hasn't been close to me for many years!"

"Now don't get angry, brother, good. Who are you chasing nowadays?"

"Sorry, sister, dear. There was no intention to get angry, but could we change the subject?"

"Yeah, sure."

"I'm really tired because of this trip, and I don't want to offend anyone. I'm not chasing up with anyone right now. I haven't had time to think about things like that on my trip. That wife will come when the time is right."

"What are you going to do next? Will you continue your studies, or have you become a deacon in a peaceful little village?" Catherine continued her prickly questions.

"Dear sister, you should know me better. I really am not going to continue my studies in theology.

I think Professor Grant has jobs for me and maybe I'll write a book about my trip."

"Would you write a book? You hate writing." Laughed Catherine.

"You can help me compile the notes. They are going to be the backbone of my science book." I looked at her with a wide smile.

"Let's see. What work did Grant promise you?" Catherine asked, leaning her elbow against the table with her right palm on her cheek.

"Well, he has not directly promised anything, but he is working hard on the "science of the future", as he calls it. I think there is enough research for me too."

"What exactly is that science of the future?" Catherine laughed in disbelief.

"Dear lovely sister. You have heard already enough. You women do not understand anything about the sciences." I said with a smile to her.

"I see. Father! Come to eat. Your food cools down!" Catherine screamed.

"I am coming." He shouted calmly from the next room.

"Catherine, thank you very much for all your help. Thank you in particular for getting Dad to send money to me. I would not have survived this trip without your support. You are dear to me." I looked straight into her eye and said it in a quiet voice as sincerely as I could.

And I really meant it. Catherine got embarrassed, blushed, and dropped her gaze on her empty plate.

"Thank you for your kind words. I don't know what to answer. I felt that was right in my heart. I wanted to help you in every way." She replied sincerely.

At the same time, our father came into the room and sat at the end of the table.

"What does home cooking taste like for a long time?"

"Unbelievably delicious." I answered gratefully.

"I am going to help the service people so that you can discuss the sciences in complete peace." Catherine said feminine in vainly as she left. I urgently wanted to break the embarrassing silence that would always follow when I stayed with my father alone.

"Have there been a lot of patients?" I asked in a seemingly interesting voice.

"Yes, there have been enough of them."

"Dad, I apologize in advance for my outspokenness, but I would like to ask you a few questions. I want to talk to you frankly now, like man to a man. Is it suitable for you?"

"Sure. Ask, please."

"What have you and Grant planned for me?"

"Hasn't Grant told you?" My father asked with an innocent look on his face.

"No clear answer. Something about some new ideology that will change the way the whole nation operates or something along those lines. I don't really understand where he's aiming for." I said with annoyance.

"You need to go to London urgently to meet Grant. He will tell you his plan for your future. At the same time, take the rest of the findings to him. A number of other scientists are also studying this matter with him. Did your eyes open during this trip?"

"In many ways, but what do you mean in particular?" I asked in surprise.

"Well, for example, the age of the earth, the development of animals and humans."

"Yes, I found some fossils, as you've probably heard from Grant."

"You don't believe the Bible's creation account anymore, do you?" My father asked in an excited voice.

"According to Grant, it seems that the earth is much older than the Bible assumes." I replied circularly.

"No sane person has believed in that book for a long time. Not a hundred years will pass, so the Bibles will no longer be found in museums at most. And it's not just about the natural sciences, but above all, the worldviews! My son, we need new values for Britain." My father said in a passionate voice.

"What could they be like?"

"Grant will tell you as soon as you meet him. However, you need to rest here at home first. Did you find evidence of human origin?"

"I found skeletons in Australia or actually dug them out of a couple of graves. I don't know if they are useful, but I took them with me. Do you want to see them?"

"I don't want to, but it's good that you also brought such material."

"Dad, how long have you known Grant?"

"We met more than ten years ago in London at an event dealing with these issues."

"Why didn't you tell me?"

"I didn't see it necessary then. Now that you are a man, you will better understand these things."

"Why wasn't I paid anything for a trip?"

"Charles, in the interests of the homeland, we all sometimes must work unpaid. The interest of the kingdom requires a sacrificial mind."

"Captain FitzRoy told me the real purpose of the voyage was to map the sea routes of our fleet. Is it true?"

"Yes, it is."

"Why didn't you tell me that either?"

"What would it have changed?"

"Maybe nothing, but it would have been fairer.

What offended me the most was when he humiliated me regularly by reminding me my job was just to keep company for him! Was that really the only reason for my participation?”

“Don't get mad now, but we had to get you on the exploration trip for free, and that's why we thought you could act as a companion to the ship's captain so he wouldn't feel lonely. Did you lack something during the trip?”

“No, I didn't lack, but I felt humiliated. The crew, therefore, treated me with contempt.”

“Charles, yes, you will receive adequate financial compensation for your ailments. You had so easy in your childhood before you left for the trip that I thought you wouldn't take the strain of the trip. If you want to achieve something in your life, as I hope, you must work hard for it. Important things do not come easily. It may be that you will become a famous scientist in your lifetime, even if you have not completed a university degree. The most important thing had your return home healthy. I'm going to sleep little by little. Thanks for the company.”

“Thank you, father, for this debate, and thank you in particular for your financial support. Without it, I would not have survived. I guess it'll be best for me to go to bed too.”

In the intoxication of the rising hop, I drank the rest of my wines from my glass. We got up from the table, and both left for our rooms. As I walked into the room, I reflected on our conversation with my father. At last, he spoke to me like his own son. Apparently, I had impressed him on my trip too. Catherine had already emptied one of my suitcases. I took my gun and cartridges to my room into a locked closet. I examined the contents of my bag and realized I needed new clothes as the old ones were almost worn out.

When I woke up at noon, I went to the bath to start. After clearing up from there, I told the maid to bring food to my room. After sorting the rest of my luggage in place into the closet, I headed to town to buy myself underwear. On the same trip, I went to the barber to cut my hair short and shave my beard. At home for dinner, Catherine praised my new style as a gentleman. I looked at myself in the mirror and noticed that the bald spot on my head was significantly enlarged recently. Am I going to be completely bald in a few years? The thought of it terrified me. The hair would drop from my head, and there was no clue about the woman. In my room, I decided to write letters to Grant, Henslow, and my brother. I told them I was coming to London soon.

I also added information about my last discoveries to Grant's letter. That information would surely get him excited. I got used to the ways of the civilized world again and started to plan my future program in London. Catherine went back to London with her husband. My father was immersed in his work, so we didn't discuss any in-depth issues before I left. We mainly saw each other at the meals. He still wanted to keep his own things to himself and did not talk about them anymore to others. I packed my suitcase again. This time it was not necessary to take the whole property, but only the necessary. I was mostly relieved because I finally found out what the benefits of those years would be. Before I left, I had a visit to my mother's grave. She certainly would have been proud of me. How much we left unexplained each other, my dear mother. I still loved her more than anyone else. I have often heard from older men that no man over twenty needs his mother if the father has taken care of his own part in raising his son. Maybe my father had neglected me because I would have needed my mother even still.

Chapter 15: Meetings in London

My father first took me to town and gave me money for a trip to London. How else would I have traveled anywhere? It was a shame to be so dependent on my father financially. I was an adult man, after all. Fortunately, the trip went otherwise comfortably. Everything felt so easy when this was compared to my experiences of traveling around the world. I had grown up as a man mentally. I no longer complained about little things as before. In London, I immediately went to see my brother. He waited for me based on my letter. Erasmus received me warmly. He was indeed a changed man. That arrogance, pride, and competitive spirit typical of him were gone. Or if not completely gone now, then at least he was much more humane than before. Apparently, his career was not as huge a success as he had imagined. Failures had increased his character in a humbler direction. He no longer imagined he knew everything. He had clearly understood his own mortality. In short, Erasmus was a broken man. His wife Caroline maintained the home, as a decent wife should. She was as aristocratically beautiful as always. Although I have always been more interested in blonde hair women, Caroline's freely hung, long dark hair made impressed me.

She had beautiful big blue eyes, a wide charming smile, a narrow graceful nose, a long thin neck, classically sculptural facial features, but a little too narrow lips to my taste. Passionately, I hoped to have an equally beautiful wife someday. I got to live in London with them house during my stay. I left most of the samples in their guest room. I didn't want to tell them all about the contents, as Caroline could have been horrified by the wild Aboriginals' bones. We also met Catherine's husband. He was handsome, confident, had a sense of humour, and was talkative. I well understood Catherine had immediately lost her heart to him. That same evening, we all went to eat at a great restaurant. Erasmus also offered me dinner with drinks. After the restaurant closed, we went to Catherine and Kevin's home to spend the evening. They told me throughout the evening how their relationship had begun. They had met for the first time with acquaintances by common. Catherine had pretended to be difficult to be achieved in the first place. In reality, she had been completely falling love with Kevin from the beginning. That night I learned more about women's plots than I did throughout my life upto that time. I felt like a love-longing creature as I watched their happiness. That was the most important happiness in human life that I had completely lack of.

I told them about my expedition, but I quickly realized it didn't really interest them. They were listening, yes, but I noticed from the bothered gaze that their thoughts wandered somewhere else. They did not waste their time contemplating layers of earth or beetles but lived a worldly, carefree life enjoying each other. Their lifestyle was as modern, secular, and carefree as urban life could be. We returned to my brother's home at midnight. I went to the guest room and slept drunk out of my inferiority.

After I survived a moral hangover-like depression, I toured the next day's different museums with samples while the cold wind accompanied me. I carried with mea few of my collections of insect and petrified mussels. I tried to offer them to museums, but they were not interested in them. The same kind of samples had already been imported from the colony. Uncertainty struck me for the first time. Had I done any unnecessary work? Did I sacrifice those youth years of my life for nothing? In my anxiety, I realized I should meet Grant as soon as possible. He has connections here. He can arrange things. So, I went to university early in the evening to meet Grant. I really had a lot to talk about with him, and not all topics were just pleasant.

I ran as fast as I could to the university, and as guidance, I saw in the hallway after Grant's entrance hall. He chatted with a couple of men who seemed to be leaving. "Professor Grant! I shouted from afar. He turned around quickly and started to walk toward me.

"Charles, you're back. How are you?" Grant exclaimed in surprise.

"Fine, thank you," I answered hurriedly, and we shook hands warmly with eachother. He asked the two men who were with him to come to us.

"Hey Henry and Bernie! Come here. I want to introduce you to this man I have told you so many times about. Grant exclaimed." They walked with dignity toward us.

"Look, here's Robert Darwin's son Charles. He has just returned from an expedition to South America. The samples I showed you are the ones he found." Grant told them about my trip. After shaking hands with them, I briefly told them about myself. They were both cool-tempered dignity government officials, albeit kind to me. After Grant said goodbye to them, we walked to his office. Grant went behind his desk, sitting in his large leather chair. I took off my overcoat and put it on the hanger. I sat down on a low wooden chair without asking permission and watched the room. On his large desk was a globe marked in red with those areas that belonged to the British Empire.

As I watched it, I realized how large areas we dominated. In the future, we will only have a chance to lose. I watched Grant as he browsed his papers. I encouraged myself. Now I would like to ask my question. I finally wanted answers to the questions that had plagued my mind for years.

"I have a lot of questions, Professor. So, at first, I would like to address you by your first name only, if appropriate."

"That's all right, Charles. There are a lot of questions for me too, though I have more suggestions for you, you can start first."

"Thank you. I want to start with positive things. I have that Negro skeletons you asked for in your letter. I dug them from Tasmania from a cemetery. It features, among other things, the skulls of a man and a child."

"Great, Charles! Where are your samples?"

"They're at my brother's apartment. I can bring them here tomorrow.

"That's good, bring them to my apartment. We can go by it today so you can come there tomorrow."

"That is fine."

"Do you take tea and pastries?"

"Thank you. I'll be glad to do so."

Grant offered me a cup of tea. I thought he was startled by my straightforwardness.

I admit I was a little aggressive.

"Well, Charles, please could you tell me about the highlights of your trip." Grant suggested with a smile.

"It would take a week. It was a heavy but, in many ways, eyes-opening journey. You were right about book writing. Interesting material is easily available for at least one book. I'm not just the type of writer, but maybe you can help me. Admittedly, first, I would like to get answers to some of the questions that came up during the trip. First, why you didn't tell me that you had known my father for years?"

"Charles, I understand your surprise very well. I received a letter from your father the other day he told me about your conversation with him. As he asked you, what would it have changed even if you knew about our friendship? Nothing, so what does it matter to you then?"

"Nothing else, but I felt like some game was being played behind my back."

"Charles, I swear by mighty Britain, nobody won't play any game behind your back! We are creating a career for you as a great scientist. You should be grateful to us for this honour. Over the years, I have spoken of your pioneering work on all the scientific occasions I have attended. I can assure you that we already have a wide range of supporters. Your name is already well known throughout England.

For the rest of your questions, you heard the answers from your father. My answers to your questions are the same. Don't live in the past. Focus on the present! In life, you must be willing to suffer for the things you believe in! Charles, that real battle is still ahead of us. Remember, we are no longer alone. Today, we are a large and strong group. Time is on our side, and we are getting stronger all the time."

"All right. I believe you. I still want to know for what you need all the plant and animal samples I sent you."

"Isn't it already clear to you? Well, with this evidence, we disprove the biblical account of creation."

"Do you mean a few horses' jawbones, petrified clams, and a couple of fossils to overthrow Christianity?" I asked in amazement.

"Yes! Exclaimed Grant, hitting the table with his fist. If not all of Christianity immediately, then at least I want to free humanity from that creation fairy-tale invented by Jewish Moses. Charles! You clearly don't realize where this world is going. Even before you left, I told you that we are, as a nation, on the eve of a new era. People are downright being thirsty for something like this revolutionary ideology. They want to be freed from the slavery of Christianity so that they get the legitimacy to fulfil their own desires. Secondly, as a kingdom, we need new national values based on British culture and race.

I have already noticed how easy this is going to be."

"This is starting to get too difficult for me. I would have one very practical request for you. I don't understand anything about most of these findings. In the last few days, I have visited a museum, but they were not interested. Could you help me get those samples to a museum to explore?"

"By no means take them to any museum but bring them all to me! Why give away such unique material for free to some idiots who have no idea what these represent? Charles, some of these species have already gone extinct. They are valuable discoveries and the best proof of the legitimacy of our cause!"

"All right. I'll bring them all tomorrow. I should probably go to my brother's soon." I said in a tired voice.

Grant's speech started scare to me, and I still didn't realize what he was really aiming for.

"Charles, thank you for visiting. Let's go the same way, and I'll show you where I live. It's not like a fair mile from here."

As we walked towards Grant's apartment, I wondered how Grant, every time so successfully appealed to my feelings. He knew I had no other reasonable optionin my life than to agree to his plans. I was a fit prey for him. I just couldn't tell him anything against it. It felt like he was hypnotizing my mind.

Grant had a marvelous ability to bend the human mind.

"Now we've arrived. I live on the second floor. Come tomorrow evening at seven."

"It's a deal. Good night."

I had to walk to my brother's apartment. It was already late at night when I got there. I went straight to my room to sleep. I packed my sample in a big bag. I left a few samples for Henslow. I came with my sacks and knocked on the door of Grant's apartment. He had worn black straight pants, and a white collared shirt with a gray knit over the shirt. He welcomed me, asking in.

"Good evening, Professor Grant."

"Call me Edmond. Come further and please have seat. Are all of your samples in those bags?"

"Yes. Will I leave a sack in this hallway?"

"Yeah, just leave them at that. Let's go to that living room to drink cups of "steeled tea". Charles, I want to introduce you to a man who is also involved in our work. We will work closely together in the future. May I introduce your namesake, Charles Lyell. Lyell, this is Charles Darwin. Herecently returned from an expedition I have told you about. He brought me more material for our theory. Please sit down, gentlemen. So, in honor of Friday night, we'll start with a few big whiskeys." Grant said with a smile.

Edmond poured all of our glasses in half. I suppose that was meant to make it easier to get acquainted with. Once again, Grant had surprised me. We had to be here, two of us. Maybe he was startled by my questions last night and didn't want to take a new risk today. Now I was at his home for the first time. The decor of his apartment was practical. The shelves were full of books, and the furniture was simple and black. The walls of the rooms were white. Practicality was looking from this apartment. One could say this apartment with its furniture is very "Grant-style". As I listened to Grant and Lyell talk to each other, I felt like an outsider. As I tasted the whiskey, I stared at Lyell with the side eye. What sort of man is he? Seems to be in his forties and a pretty serious-looking man. Lyell sometimes looked at me as judging my suitability for this mission. I decided to make it easier to get acquainted and drank my glass blank with one sip.

"Shall I pour more?" Grant asked.

"Yep, just pour," I said in a low voice.

Lyell, please, could you tell me a little about yourself?

"Sure. I am married and have two children. I am a lawyer, and I like my work. I'm good at arguing. Recently, I have become acquainted with different types of rock in the soil. I have already studied the soil layers in particular. In my research, I have come to the conclusion that the age of the earth is several million years.

I can prove my claim with my research on the slow subsidence and rise of the ground. Here I briefly about myself."

Bored, I listened to Lyell's analytical monotonous presentation. Be it a formal-styling man. However, I decided to answer him politely.

"Thank you. Indeed, I recently returned from a trip around the world during which I made observations of the different layers of earth. I was particularly reminded of the case where petrified wood had split different layers of earth, the formation of which I thought was the result of millions of years. I still do not understand it today."

"Sounds weird." Lyell said seriously.

"How do you explain the large mass graves we found there, which were full of all kinds of animals? My local guide muttered about some great flood that happened a long time ago that may have caused its destruction. Do you have any information on what really caused such destruction?"

"It's hard to take a stand when I haven't seen them, but it's probably caused by a quick earthquake. Had the animal carcasses already rotted?"

"Some were, some were not. What amazed me the most was the fossilized fish we found. After all, a fish cannot fossilize in water.

Instead, it must have covered itself in the airtight mud very quickly so that other fish do not have time to eat it or it does not have time to rot. I am still very annoyed because I don't understand anything about paleontology. I wrote all my observations on paper and tried with poor results to draw illustrative pictures of them."

"Sounds really interesting. I have never heard of anyone finding fossilized fish. About the fossils that came to mind, would you like to explore with me the fossils of giant animals on the Royal of Surgeons' premises?"

"Yes, very much. That would be great. What kind of animals are they?" I asked enthusiastically.

"They are already extinct large lizards. I have called them dinosaurs. It is anancient Greek word." Lyell opened the secret.

"When are we visiting those creatures?"

"Is it suitable for you next Monday evening?" Lyell asked mysteriously.

"Yes, it does. Where is this Royal of Surgeons located?"

"On Lincoln's Inn Field. Come to college, and we'll go from there together. By the way, could you give me some of your samples for examination?" Lyell asked in a cautious voice.

At the same time, Grant stood up quickly in front of his eyes, a little drunk to stand, saying:

"I think it's better that the samples stay with me. They're in better safety in one place. Can we take a quick look at them, even right away, or what, Charles?"

"Well, yes, it is fine by me."

Whiskey influenced my enthusiasm; I fetched the sack excitedly from the hallway and dropped it on the living room floor.

"Here are the rest of my findings. I left my drawing in my home in Shrewsbury. I can get them quickly from there if they are needed."

Grant started dicking the sack, and, as you might guess, the bones of the Aboriginals interested him the most.

"You look at the boy. You're really found a real wild man's skull!! This is especially important evidence to support our theory. Here is clear evidence of the differences between the white and black races. Great Charles!" Grant exclaimed.

"Human bones are not my field, but it is interesting to study them." Lyell stated in an analytically cool voice.

"Yes, my findings are not related to geology. Those things may be found in my notes." I replied cautiously to Lyell.

Lyell sipped his whiskey glass empty, after which he slowly stood up to look at us.

"Time is running out, and I think it's best for me to leave my home because my family is already waiting for me. It was really nice to meet your namesake, Charles.

Thank you both for your pleasant company. Charles, see you next week at the university. Good night." Lyell said in an official tone.

We escorted him to the hallway and wished him a good trip home. After Lyell left, we went back to the living room to continue examining the skulls.

"Can you describe what these sub-humans looked like? Was their beak like a pig's snout?"

"What do you mean?" I asked in amazement.

"Low nasal bridge and big, wide nostrils?" Grant asked in an interrogative style.

"Yes, most of them looked something like your description. Low-headed and round-faced." I replied in amusement.

"Such facial features indicate that they are mere prey to a stronger white race. Did you draw pictures of them?"

"I didn't draw. I'm so bad at drawing people that I didn't even try, but there was an artist on our ship who drew pictures of everything possible. He gave me a couple of his drawings from the Indians. Those are also at home."

"Charles, you must move here to London. Here that science is done, and not in any small villages." Grant advised me in his paternal style.

"That is an incredibly good idea. I can ask my brother if I could live in their corners at first." I exclaimed excitedly.

"Do it. Your move would make a huge difference to our cause." Said Grant coolly while looking tightly into my eyes. That look always made me feel fear.

"I guess it's also best to leave for my brother's apartment. I promised them to come no later than 7 p.m. Will I leave these samples here with you or?" I asked as I walked into the hallway.

"Leave them here. I will sort them over the weekend. What are you doing this weekend?"

"I promised to meet Professor Henslow." I said in a slightly scared voice because I didn't know how Grant would react to it.

"Well, that's a great thing! Tell Henslow my warmest greetings!" Exclaimed Grant. I looked Grant in the eye, stammering that I would convey Henslow his warmest greetings.

"Don't you have a constant arguing with Henslow?" I continued in a surprised voice.

"Who said so?" Grant asked, questioning with a serious look on his face.

"No one lately, but before my trip, I heard all kinds of rumour's." I replied circularly.

"It's not worth listening to the gossip. We may have had controversy before, but it was purely scientific matters. And it wasn't because of me. Henslow just envied me.

It's human because he's not as respected a scientist as I am, but I don't let that bother me. That was in the past. Please come to college when you have time. How long are you staying in London?"

"At least for another week." I said as I put on my jacket.

As I went to my brother's apartment, I thought about this evening's meeting. Now, for the first time, I saw Grant in my spare time and even a little drunk. He apparently seems to trust me when he once invites me to his apartment in his spare time. Who is all involved with Grant in developing this theory? What are Grant's real motives for questioning the Bible? How did my father end up in this group? What did this Lyell think of me? Grant and Henslow reportedly competed fiercely against each other. Although they are opposites of each other in their worlds of values, they are both united by a fierce fire in the making of science. As I pondered all of this, I felt great pride in being able to belong to this group. It might be central to see how history is made.

My brother also had a day off and was in no hurry to get up next to his wife early in the morning. I ate quickly, took the rest of my findings with me, and left for the city. Henslow had asked me to come in front of a church at noon. I was there in good time enjoying the sunny, cool weather. Henslow arrived at exactly twelve.

He was in a happy mood, and for a reason. He had just become the father again of a healthy boy the previous week. I warmly congratulated him, and we took a walk towards the nearby park.

"Hello Charles, nice to see you for a long time. You are now an adult man."

"Hello John and thank you. Nice to meet you too a long time. It may be that I'm a little more manly now, at least externally. I think I'm probably always the same boy mentally as before. I'm really glad to meet you. How is your family?"

"Thank you for asking. My older son can already read, even though he is only five years old. He is quite intelligent for his age. I really enjoy being a father. It is the best a man can experience in his life. As a family man, there is some reason to work. Do you still remember my wife, Elisabeth?"

"Yes, I remember her very well."

"She sends her warmest greetings to you. It feels like time goes by faster than the older you are. Can you imagine I turned forty last winter? Feels like we just got to know each other. How are you doing?"

"Quite well. I came to London early this week and lived with my brother."

"What are you going to do next?"

"I do not know yet." I said in a cautious voice.

"I guess you have some plans for your future anyway?" John asked with anastonished look on his face.

"Grant offered me some work in his field. I'm going to try it."

"However, I recommend that you first find out what he has to offer you." Henslow advised.

"I've already talked to him about it. I answered sharply."

"Will you tell me about your trip around the world? How did it go?"

"First of all, it was a really heavy trip. I collected some animal and plant samples, which I mailed to Grant. In fact, I have a couple of samples included that I'll be happy to give you as a gift." I said with a smile.

I dug a petrified mussel and a beetle in a small glass display case from my pocket. I handed them to John.

"Thank you, Charles. These look interesting." Henslow said in a slightly bored voice while putting the samples in his pocket.

"Where did you find these?"

"From South America. I found a seashell on the seashore and a beetle in the rainforest."

"I see. What else will you learn along the way?"

"At least that the world is a really unfair place. My belief in human goodness was hit hard. I saw a lot of terrible things I couldn't have imagined. There was death, disease, wars, Indifference, and poverty everywhere."

"Yes, that kind of place this world is. How is your Faith Life going?"

"When I see all kinds of violence in nature, I often think about the possibility of God's existence. If He exists, then why is there so much evil in the world?"

"Good, when you have also thought about spiritual things. If you want to reflect on evil in the world, then you should first define what is evil and why it is evil. How do you define moral evil? Where did you get a concept like evil? Predators do not feel guilty for killing other animals or even offspring of their own species. Do you use the Bible as a yardstick, some religion, British law, or just your own feelings?"

"I haven't thought about it that far, but in the name of honesty, I have to admit, I have probably defined evil with my own sentimental feelings."

"That's how we humans usually act, but it doesn't work because we are challengeable to define evilness with our own feelings. Someone else may feel the opposite in the same matter. Just think of slavery. From a slave, it probably feels wrong, but the master may disagree with that. We humans cannot implement justice in any part of anyone's life. We don't even understand what justice really means. If justice is ever to come to pass, then it must affect all people, including those who died hundreds of years ago.

There is no way we can make a difference. In order for such a situation to materialize, one must be some being who is eternal, omnipotent, omniscient, and completely independent of men. Let him then be called God. Only such a being can bring justice to all of humanity. You are right about the evil of the world, and its amount only seems to be growing all the time. Humanists have lied to us for years about how man is supposedly morally good, but they have not bothered to present evidence to support their claim. Man is a wise and existence-conscious being but completely immoral. The Bible clearly states that the prince of this world is not Jesus Christ but Satan and his demon. Mankind has lost touch with God because of the Fall. Hardly anyone wants to hear it because it doesn't sound nice. It makes us Christians ask ourselves, why do we thrive in this world so well? Is this life dearer to us than the kingdom of God?"

"Honestly, haven't thought so deeply. You should write that on a piece of paper so I can study it in complete peace. I guess I dropped off in the middle of your narration. In fact, the more I study nature, the less I think it requires a designer or Creator. The earth seems much older than what the Bible says. I did a lot of excavation, which led me to conclude that the earth is probably millions of years old."

"Have you given up your Christian faith?"

"I don't know if I've ever even been a believer. Maybe it's been more so that society has grown me to believe in a certain way, and then I've tried to follow those norms of behavior in my life. I don't think I could work as a deacon. I couldn't tell anyone anything about Jesus." I said in frustration.

"You get power from God if you really want it unconditionally. I have grown in my faith a lot during these years. I'll be happy to tell you about it, but I don't require you to believe as I personally believe. You are my good friend just the way you are."

"Thank you. That means a lot. How have you noticed those things about justice that you just told me about?"

"In His grace, God has sometimes taken me to lonely wilderness moments. In those times, I have had to think of things that nobody usually wants to think about. Those times have been times of great spiritual growth, and growth is always accompanied by pain and loss. We had to think about the purpose of the Creator in our lives when one of our children died a couple of years ago."

"I am sorry. How did you recover from it?"

"We treated it honestly with my wife and talked about it together also with our friends. There is nothing man can do about such things. Life just must go on." Henslow said seriously with a hopeful look on his face.

"I hope you don't have too high expectations about me. You will probably remember that I am by no means a particularly intelligent man."

"Don't worry about it. I'm not looking for any benefits from you. Can you tell me more about the work Grant has to offer?"

"I believe so. Grant wants to develop a kind of theory of how the whole universe is born out of nothing on its own without a supernatural creator."

"All right. That's a big deal. As I warned you, he is a megalomaniac man. How is he going to prove this theory?"

"I do not know. Apparently, with the findings I posted."

"Has he told you about his goals? For what is he really aiming?"

"Not for me, but there are others involved. My father knows more about this. He has been familiar with Grant for years."

"If Grant wants to overthrow Christianity, what values will he offer instead?"

"I don't know, but I think he's telling me his plan." I said carelessly.

I did not understand the importance of the Henslow question at all.

"Do you want to come to visit our home? It's close here.

My wife has already brewed tea and baked something delicious." Henslow proposed.

"That's perfect. I don't have any special program for this day."

"Good. Then we should walk in that direction." Henslow said calmly.

As we walked through the park, I thought about the conversation we had. With those sailors, I had almost forgotten how profoundly wise a man Professor John Henslow is. I felt like a really light-level conversationalist with him. He had indeed had to think about these things. These were such heavy subjects that I got a headache again during our conversation. We soon arrived at Henslow's home. John's wife, Elisabeth, came into the hallway, welcoming me warmly. She wasn't the most beautiful woman in the world, but she was very cordial. Their home was warmly decorated. There was a huge difference in comfort compared to Grant's apartment. Yes, you will notice it when a woman lives in the house and is in charge of the interior. The woman brings a spirit of coziness to the apartment. Their son George was playing with his toys in the living room. We drank tea and ate pancakes with strawberry jam. It felt good to be with them. It was easy to be with them. I didn't have to perform anything at all. I just let me be myself. We discussed religious matters, family, and relationships.

The best thing about our conversations was the openness with which Henslow's talked about their own life. Elisabeth asked a lot about my plans for the future. I openly told her about my own wishes. She could not understand how a soft, calm, fluffy, quiet, and reputable young man like me was still unmarried. Besides, I came from a rich family. Elisabeth promised, with a sly smile, to keep her eyes open for a suitable wife candidate. I asked them how they had met each other. John said during his studies at the university that he had met Elizabeth's older brother, through whom they had met each other. It seemed that they had also had their own difficult moments during the marriage. I told them, liberated, that I had not yet felt drawn to the girls in my youth. Instead of girls, serious religious thoughts took over my mind at the same time as boys my age spent their time teasing girls. I was melancholy by character at the time, and girls are not interested in such boys. Elizabeth laughed in embarrassment as I shared my own opinions about the girls. As if I had revealed her thoughts too. John asked about my spiritual life at a young age. I also told, without feelings of shame, how I often thought alone by myself what my eternal destiny was going to be. If I had died young, would I have gone to heaven? Sometimes I was haunted by the thought of hell.

Could it be eternal suffering without any purpose and end? Was my mother already in hell? When I finished my speech, they encouraged me to continue on the path of honesty no matter what it would cost. As we spoke to each other, I realized that these years had changed people's attitudes towards me. Now I was treated like an adult man. With them, I realized how little I had experienced true love in my life and how alone I had lived my life. It had been the over-protected and carefully guarded life of a privileged child. During this visit, I made the decision to move to London. If I want to do science, I must move here as soon as possible. Here are all the best possibilities in life. If only my father would agree to finance me one more time. When I left, John asked me for tomorrow's God service. I hesitated at first, but when I heard the venue of the event was other than the church, I agreed to their request. John promised to come to pick me up from my brother's apartment. They came in the morning and he had a short conversation outside with my brother at the outside. We left soon, as the worship would start at ten. For some reason, Henslow didn't ask my brother to come along. I felt excited when I accompanied them to worship. We arrived on time. At the front door, a man shook hands with us, welcoming us. We walked into a building with a large hall they had rented for their use.

I didn't see any religious plaques or crucifixes anywhere. There was no special altar in front, only a podium. The apartment was bright, spacious, and warm. There was a mentally lower threshold of coming to such a place than to the traditional stone church where no one would pay attention to you. There were people from all walks of life here, and they spoke freely to each other regardless of their social status. These people did not seem to be overwhelmed by the sorrows of this world, as if their minds were attached to something other than this materialistic world. We went to sit in the middle of the hall next to the Henslow acquaintances. After the opening songs, the children had their own program, and an older woman led them to an adjoining room for Sunday school. The speech was given by the same man who welcomed us at the front door. He was wearing a plain dark suit. The man was in his fifties but physically fit. He was a gentle but determined-looking man. This speech was as it should be for all speeches. The speaker believed what he was saying. He understood the meaning of his speech, and according to Henslow, that is, he also lived to it. The speech lasted only half an hour. I didn't feel bored. Instead, I would have loved to hear more. For the first time in my life, I began to understand what Christianity really all is about.

It is not some moldy religious culture that has stuck to its formula, but a living relationship with Jesus Christ who defeated death. Now I understood the opinion of those missionaries that my studies as a deacon had no value in spiritual work if I did not allow God to prepare me for work. You can't really even study it, but would I have wanted to pay the price involved in following Jesus? As I thought about those things, the choir sang the final song. It didn't touch me because I never understood anything about music at all. The man giving the speech sat in the front row next to his family. I would have liked to go talk to him, but I just didn't dare go to him. I made excuses in my mind that I didn't want to disturb his family. The truth, however, was that I was afraid of mental breakdown in the same way as I was there on the ship then. I would have died of shame if I had burst into tears in front of strangers. I gave myself a false escape by thinking about the time after my move when I could set aside talk time for him. I already knew then that this was just one more miserable excuse to continue my past lifestyle. Frustrated by my cowardice, I said piece in my throat to John that I was leaving to home. He thought I was offending my mind about something, but I told him it wasn't that. After saying goodbye to them, I set off to walk in gloomy thoughts towards central London.

I felt similar to when I was young, then, I was embarrassed by the interruption of my own studies, but now I was facing a much bigger crisis. I couldn't help but think about my attitude towards life. How long did I postpone important decisions in my life to the vague future? Whether it's a job, a life partner, or a faith to God, at some point, I would have to take a stand on those things, whether I wanted to or not. I did not understand what I was fleeing. From downtown, I got a ride to my brother's apartment. I arrived just before the rain. I felt happy about the new understanding of Christianity. On the other hand, I was depressed by the fact that I did not dare to go talk to the pastor. If I had continued to attend their events, would I have been born again from the Holy Spirit, as they said? On arrival, I got straight to the dining table. Caroline had prepared a delicious dinner for us that really came in handy. After that sailing trip, I realized how much good, varied, and nutritious food affects my mood.

Chapter 16: Dinosaurs

I left for the university in good time to wait for Lyell. I was excited about those dino creatures or whatever they were now. As I approached the university, I once again felt that deep, bitter sense of contempt within me for all theoretical bookwisdom. It remarkably reminded me of the shipwreck of my medical studies. I shook those grim memories out of my mind as I walked straight to the office to ask for Grant, but for some reason, he wasn't at university today. While waiting for Lyell, I watched the hustle and bustle of young people at university. I no longer felt envious of them, for I felt intellectually like a natural scientist and fully equal among them. There were paintings on the walls of the hallway about the great men of the past. Maybe my picture would sometimes adorn these walls as well. In the midst of my fantasies, Lyell arrived a little late. We set off immediately for the Royal of Surgeons. Lyell told us as we walked about these creatures. I thought he had slightly exaggerated the size of those creatures. In the beginning, he introduced me to the skull of a giant rhino that lived in ancient times. Its horn alone was just over four feet long. Such an animal must have aroused fear in its environment during its lifetime.

At the same time, I wondered at the core of Grant's theory, where he claimed that everything was constantly evolving for the better. If that was true, then why are rhinos smaller today? Is there any selection advantage for them from atrophy? We continued on our way forward cause better was coming. As we came to the door of the great hall, Lyell stopped, turning to me, surprisingly saying. "Now you see something you could never have imagined." Lyell pulled the door open, and I looked inside the hall. Opposite me was a gigantic creature I really couldn't have imagined even in my wildest dreams. This petrified fossil was several yards high. Its head was sloping down, and it seemed to look straight at me with its empty eye pits. I stared at it, mesmerized. It felt like I was in some fairy tale. That monster looked completely unreal. I thought that there could not have been such big animals. I walked inside in the power of hypnotic admiration without being able to detach my gaze from the remains of that big incomprehensible animal. I walked to its right side, looking at the fossil and its astonishing length. I stared at its long neck, which was as long as its tail. I thought it was over a hundred feet long overall. The bones of its legs alone were thicker than my waist. After returning to my senses, I began to analyze this creature part by part.

Its head was inconceivable small compared to the rest of the body, due to which the brain activity of this lizard could not have been very remarkable. Likewise, its mouth was surprisingly small, presumably in proportion to its great need for food. About a long neck has certainly required large lungs. How in the world has that animal been able to oxidize its body? Judging by its teeth, it has had to be an herbivore. Lyell came after me asking my opinion on this creature.

"Well, what do you say? Aren't you believe your eyes?"

"This is absolutely amazing! You were right. I really have never seen anything like it. Has that really been a living lizard or some sculpture?" I asked with astonishment.

"Yes, that's a real lizard. It was discovered in the United States a couple of years ago."

"Do you know how much that creature weighed?"

"I have no idea, but I would assume it weighed tens of thousands of pounds.

"It has had to eat huge amounts all the time to survive. What has it all eaten?"

"We don't know, but I think it was completely herbivore."

"How in the world can herbivores grow so big? How long ago was this animal extinct?"

"Probably millions of years ago. Finding it as a whole is a downright miracle. It's skeleton had petrified into fossils within the earth."

"How could it have soaked into the airtight mud so quickly that it has not had time to rot?" I asked in amazement.

"Probably some huge natural disaster has caused it." Lyell analyses.

"Can anyone come to see these dinosaurs?"

"Not yet, but in a few years, we thought we would open this department to the common people as well. We must first take care of the safety of these fossils, and we also need more information about these creatures. At the moment, we know so little about these lizards that we are unable to use them to support our theory. I assume there have been dozens of different species of dinosaurs, some of them probably hunters and scavengers like the current beasts. Most importantly, these creatures play an important role in shaping the new worldview. When we make more such lizard discoveries, we will have great evidence in these to support our theory. We need to present these dinosaurs, especially to children. Old people we can forget. They are unable to develop their minds. Our hope is for youth people. Think how excited the kids are going to be about these dinosaurs. After seeing these dinos, no child wants to go to any boring Sunday school."

"True. Does Grant know about these dinos?"

"Of course, he does. He has visited this museum many times." Lyell replied carelessly.

"Why hasn't he told me anything about this?" I asked in annoyance.

"Charles, we each have a role to play in building this ideology. Grant isn't interfering with my industry, and I'm not his. I am not interested in studying human skulls or different human races. He will tell you everything essential about what he does best. Yes, you will get enough information. All in time, be patient.

"Exactly, you're right. One man cannot understand all this. I was not meant to blame anyone. I'm just so excited about this creature I've seen. What is the name of this animal species?"

"I haven't come up with any separate name yet. My intention next summer is to do excavations all over England to find more of these lizards." Lyell said seriously.

As I listened to Lyell's performance, I wondered about this paradox in my life. Yesterday I was full of enthusiasm for Christianity, while today, science seemed to sweep the whole Bible into the rubbish bin. Does the Bible mention any of these dinosaurs? Would Grant be right anyway? Now I understood why museums were not interested in my collections. Who cares about petrified mussels if such giants are on display?

Hell, why am I never in the right place at the right time? If I had found some creature like this one in South America, or even a single bone, then my reputation would at least have been guaranteed. Should I try to get Lyell to look for these dinosaur bones with me? Would he want to take me with him? It could be another option if Grant doesn't offer me any jobs. We left the museum. As we walked toward the city, Lyell suggested to me to visit the zoo with him. I gladly agreed to his proposal.

The next day at the zoo, I told Lyell about my desire to see cat beasts right away, so we went straight to that department. To my disappointment, those didn't give joy because they slept. Looking at the lions, I wonder to myself, how these big animals thrived in such small cages? Lyell minds it was more important to go straight to the monkey ward. For me, it didn't matter, as I could come back here again sometime. First, we went to see the gorillas glancing at us, gloomy-looking from their cages. I remembered Captain FitzRoy when I watched a roaring male gorilla pounding his own chest with his fists. We continued our journey to look for the chimpanzees. It was affectionate to watch as the chimpanzee mother breastfed her son. There was something very human about it. I knelt on the edge of the cage and watched the young chimpanzee.

It came to the edge of the cage, scratching its own head. I also started scratching my bald head, grimacing at the chimpanzee. In it, we two lonely entertained each other. I liked this little monkey. Too bad when I didn't take anything to eat, I would have been so happy to feed this little creature. In it, while I was playing with the monkey, I noticed Lyell coming beside me. I looked at him and saw him look down at me contemptuously along his nose. Apparently, my innocent play with the monkey didn't amuse him. He looked at me for a long time as if measuring my intelligence. I got up slowly, breaking the silence while proposing to move on to the next section. Lyell answered nothing to me but went for a walk towards the front door. As we left the zoo, Lyell asked me about my observations of monkeys. I said those were surprisingly human. To this, he replied gracefully that they were our close relatives. I was shocked by the allegation and protested vehemently against it. After all, we are on a completely different level compared to monkeys. I urge him, excited, to prove such a wild assertion. Lyell laughed contemptuously at me and said he would show me the evidence to support his claim. He said with a mischievous smile. I looked surprisingly much like a chimpanzee while squatting, scratching my balding head. I didn't comment on his prickly throw in any way as we walked into central London.

In the university yard, I thanked him for the guidance. Lyell continued home to his family, and I went to the nearest pub for a beer. I had seen so much of everything new in the last few days that I felt I had earned a few beers. I hadn't been on a beer for a long time, and now I wanted to relax a bit. In the pub, when I ordered a beer, I remembered the studying time in Edinburgh, when guys older than me went to the pub in the evenings, and I just had a chance to watch them as they drank beer. Now there was no more than fear. My intention was to have at most a couple of beers. As I sipped my beer, I pondered Lyell's argument about the kinship between man and ape. Why did they want to prove such a silly claim true? That would be a disgrace to all of humanity! As I drank, I pondered Lyell's idea presented, so those couple of beers went so quickly. I smoothly ordered more. I've always loved the feeling of rising hops because then and only then do I feel free from all the silly shackles of customary culture invented by society. When I got drunk, I tried to discuss these things with other drinkers, but they weren't interested in a drop of my subject's human-monkey issue. They treated me like some farmer. It didn't bother me as I was too drunk. London had the right urban vibe. I looked out the window of the pub out onto a street adorned with bushy trees. People walked down the street all over the place.

I really wanted to move to London, because here there is every opportunity for a stimulating life. I sat in the pub, tippling beers up until closing time. When the waitress came to rush me out, I was very annoyed by the early closing time in my mind because I would have liked to get drank until morning. After closing, I left to shuffle for my brother's apartment. I went for a couple of beers, and that's how it happened again. Maybe I shouldn't drink alcohol at all because I completely lack control. Either I don't drink it at all, or I drink myself right completely out. Along the way, the beer started pissing, so I had to empty my bladder into the street. Like miraculously, I avoided the cops and found the right address. Fortunately, Erasmus had given me their spare key so I to get inside after a long attempt. My rumbling in a dark apartment woke them up. Caroline was angry because of my drunkenness. She nagged at me like her own husband. Now, for the first time, I saw her bad sides. I reportedly was no longer with the sailors on the ship, where everyone lived how they wanted to. If I still wanted to live with them, then in the future, I could come to people in time to sleep and sober! In her opinion, it was incomprehensible how a young man of the best working age could come to them in a drunken place on a Tuesday night. Worst of all, I didn't even pay them any rent for my living.

My brother tried to control the anger of his beloved wife but to no avail. Her rage only intensified as I began to sing in a loud voice the song I had invented on the way, "Oooh... noooo... no... no, we are not monkeys! Ooooh...no... not to be monkeys, but civilized Englishmen!" Caroline did not fall in love with my singing. Maybe I sang about the wrong note. I had turned off on the guest room bed with the outerwear on. I woke up at noon with a creepy hangover. Thanks for the that I didn't live with Henslow's. It would have been embarrassing. My head ached, my stomach was spinning, and my mouth felt dry. My mind was depressed. I was lying on my back on the bed. In hangovers, I always suffer from a state of depression, and that's when some unpleasant memory of my past life often comes to mind. This time, a nightmarish memory came from the year of Edinburgh. That cold winter evening in Edinburgh jumped from the dump of my memories when I drank the first hops of my life. I had met a young Scottish man in the university library who had been studying medicine for his last year. We drank a bottle of Scotch whiskey at Malcolm's apartment in honor of his birthday. I felt really liberated and happy. Those feelings still make me crave a state of drunkenness. Still, that night, after Malcolm had already turned off the couch, I vomited out all the whiskies I drank from the window.

At night I saw a nightmare where I got into an argument with my father, and in a rage, I shot him. After the death sentence from the court, I was hanged on a branch of a large oak tree in the yard of our home. My mother was also watching with big smile my execution. In the hangover, it felt as if the rope had once again sunk into my neck, strangling my throat. When I woke up, I felt a strange guilt. I didn't know if it was because of drinking alcohol or because I had spoken openly about my feelings and mocked all my relatives at the same time. It felt like I had committed some big crime. As I lay there on the couch of his apartment, I noticed our drink on an empty whiskey bottle on the table. The smell of whiskey coming from it caused an unpleasant spin in my stomach. Instinctively, I snatched the nearest boot from the floor at lightning speed and vomited there. It was such a raging cramp In my stomach that I thought my guts would come out with the vomiting. Luckily, it was my own boot, so I didn't mess up the floors of Malcolm's rental apartment. I hadn't vomited for a while, but in that situation, there was no alternative on that thing. It was a really bad-smelling dark yellow burning, acidic crap. It also flowed from my nostrils. I tried to drink water, but the result was the same. I walked to my rental apartment with a vomit-smelling boot on my foot. My voice was on the ground the whole next week.

I had to ask my father for money to buy new boots, as the old ones could no longer be used due to odor nuisances. It was the only new social event of that winter in my student life at the time. Now I would not be able to afford such vomiting. I tried Malcolm's old recipe and asked Caroline for a cup of cold milk. It usually made my stomach calm down in a hangover. I swayed with trembling hands into the living room. Erasmus had gone to work. Caroline had cleaned the apartment. Fortunately, Caroline's anger had quickly passed, so she no longer recalled my last night's foolishness. She brought me a cup of milk, which I drank quickly. I apologized to her with a cup in his hand, swearing that I would never again cause them such shame. I even got her to laugh when I told her about my adventure at the zoo. She didn't believe my story about the giant lizard. I told her I was going back home soon. She was barely able to hide her joy from my departure. I didn't mention anything about my idea of moving to them to live again. Why take such a risk in vain? Now I can safely plan my move to London. They would no longer dare at that point to deny me coming to live with them as I stand behind the door with my moved luggage. When Erasmus returned from work, we ate well. After dinner, I left for the city center to arrange a ride to Shrewsbury. This time I was relieved. This visit to London was really successful.

I would move here in good vibes. I was relieved as the ride left for home. During the trip, I met a young woman with wheat-blonde thick hair. Her face was roundish with a big-eyed. She resembled Fanny a bit. The name of this talkative and immediate woman was Emmy. She was working at a bakery and was now going to visit her childhood home. I liked her right from the first very beginning. Her hearty speech, spiced with humor, got me in a good mood. I told Emmy I was a scientist, to whom he laughed sweetly. She thought I was joking. I reportedly did not seem to be any kind of scientist but an ordinary farmer. I went on to tell her I will moving to London so I could get better acquainted with nature research. She said she was pleased with her work at the bakery. I secretly tried to ask Emmy what women really want from a man. What kind of men do women like? Why were women always so mysterious? I wanted to test whether the claims I heard from other men about women were true, but Emmy didn't respond to my curiosities, laughing at me with a cunning look on her face. Her mother had said it was not good for the human mind to think too deeply about things, so Emmy, in her own words, took life lightly. She thought life was meant to be enjoyed, not worried about difficult things. I liked the relaxed immediacy of this young woman. It was easy to be with her.

Emmy stayed away before my hometown, but before that, we exchanged our contact information. I sincerely wanted to meet her again. The rest of the journey went slowly when there was no one to talk to. At home, I told my father I would move to London. That was a great thing, he thought. My father went on to ask in an ironic tone about financing my move and housing. I replied, embarrassed, having calculated his money again in both cases. He once again agreed to help me. I will regret myself mentioning to him about baker-Emmy. He found my acquaintance with some of the baker's assistants completely inappropriate. My father told me to end our beginner acquaintance immediately, or he would deny me my inheritance. I felt humiliated. Even at the age of thirty, could I not decide with whom I spent my time? My father interrupted my grim reflection by saying he had already chosen a spouse for me. According to him, when choosing a life partner, the most important thing was the same class status and the opportunity to increase wealth. I could postpone my move for a couple of days as we would go to see his chosen wife tomorrow. I was amazed. My father had chosen a spouse for me without bothering to ask my opinion on the matter. Who is this princess, then? I almost fainted as my father said that my cousin Emma Wedgwood would be my wife. I had last met her years ago.

Then, she was boyish, stout, serious, distressingly quiet, and boring. She is older than me. Worst of all, she's my cousin! As I snorted at my father, this was already approaching incest. He reminded me that he had to marry his cousin too, so that's about it. The most important thing was the preservation of wealth in possession of the family, not the emotional connections to the spouse. Emotions will then come in later if they are to come. Shocked by the news, I went to my room. I wasn't asleep a minute because I was so frustrated to hear that announcement. Disgusted, I packed my stuff to move to London. I wondered how quickly my good state of mind turned into deep shit. I am lying at night on my bed, hungry in my stomach, without getting any sleep, thinking about my own possibilities and options in my life. Basically, I had no worries, but on the other hand, I couldn't control my life in any way. I was completely under my father's will. When could I break this humiliating dependence on my father? When would I make it on my own? One possibility would also be suicide, though not a pleasant one. I had secretly dreamed of being hanged for a long time. There's something brutally manly about it, as a man is hanging high in the log at night from a cloudless sky against the brilliant moonlight. There is no need to explain anything in it. You can see at once glance what it is all about.

The thought fascinated my mind, but I was afraid of the pain. I wouldn't want to suffer when I die. Death should come quickly. However, perhaps this situation was not quite so serious. Maybe Emma has been beautified in recent years. On the other hand, she is older than me, so if she were beautiful, I guess she would probably already be married. How would I perform my husband's duties if she didn't charm me? Who do the kids with her? My thoughts haunted me. No hell! It's already morning, and I haven't even slept at all. In a panic, I prayed tothe Israfil to bring peace to my mind. With that, I finally fell asleep.

Chapter 17: Emma Wedgwood

My father came to wake me up early. After eating quickly, we went on a horse carriage towards Maer Hall, as riding has been impossible for my father for due to his obesity. The weather was cold and humid. This wasthe typical weather in England this way towards the end of the year. My father told me on the way about the purpose of our visit. Everything, he said, was arranged so that Emma and I could sort things out in peace alone. We arrived hungry in the afternoon. Emma's father rode in the yard of the house when we arrived. I shook his hand quickly. My father stayed with him to talk, and I was told to get inside to do my duty. The building was almost empty. Only the kitchen staff was present. An older woman who worked as a chef in the house advised me to get to the right upstairs room. After leaping up the stairs in quicksteps, I knocked on the door. A dry, monotonous nasal female voice asked me in. I opened the door and saw Emma sitting on the edge of the bed, caring for some old woman. Emma really wasn't beautiful. However, I decided to introduce myself because I couldn't cancel, even though my mind did. Embarrassed, I gathered my courage to walk to her and held out my hand to greet her. "Good afternoon. I'm Charles Darwin. You must be Emma Wedgwood?" I asked seriously.

"Yes, nice to meet you for a long time. How are you?"

"I am fine. Thank you for asking. So, time goes by really fast." I replied in an afflicted voice.

"Are you hungry?" Emma asked in a patronizing way.

"To be honest, I'm really hungry." I said with a relieved.

"Please take an apple from this. It is picked from our garden. These are good."

"Thank you." I replied with delight. When I bit a piece of this little green apple, it felt like my tongue had dried into a crumb, for it tasted so bitterly sour. When Emma asked about the taste of the apple, I lied. My face curled up to make it taste really healthy. Did this bitter taste describe our common future? An old woman sleeping on the bed woke up mumbling something not understandable.

"Who is she?" I asked Emma, referring to the woman.

"She's my father's big sister Emily. She has been disabled since birth. I've been taking care of her lately."

"Well, it's good that someone bothers to look after her. What else are you doing?"

"I don't really do anything else. On weekdays, I help the service staff in the kitchen. On Sunday after church, I have time off, and that's when I usually play the piano myself." Emma said in a quiet voice while looking at the bedspread.

Oh, hell, how boring life Emma spent! I decided to talk about myself and my own dreams.

"I want to be a scientist. I was on a world tour for almost five years. I study nature and animals extensively there." I proudly told.

Emma severely interrupted my presentation before I had time to tell her more about myself.

"I know about your trip. My father said you were there as an unpaid captain's companion." She said, looking out the window.

"It wasn't exactly like that. It wasn't just a trip; it was an exploration trip, and yes, I had a really scientific mission there. On my exploration, I made a lot of discoveries that I took to London for a professor who is currently researching them. He said my findings are unique in the world. This professor has promised to arrange for my work in his field. I want to advance in my career, so I'm moving to London this month." I said excitedly in defense of myself.

I cursed that hefty cheeky woman in my mind! How did she dare to try to evaluate the results of my trip without understanding anything about the natural sciences? With her, life can become really awkward. I will say direct words to her and my father about the future of this marriage.

"I've been to London, and I didn't like it at all. A terrible stench of human feces rose from the river Thames.

There were too many people there, and they all seemed to be in a terrible hurry to get everywhere." Emma continued in a negative voice.

"I see. When do you eat dinner?" I asked indignantly.

"Soon. By the way, why did you come to visit us?" Emma asked in acontemptuous voice tone.

After hearing the question, I felt my heart start bouncing in panic as blood rose to my head.

"Uh… it was thought that…heh…heh….it would be nice to visit relatives for a long time." I lied embarrassed on blushed.

"Oh really. Or so you did think about it. My dad said you were going to offer to marry me!" Emma screamed.

"I didn't know that. Shouldn't we… at least initially… should… that… get to know each other first or what? I hardly immediately saw it at the first meeting to know if you or I wanted to get married or not." I explained embarrassedly.

"Oh really!" Said Emma proudly with her nose upright.

"Could we go downstairs already? Dinner is probably already set on the table."

"Alright. Aunt Emily get back to sleeping, so I'm going to eat quickly. I'll be back soon." Emma huddled with her aunt.

The old disabled woman only mumbled again at something incomprehensible in response.

If I had a chance to be a dictator someday, then such kinds of people would get a poison spike in their ass under a unit of time. Is that disability hereditary? What is bothering them? It would be quite a risk to marry a woman in her thirties. In the worst case, at least some of our children may become disabled. I stared at Emma as she walked down the stairs. She was quite thickset in the physique. She walked like men. By nature, she seemed like a neurotic bitter woman haunted by her feminine care. Neuroticism might decrease at a later age, but that sick codependency would probably remain the same. Had loneliness hardened her? Did the lack of a man make her cling to her disabled aunt? This marriage issue needs to be really seriously discussed with my father. When we entered the dining room, our fathers were already there eating. My father said to me: "You felt so comfortable with each other that you hadn't remembered coming to eat at all." I was shocked by the prickly comment. I glanced at him angrily. It was awfully close that I didn't tell everyone the truth about us. The food was good, but I ate quietly and quickly.

On the way back, I expressed to my father my dissenting opinion about Emma's suitability for me. He didn't think my opinion mattered. He had already settled the matter with Emma's father.

My father promised to give me fair financial compensation as a wedding gift. I did not comment on his bribe suggestion in any way but went on to ask about my siblings. Why had they been free to choose the spouses of their choice? Why isn't that the same right given to me too? My father responded harshly: "You have already slept over your happiness in these marriage things. Your siblings are charming people, unlike you. It is easy for them to meet new people." He went on to ask me, did I think I was some kind of prince to whom all the young women queued up competing for my favor? What exactly did I imagine about myself? This is not easy for Emma either. If, in general, I wanted to get married, now was the moment. He promised to bequeath most of his assets to me if I would agree to his plan. Emma's father also planned to donate Emma a large sum of money for marrying me. For the rest of the journey, I thought in my gloomy mind about my situation. I felt like a whore who could be bought into any activity as long as the price was right. What options did I have? Once again, nothing. My father would not fund my move to London unless I agreed to marry Emma. The situation was tragicomic. At worst, he could deny me my inheritance. In that case, I should go to work for some lousy job because I have nothing but that damn deacon's degree.

I really wouldn't want to experience that kind of horrible fate, so quietly in my mind, I accepted my destiny. I would continue the inbred tradition of our family by marrying my cousin.

At home, I finally got to pack the rest of my stuff for moving. I also took Conrad's drawings and some of my research tools. I got my father for £ 150 to start with. That amount corresponds to the gross earnings of the month of the average lawyer at the time. These would get me started. He promised to send more money later. In London, Erasmus met me. Together, we dragged my bag in the sleet to his apartment, where Caroline welcomed me with a smile. However, her beautiful smile froze soon after hearing from her husband, that I will live with them apartment until spring. She had thought I would come to them for at most a week. Apparently, my father had also bribed Erasmus because, so favourably, he agreed to live with me. That's how I got to London. In the end, it went pretty painlessly. Now I just had to meet Grant as soon as possible to find out what job he had to offer me. Full of enthusiasm, I headed for Grant's apartment. I climbed the stairs and knocked on the door.
"Look who's there. Hey Charles. Come on in."
"Thank you. I just moved to London. I now live in my brother's apartment again.

"Good. That's how those things go forward. Grant replied calmly with a smile. I wanted to ask Grant for help to find some meaningful work done. I just didn't know how I would have intelligently put it. I finally encouraged myself and put it forward.

"I should get a job somewhere. Would you have any research work to offer me?"

"Well, I don't know about the research work, but yes, I have a clear plan for what we need to do. Let's go talk into living room." He said casually.

Grant was in a hilarious mood. Judging by his eyes, he had apparently drunk acouple of whiskeys again in honor of this weekend.

"I also included my notes and Conrad's drawings that he made in South America." I said in a quiet voice.

"Good. First, you get to write down your notes. They are made into a small booklet that is easy to sell at our events. It has to be a short, concise adventure-type book for people to be interested in. The second work needs to be more scientific, focusing on some discovery that supports our theory. For example, you could write about the earth's surface changes over a long period of time. Lyell can help you with that."

"I've never written anything scientific in my life. You must help me with this project. I can also ask my brother's wife to be a secretary. She hardly has anything else to do."

"I can help, but you don't have to come up with anything new. You just write what you remember. Don't think about it too much today as I have great news for you. Tomorrow is a celebration at the university where I want you to be involved. I will introduce you to the important people there. Can you get there early in the evening?"

"I believe so. What kind of event is that?" I asked curiously.

"Then you'll see it. The main thing is that you are there."

"Will I come here to your apartment?"

"Just come here, then we'll continue from here to the university." Grant said as he escorted me to the front door. I left excitedly for my accommodation. I felt involved in something really important. I finally got inside to meet scientists.

Chapter 18: Celebrations at the University

Grant was waiting for me in the yard when I arrived. We left immediately to walk to the university. Grant was in a good mood but mysteriously quiet about the events of the evening. He only told us that we were going to our own kind of people. We soon arrived at a university that was dimly lit. There were already a lot of people there, and many of them greeted Grant with real respect. It made good for my self-esteem to move together with Grant because with him, I felt important. We went to the large ballroom that was reserved for us. The official occasion began when Grant went in front of the hall to utter the opening remarks, after which we drank the welcome toasts. Before we drank toasts, Grant asked. "In what honor are we drinking these toasts!?" Some shouted from the crowd in a slightly drunken voice: "For Great Britain!"

"Right answer! Let us raise the toasts to our homeland!" Grant shouted.

So, we drank the glasses empty by one sip within a devotional atmosphere. Grant then walked to the stage, opening the event.

"Gentlemen! Welcome to this celebration! This is the first time we have met such a large group in the spirit of our ideology.

The last time I mentioned to you was a young man who did valuable pioneering work in front of our new worldview on his expedition to South America. Today I want to introduce you to this new hero of our nation. He is Charles Darwin. Charles, please come here on stage. Please, tell us briefly about yourself and your trip." I began my presentation with tension: "Yes, I am Charles Darwin, and I have graduated as a de...de...deacon. Indeed, I was on a sailing trip around the world for almost five years..." That beginning is the only thing I remember from my short pathetic speech. I was so surprised by Grant's invitation to the stage that I couldn't get many of the sensible words out of my mouth. Damn Grant, he could have warned me in advance of his intention to invite me to the stage to speak. Fortunately, Grant quickly took over the situation, interrupting my confused stutter. I walked down from the stage and fetched myself a couple of glasses of wine. I quickly drank the first glass of wine. I went, embarrassed to sit with another glass in hand to the back of the hall. Grant continued his speech, painting great images of the future for his theory. At the end of his speech, the hostess of the event said the dining room was already covered for us. I had been waiting for this moment. We got to eat. Already at this point in the evening, a few men who were already completely unknown to me came to congratulate me on my trip.

I was reportedly on the front lines making history. They claimed that I was already an equal scientist to Isaac Newton. It sounded more like a drunken man speaking, for I hadn't done anything significant yet. Accompanied by these fellows, I walked into the dining room, which had tables set for an estimated more than a hundred men. Grant grabbed me by the arm and asked me to sit at the same table. It suited me well because I felt like an outsider and out of place here. There was dim lighting in the hall. The delicious smell of meat food meandered through my nostrils. Large green plants in their pots had been brought to the edges of the hall to bring atmosphere to the hall. There were also flowers in small crystal vases on the tables. There were paintings on the walls and a large Union Jack flag on the end wall. In the front of the dining room, the orchestra played calm classical music. Lyell, a colonel, and a couple of government officials from the Ministry of Education came to sit at our table. They said they had already met my father on a similar occasion. My father seemed to be deeper into this thing than I realized. As an appetizer, we were again offered whiskey. It awakened the stomach acids to full action. We started the meal lightly with soup with potatoes, pheasant meat, and vegetables. I gobbled it up quickly because this was only my first hot meal of the day.

The atmosphere was clearly relaxed as the alcohol rose to the head and the stomach filled with delicious soup. I waited impatiently for the main course to be served while others discussed work matters. The rumble of the speech filled the hall as the men got excited to chat. I looked around the other tables. I didn't know anyone here. Were they all involved in this great Grant's plan? That, too, would probably still be talked about vigorously this evening. The waiters collected deep plates, after which the main course of the evening was brought. It was delicious roast beef tenderloin with cognac sauce. There were garlic potatoes stewed in cream with vegetables. As a food drink, we were offered Italian red wine, which was really good. During that meal, I got to know my table members better. Grant made me realize he was going to have a lot to do in the future with these men in the hall. They were all from the top of society. The future of Britain depends on men like them. These men decide what Britain's future will be like. To finish the official part of the evening, a young female friend of Grant's played a song for us on the grand piano. Grant introduced her to us with a glass of whiskey in his hand. That woman was in her twenties, almost a girl. She was not spoiled with beauty. She was a skinny-looking girl with short, dark hair.

She started her playing, which was fast, aggressive, modern, unmelodic, and therefore difficult to understand. I couldn't stand her piano playing longer than a few seconds. I was relieved as she finished the termination of her distressing playing. Grant praised the composition as the music of the future that would break the old-fashioned, conventional style of music. He analyzes this to have been national music exuding a new British pagan power of nature. That composition really broke all the old melodic, easily recognizable music with aggressive style. According to Grant, we should be creating everything anew. It was primarily about national values but also about culture and art. Everything must be British, with roots in ancient Germanic traditions. He ended his speech with a triple long-live cry for Britain, which everyone agreed with. At the end of the last cry, the hall echoed handsomely for a moment. After the echo disappeared into the walls, an ominous silence remained in the hall. Grant broke the silence by ending the evening's official leg. Now the informal part of the evening began, during which I had a chance to come to get to know guests. I drifted into the hallway with the men. I came across a group of men who were already drunk. They greeted me with joy and asked me to join them in their company. I thought, why not, so we walked into the hallway.

They smoked cigars. One of them also offered for me. I hadn't smoked such a one before. He offered me fire, and I pulled my lungs full of smoke. As a result, I got a horrible cough. My guest friend patted my back while praising profusely my courage to embark on a long expedition journey. The desire to leave such a journey did demand the man for courage. He asked me good questions I hadn't thought about. Was I not afraid of sinking the ship or a possible shipwreck on a desert island? There I would be able to get into a savage's mouth or get some dangerous disease. Or worst of all, when I was on the trip, all the beautiful women would have already had time to get married. The last comment was followed by loud laughter, as these men had been married for years. I said with all the courage brought by the hops that I, too, had already found the love of my heart. They burst out laughing again as I told them that woman of my dreams was my cousin. They once thought I was joking. I tried to save my leather and started pretending to laugh at myself. These men considered me a fun chap. After the chatting topics were over, I continued my journey forward. After I tossed a piece of my cigar around the corner on the stone floor, I looked and saw Grant arguing fiercely with Lyell for a long time. They didn't notice me, so I walked secretly closer behind the pillar to listen to what they were really arguing about.

"Calm down, Lyell. We stay on schedule. We analysed Darwin's samples, and we will obtain more. If we don't have enough evidence, so it is always possible to falsify research results."

"I would have liked to have talked more about Darwin. Why did you choose him? That man is a complete fool! From the very first meeting, I doubted his abilities. He lacks an in-depth understanding of this matter. What degrees does he have? Deacon's degree! Then he still dares in front of this audience to stammer that he is a deacon! What the hell benefit is for us about some a deacon!" Lyell shouted.

"He's the best option for us." Grant said in a calm, low voice.

"What! Have you lost your mind? Justify your argument!" Lyell demanded.

"First of all, he has no choice but to agree to everything we demand of him. He is lazy, and it guarantees that he will never leave us. Otherwise, he has to get the right job! Secondly, with the help of the deacon, we can more easily get churches on our side. By him, we can justify our cause to believers, if necessary. Thirdly, if it happens so unfortunate that this ideology of ours did not take the wind under the wings, then at that point, there must be someone on the of which this soup can be poured.

I won't risk my career as a scientist for any reason, and that's why this theory is named after Darwin. This does not mean that I would not fully believe our cause, but it would be foolish not to consider that negative option as well. Were you satisfied with these answers, Lyell?"

"Well, maybe a little. So, you're going to name this theory after him?"

"Yes. It's justifiable for him because Darwin has done the hardest work. Consider now, five years with fleas and in the company with low-intelligence sailors prone to sadomasochistic homosexuality. Sounds appealing? Besides, if we were to exchange him for something else now, would we again have to send some young man to travel around the world for a year looking for samples? We no longer have time for that. We are getting older, and these issues are being explored in other countries as well. I have already heard someone from France's moron investigate this same matter." Grant justified my choice. By this point, I had already heard enough to come out from behind the pillar. They were startled to find that I had heard everything, and I guess they were afraid I would withdraw from their play. I'm not so stupid that I wasn't to suspect something like that. This time it was my turn hit back.

"So here those dear friends spend the evening hiding from others!" I yelled with a confident voice.

"What, Charles? Good when you came. We were just leaving to look for you." Grant tried to explain by pretending to have a sincere voice.

"Well, here I am now. Yes, I thought I'd leave home soon, so thank you very much to both of you for this party."

"No, Charles, you can't leave yet. The evening is still young, and the best part of it is just ahead." Grant hurried to block me.

"What events are left here?"

"We go with the core crew to spend the evening in a big living room where we can discuss these things under real names. At the end of the evening, you get to swear an oath on the flag."

"For which flag?"

"To Union Jack, of course. Come on, let's go."

At this point, I was already so drunk that I don't remember all things very closely, but we still found our way to the living room, where there was already a gang in drunk. It was more of a warmly decorated meeting room with a large bookshelf made of dark beech at the back. In front of the tall windows were dark green, thick curtains. In the center of the room was a long table made of oak, full of drinking glasses, different brands of opened liquor bottles, and playing cards. The room had gorgeous loungers upholstered in high-quality burgundy leather.

On the floor was a large carpet full of pagan symbols such as swastikas and old images of Viking symbols.

"Charlie boy, do we start on spiritism?" Grant asked.

"Maybe, but though, you should first teach me the rules. My mother practiced it a lot with her female friends. I was still so young at the time that I wasn't allowed to participate."

"I'll skip it. It takes so much time." Lyell replied in a tired voice.

"For what are you in a hurry? Tomorrow is Sunday. Are you going to church?" Grant asked with a laugh.

Lyell didn't answer anything, just glared angrily from under his eyebrows.

"Listen, Charles, there are no very precise rules in this game. The most important thing is that you do not pray and do not read the Bible. Those are ruining this game. For starters, we can contact your dead mother, for example."

"I don't think that's a good idea. I mumbled, scared."

"Well, not then. The last time we asked for advice from the spirits here, in the end, the cups flew into the wall by themselves." Grant bragged with laughter.

The assistants next to him belonged to a student organization called the Skull and Crossbones. The first of them started reading some foreign language spells from the book, and his friend spread the cards face down around the table. They were no ordinary cards, but there were strange symbols behind them. We were around a table where every one of us was dealt one card. Every one of us turned the card to turns. I was terrified when I saw the picture on my card. It featured a beautiful female angelic with a headless baby girl dressed in a pink dress in her arms. I immediately remembered the witchcraft ritual I attended in Tierra del Fuego islands. I was so out of my mind that I couldn't look at other people's cards at all. My heart was pounding. I went to sit in a leather chair, drinking whiskey from my glass. Now I regretted that witchcraft ritual. I made up my mind not to cry. I bit my teeth together, suppressing all my feelings. Was that baby sacrificed because of me? I felt guilty about the death of that baby. I tried to reassure myself by saying in my mind that this must be a coincidence. This must be a coincidence! At the same time, there was an inconsolably gloomy voice in my head saying that the image on the card proved that I had been consecrated to her. Grant looked at me strangely when I hit myself with my fists on my forehead, and at the same time, I cursed myself. At the same time, Tilley lamps that were with us exploded, spreading burning liquid around the room. That spread to the carpets but not to the curtains.

Grant shouted to others, telling them to suppress the flames with their coats. After they put out the fire, I decided to go home. I stood up, but Grant would tear me down by sleeve back to sit. He looked furiously into my eyes. "Charles, where exactly do you think you're going? Don't go anywhere because now I inaugurate you to become a full member of our organization!" He then landed on his knees next to my chair, continuing between his teeth in a hissing whisper, "Needless to say, you keep everything as your own knowledge. Is it clear?" Frightened, I glanced at him, nodding quickly as a sign of consent. Grant pulled a chair next to me to sit down. He then poured more whiskey into our glasses and began to tell in a creepy drunken voice about his visions that would come true by our theory in the next century. Some of the others present laughed mockingly at Christianity and sang war songs. Grant dragged me to the back of the room to the Union Jack flag. He leads me to grab the flag and swear an oath after him. "I, Charles Robert Darwin, through my life, I swear to be forever faithful to the kingdom and to serve the British Empire by all available means." After I took an oath, Grant shook my hand. He whispered in my ear that there was no going back after that. Others also came to me to congratulate me. At some point in the night, we set off on a ride arranged by Grant, and as if by a miracle, we found an Erasmus apartment. This time I tried to come in as quietly as I could, but Caroline was already awake. She stood in the doorway with her hands crossed over her chest and an angry look on her face. I began to explain to her that I was coming…. from an important occasion…. with only important men. I am important… I had to behave with dignity there… that is why I am an important man… I feel my value… it is valuable to be important… I am a famous scientist … they only drink great drinks…Before I had time to slobber more, Caroline slapped me on the left cheek with her right open palm. Shouting, she told me to go to sleep. "You haven't lived with us even a week yet, and now you're already drunk again!" She screamed. This time I was out to the floor of the guest room where I woke up in the morning. The next couple of days went by as I cleared my head and listened to Caroline's demands. She demanded that Erasmus evict me from their apartment, but fortunately, my father's money weighed more on the requirements of the sister-of-law. After this celebration, I held a quiet life, trying to take stock of my notes. I wrote them clean at a rate of about five pages a day, composing the parts from my head that I couldn't figure out. Even I wondered about my diligence. I had a compelling desire within me to do this work as quickly as possible.

Chapter 19: The first scientific publications

When I met Grant in college, he didn't say anything about the party where we acted like we were possessed by demons. He just inquired about the pace of my writing. After I told them it was going well, he said he trusted me from the beginning. He already had new jobs to offer me. Namely, Lyell needed my help. I should give a presentation at the university based on his research work. Frightened by the announcement, I asked about the schedule for the presentation. Grant comforted me, saying there was no hurry with the preparation. He went on to promise that the audience would be made up mostly of Lyell's students, so they wouldn't cause problems with too difficult questions. There may be a few who are familiar with geology among them, but Lyell would respond to them. He had promised the same thing years before, yet I had to give my performance alone. Sometimes I felt like Grant had a desire to humiliate me in front of large crowds. As I walked around town, I remembered when Grant asked me to give a presentation to the Plinian Society in Edinburgh. His notes were the body of my presentation at the time. It was the first public scientific presentation of my life. Even though it was based on Grant's notes even then, it still didn't alleviate my tense feelings at all.

I remember tensing the presentation so much that I didn't sleep for even a minute the night before. It would have been a tough place for a much more experienced performer. Unfortunately, I arrived a little late at the university, where the association had rented a hall for the event. I walked briskly through the lecture hall, watching carefully at those present. To my horror, I found them all older than me. A few of them made long glances at me as if measuring my qualifications. At that time, it was estimated that there were less than 50 people present. As I got up to the speaker podium, my hands trembled and sweated. I tried to find Professor Grant in the audience, but I couldn't find him there. I forgot him soon when I started my lecture. My topic at the time focused on the life of beetles in the vicinity of barns. Because I hadn't given performances before, I read the entire presentation from my papers without realizing ever making eye contact with the audience. Judging from the bothered applause, the topic of my lecture apparently didn't interest just anyone. I didn't let it distract my enthusiasm. Right after my presentation, I felt really relieved. I left to my home after thanking the secretary of the association for the opportunity they offered. When I walked I got some kind of emotional burst, and I would have liked to talk about my experience with someone.

I just didn't dare go talk to anyone. Afterwards, all I remember from my lecture is how my voice was whining about the excitement. However, that occurrence had a large positive effect on my low self-esteem. I later heard malicious gossip where I was said to be just Grant's ass licker. They claimed I had the possibility to speak and to attend lectures in general only under the name of my grandfather. At the University of Edinburgh, I was considered stupid. Now, I have shown those envious of my greatness. Grant was worthy of my trust this time, and so I gave a short presentation at the university about the rise of the South American ground. On the advice of Lyell, I quoted this scientific discovery that we which help us to prove the nullifying account of the biblical creation. The students were excited about my presentation. They asked me questions about the animal discoveries I made along the way. I answered the ones I could, with Lyell taking care of their most difficult questions. At the end of the event, I thanked Lyell from the bottom of my heart for this presentation opportunity. After leaving, I walked aimlessly in the city and felt inside me as if on fire. I realized I was now doing the things I really believed in. My heart was on fire for our cause. I realized I was on the right track in my life.

Soon Grant contacted me again, saying that even better was coming, for he had arranged for me to speak to the Zoological Society of London. There I could present my research findings on bird development. We had plenty of time with Grant to prepare for it. I also invited Professor Henslow to listen to my lecture. This time the lecture was already much more demanding, as this was based entirely on the observations made by McCormack and me from the Chiloe Islands. I didn't tell Grant I bought the research results from McCormack. Grant helped structure the presentation, but the content was written by me. In my presentation, I aim to show, on Grant's advice, how different Bird Species have evolved over the millennia. As proof, I used different beaks of birds. After the presentation, Henslow came to congratulate me. He asked to get a closer look at the material I used in the presentation. I gave him permission to do so, even though Grant opposed the idea. After getting acquainted with my performance, Henslow asked me to come to the university. He had made additional observations about my performance. First, he said all the birds I found were finches, not pineal birds, or some other birds, as I had claimed in my presentation. It was true that the beaks of the birds were different, but it proved nothing of evolution but adaptation to different living conditions. No new species had been born.

Instead, the birds had remained finches. I also had no evidence of which animals the birds had evolved from. The beaks of the birds were different because their diets and habitats differed greatly. This, in his view, explained why the beaks of some birds were larger than those of the others. It had never occurred to me that the bird's habitat or food had a bearing on the size of their beak. Henslow said I had also been careless in tagging the birds. After telling Henslow's comments to Grant, he just advised me to forget about Henslow's nonsense. He had more good news for me. Lyell was a member of the London Geographical Association, and he thought I should be nominated as a member of the association. Lyell had gotten us involved in the next meeting where new members were decided. We were there in time before the meeting began. Grant and Lyell had done a tremendous amount of propaganda work for me. Thanks to that, I was unanimously accepted as a member. The biggest surprise was when at the end of the meeting, a new board was voted for the association, and I was also elected to it. I was excited about it! At the time, I wasn't still wondering what responsibilities the new task would bring to me. I was interested in power, not in responsibility.

Chapter: 20 Missing link

I finally got to move into my own rental apartment with my father's financial help. I got along quite well with Erasmus, but with Caroline, time went by in quarrelling. She did not forgive the promises of sobriety I had broken. After much hard work, I was able to write down the notes I made on the voyage. Grant arranged the cost for that booklet and paid the expenses through his association. This is how my first scientific publication saw the light of day. I was happy. I felt relieved as I walked the streets of London. The sun was shining, the trees were green, and the birds were singing. The heavy winter was finally behind me. I had accomplished a lot in my life after my move. Grant invited me to the university to explore a new discovery that he thought would prove our theory true at the latest. I left excited to listen to what Grant had to say. He and his partners met me in the university lobby. We went straight to Grant's study. There were bones spread on the desk that seemed to belong to the monkey. It had the upper part of the skull without the lower jaw and a few pieces of bone that may have been parts of the limbs. Grant was excited about the bones.

"Well, gentlemen. There it is now! The missing link between humans and monkeys. This skeleton proves man has evolved from a monkey.

We have probably had a common ancestor sometime in the distant past. This is yet another piece of evidence to support our theory. No one can argue against us anymore." Grant explained confidently.

I couldn't believe my ears. I don't know if I was envious of the men who made the discovery or if I doubted the true origin of the bones. The fact was, however, that there were only a few pieces of bone from that one monkey. You would think there are more intermediate forms needed between a monkey and a human. I watched others in amazement as they swarmed excitedly around the bones. I encouraged my mind and asked Grant a critical question that came to mind.

"When and from where were these bones found?"

"Three months ago, from East Africa."

"Who found these bones?"

"Expedition sent by the government."

"Do you know how old these bones are?"

"I have no idea, but these are at least 50,000 years old." Grant replied uncertainly with a laugh.

"How and who did the age determination?" I continued to challenge.

"I don't know, but I personally think these bones are at least that age." Grant replied in a slightly nervous voice.

"Where exactly are these found?" Lyell asked in a calm voice.

"I heard that from near the creek." Grant said insecurely. "We can't say that because it raises doubts about the age of the bones. It's better to say, even if they were found in some cave on a high mountain, then no one can question our age determination. In that, Edmond, you are right that these bones must be at least 50,000 years old or even older to credibly support our theory." Lyell said.

"I think it is too early to draw conclusions from one discovery that this is where the remains of the human ancestor are. Where are the intermediate forms?"

"Don't you Charles doubt about that. As these excavations are carried out around the globe for the next decades years, there will surely be found millions of different monkeys 'skeletons that will unequivocally prove our theory to be true. We just need to get some good artists to draw a picture from these bones. It will be important when this ideology is sold to the people. Its creature must be hairy like a monkey, but it must stand on two legs. In addition, we need to draw a gavel into his hand. The weapon proves that such creatures were capable of systematic hunting."

"How do we prove the age of these bones? How do we even know if these bones are from the same animal? I guess we have some evidence?"

"Not necessarily. Rely on the authority of our scientists.

Yes, people believe when enough professors swear by the name of the same thing. What evidence do Christians have to support their own faith? Nothing, and yet people believe them. Yes, we will come up with some reliable way for age determination in the future. It is not a problem. The key is to just make more of these human-monkey discoveries. Perhaps we will soon find the first British Primitive Man, it would prove that man evolved on all continents at the same time, and as a result of interracial competition, the white race has become the master race in the world."

"What about those scientists who don't believe in our theory?"

"It's hard to imagine such, but it's certainly possible. First, they must be made ridiculous in the eyes of the whole nation. As a result, they lose their credibility as scientists. The logical consequence after this is to dismiss them from their posts, and the reason is the use of unscientific research methods. It guarantees the destruction of their research career. That's right for them because they are heretical."

"How do you think the churches will respond to our claims?"

"It doesn't matter how they react to this. We will hit such arguments on the table that every sensible person believes in us.

If they dare to oppose us, we will disgrace them completely. We have our own men in the Ministry of Education and the Board of Education. Soon these things will be taught as scientific truths in all schools to children. When they grow up, then we have the first generation that has been raised based on our theory. That generation is independent and free from the superstitious Jewish fables of the past. That generation is capable of fighting for the British Empire! That generation will survive as a winner in the battle between nations!"

I listened quietly to Grant's passionate sermon. Indeed, he seemed to believe in his theory completely, and in that same belief form, he wanted to force all of humanity. There were a lot of questions in my mind, the majority of which were questionable about Grant's theory, but I no longer dared to ask them. I was left alone in my deep thoughts to walk towards my rental apartment. Why and how would a monkey-like creature begin to change into a human by itself? What would force it into such an evolution? Are monkeys still changing? And is man still evolving? If so, in which direction? We have a written history that is less than 5,000 years old. There are no mentions of any great apes. This issue should be discussed with Henslow. I went to see Henslow and told him about Grant's latest discovery.

Henslow listened seriously to my narration. When I finished my report, he reminded me that he had warned me of Grant's ideas. According to Henslow, there are many things in nature that we do not understand, but that does not mean that the God of the Bible is not behind everything that exists. The Creator had first created the laws and elements of nature. In this way, He has enabled favourable conditions for life on earth, as a result of which a diverse life was possible. I listened intently to Henslow's arguments, after which I told him about the dinosaur fossil I saw. John had never heard of such a being. Henslow did not know whether these dinosaurs were mentioned in the Bible or not. The Bible, in his view, is not merely a scientific book, instead primarily a letter of love from God to mankind. Its purpose was not to answer all the scientific questions but to bring eternal hope to humanity living in the midst of death. In his view, the birth of life on its own was impossible because of its complexity. He continued with challenging arguments. According to John, everything living or inanimate needs material, energy, knowledge, a designer, know-how, a builder, and some reason for its existence. Henslow repeated the familiar mantra that only life-produce life. Philosophically, Henslow thought there was no meaning in life without God.

Whole life would be just a short moment that would quickly disappear forever. Once again, he asked how atheist defines morality. If morality is defined by one's own feelings, then it is the same as trying to build a stone castle on a swamp. Why does an atheist want to live a morally high standard of life? Everyone wants a reward for their refusals. An atheist will live moral conduct only if it is of some use to them. Finally, he asked an unpleasant question: "Do you think the behavior of Grant and his partners is morally correct?"

I knew it wasn't, but I couldn't tell Henslow the truth about Grant's plans. I had sworn an oath of obedience at a university party. Henslow succinctly concluded our meeting with a crushing prophetic statement: "*When mankind has lower themselves as a monkey to among other animals, the justification for the genocides has been obtained.*"

I left Henslow's home in a confused mood. What is the truth about these things? Who is right? Who is lying and why? If Grant is wrong, then why would he lie? What do I do then if Grant is a cheater? I can't endlessly live with my dad's money. I'm not interested in studying, and what would I study? At some point, I got to get some meaningful work. Henslow had nothing to offer me other than studying geology or the work of a deacon. I didn't want either of them.

Grant, on the other hand, offers me scientific work with the country's leading decision-makers. The moral difficulty of choice crooked my mind. I felt deep anxiety inside me and wanted to start drinking booze again.

I went with Lyell to look for the remains of a dinosaur in the south of England because he thought it would be the most potential place where we could find them. We also desperately wanted to be the first to find a British monkey man. It would have tremendous propaganda value in Lyell's view. I was frustrated with this project from the start because we didn't have a clear plan of where to carry out the excavations. This was like looking for a needle in the woods. Needless to say, we found nothing but a couple of fox skeletons in the rain, and with these, we would not make history. I said irritably to Lyell that the British Isles might not have been the most favourable place to make these discoveries. However, neither of us wanted to leave for Africa because of the monkey bones. I returned home disappointed and chilled. My relationship with Lyell became even cooler with the failed expedition. After recovering from the horrible flu, I received, I began working with Grant to investigate the causes of the evolution of the organisms.

Grant had drawn a preliminary picture of some tree of life that described the evolution of species from simple organisms to humans. As I watched that drawing, I suggested to Grant that we consider a few scientific questions that Henslow had asked me. Why would species become other species? What evidence is there of this change? Where are the intermediate forms of different animal species? What is the smallest living organism? How was it born? And so on. I had a lot of "why" initial questions. Grant thought that those were silly questions. In his view, only little kids ask "why" questions. Our job is to tell people how things had happened. The word "how" starts from the fact that things have already happened, and it makes the sentences true for the listener. It convinces listeners of the veracity of our theory, and therefore the word "how" must be used in front of answers. We just will tell how species are born. How species evolve and how they become more advanced species. How different species have spread from the continents to distant island. Grant thought there was no reason for the species to change, it just happened. He stressed that we are not philosophical clowns but makers of practical science. We don't have to think about unnecessary "why" questions. We'll just tell you how things had happened.

According to Grant, the correct arrangement of question-and-answer words was a psychologically important issue in a debate situation. I was intimidated by the thought of debating with someone much smarter than me. Grant said there was no longer an alternative to it. He thinks we would certainly be subjected to malicious attacks from some quarters at some point.

Chapter 21: First symptoms of my diseases

At Grant's command, I continued to write a book about my voyage. In that work, Catherine was an invaluable aid in reviewing my writing. Catherine spent a lot of her time correcting my grammatical errors, and because of this, she wanted to write some of it herself according to my dictation. Just as I was struggling with running out of money, Grant had arranged for me a grant of a thousand pounds for my written work. It was like a gift from heaven. He didn't tell me where he got it, and it didn't matter to me. The main thing was money income. I was really grateful for that because now I didn't have to beg for money from my dad. He did usually give me money, but recalling how pampered, lazy, and ungrateful a child I had been. This time I was spared his discouraging complaint. By those times, my body was giving the first serious warnings about my health problems. I was my home for several days due to severe heart pain. The doctor ordered me to take a holiday. It sounded weird because I hadn't done much other than take a holiday in my life. I didn't start arguing with him but decided to laze for a couple of weeks. I wasn't sure I was in better shape, but at least the heart pain was gone. I had one skill well under my control, and it was laziness. It would end soon.

For now, I would have a busy time ahead of me on the board of the Geological Association. Our study of species change had already been criticized by some naturalists. For some reason, all the charges seemed to fall on my neck, even though Grant was the director of our scientific research. They were most annoyed by our speculation about man as only one animal species among other animals. Due to the tremendous amount of criticism we received, we decided to slow down a bit in terms of developing our theory. First, it was better to make people's minds more conducive to our theory. According to Grant, the criticism we received showed well how Christianity had corrupted the British. We urgently had to find conclusive evidence somewhere for this mechanism of nature that guided the evolution of life. The criticism we received from scientists wavered my faith in our theory, and as a result, my health began to fall again. This time I lost my appetite and was unable to eat solid food, and as a result, my stomach started to show symptoms. Stomach upset was the most vicious because it was accompanied by profuse diarrhea. I must sit many times a day in the toilet, emptying my gut. I lost weight again. I went to several different doctors, but they were unable to give any diagnosis of my illness. As a result, treatments were scarce. One of these humbug swindlers dared to even doubt my mental health!

Personally, I suspected I had contracted my illness on my way through the jungle. I must have been bitten by an insect. Maybe I had gotten some disease from it. These ailments appeared whenever I experienced severe stress. Grant visited me regularly to encourage me. At the same time, he brought me his books to read. The best of those books was Malthus's work, which dealt with the relationship of population growth to food adequacy. Malthus realized that the weakest individuals would die in the struggle for their existence. In his view, this theory was valid throughout the world. People fought for living space, food, and a spouse. Grant shared his own thoughts as a sequel to the book. In his view, the increase in species depended on the resources available, so the species best adapted to the conditions would produce the most offspring. It would lead to the victory of the species best suited to the prevailing conditions. As a result of these increases, more advanced species could emerge. This will soon lead to the spread of the best features and the disappearance of the weak ones. I wondered if it could be that simple? What would be the mechanism that would produce the necessary changes? In addition to my travelogues, I wrote in my diary for myself goals for my future. Did I want to get married or not? What benefits would I get from getting married?

A woman would be of help in household chores, but as companion, she is no better than a dog, although the life expectancy of a woman is considerably longer than a dog, but you may have to talk to a woman. On the other hand, it is not possible to discuss scientific matters with a woman, but no one who has a full head will marry because of it. A woman has to bring joy and pleasures to a man, they compensate for the expenses that she incurs, but on the other hand, the time spent with a woman is a gruesome waste of life. A woman is like a dog who needs a master for herself so that she can live a rational life. If I got married, with whom? What options would I have besides Emma? Probably no others. In this matter, too, my father's will weigh more than my own will. I wrote a letter to Emma telling me more about myself. I let her understand that my religious views differed from her own. Perhaps that would make her back away from this marriage. I received a letter from my father in which he was telling me to come to my childhood home immediately. My dad told me about his planned wedding schedule. Now was the high time to marry Emma. With my mind numbed, we went to my uncle in Maer Hall. Everything was again pre-arranged. I walked from my old habit to their large living room, where she played the grand piano. This situation did not excite me at all. Nothing mattered. I felt indifferent.

I walked next to Emma and presented my case. I asked her to be a wife, to which she seriously replied in the affirmative. We did not kiss but shook hands as a sign of consensus. Apparently, she, too, had already succumbed to the idea of our marriage. After my proposal, I walked over to my father and said the job had been taken care of. After many heavy years, I saw how wide a smile spread on my father's obese face. He patted me on the shoulder and said he was happy with me. Apparently, this was an important thing for him. Now that the wedding was certainly known, I could focus on getting an apartment in London. A bribe of almost £ 10,000 from her father had made it easier for Emma to make a decision. My father promised me another ten tons more for dowry. That amount corresponded to the five-year gross salary of a top lawyer at the time. After all, it was a tremendous amount of money from the marriage. My brother Erasmus only received a gift of over a hundred pounds from our father for his own wedding. Admittedly, he was allowed to choose his own spouse. While looking for an apartment in London, I gradually got used to the idea of marriage to Emma. I started to see Emma's good sides. She was practical, quiet, modest, good at housework, and good at playing the piano. I quickly found an apartment of my choice near the university that would suit us well.

I quickly went to college to tell Grant about my future life situation change. He congratulated me warmly. He had much better news for me. Thanks to their hard propaganda work, I was chosen as a member of the Royal Society of the British Scientific Community. I couldn't believe my ears. By what miracles did I have been chosen there? Apparently, in this world, anything is possible as long as you get into the right circles.

A related celebration will be held before the wedding. I have to be there. Grant would spend a few weeks in Germany vacationing and visiting local universities. After returning from Germany, he promised to help me by all possible means to cope with the Royal Society's ceremony with honor. This time it was also about his own reputation. There was enough reason to practice my thank-you speech at the end of the celebration ceremony carefully. I went to see my brother and asked him for help moving our goods. At that time, I told him about the upcoming wedding. He surprisedly laughed a little contemptuously when he heard the bride's name, anyway, they promised to come to celebrate our wedding. In the drizzle, we left for our future apartment to arrange the goods. In our apartment, Erasmus provocatively wondered out loud how I was able to move into such a large apartment without a regular income.

Envious is an inexhaustible resource. Yes, Erasmus knew who I had received the money from, and that annoyed him. The biggest shock to him was when I asked them to come to celebrate when I would be admitted to the Royal Society. Erasmus by no means believed me but laughed in disbelief at my face. I took the invitation letter from my chest pocket, and without saying a word, I slowly handed it in front of his face. The arrogant laughter echoing from the stone walls of the apartment ceased as if cutting with a knife. A calm silence descended on the room, and that silence was manna in my ears. I slowly lowered the invitation letter from the front of his upset envious face. I asked in a confident vengeful audible voice: "Don't you laugh anymore?" Erasmus raised his eyebrows and shoulders, pathetically saying:

"Congratulations, Charles. This is a great honor.....for the whole family."

I didn't answer anything but folded the invitation letter briskly back into my pocket and walked quickly out of my apartment. For the rest of my life, I will remember that sweet feeling of revenge on my chest as I leaped down the stairs, and at the same time, I squeezed my hands into my fists happily, cheering quietly in my mind. Poor brother was so upset that he didn't even ask why they chose me there! After a while, he came after me in the yard.

I paid Erasmus a couple of pounds for moving aid, and finally, once again, I reminded them to come to both of my inaugurations. I received a letter from my father telling me that the wedding would be held at Maer's local Anglican Church. I was responding to his letter to tell my other inauguration as a member of the Royal Society. I prayed for him to come there. In my mind, I was sure of his arrival. He certainly wouldn't envy me but would be proud of me. Anyway, I had proved my genius to my whole family. I also mailed a letter to Emma telling her to pack her stuff by the wedding. We would move to London right after the wedding.

Chapter 22: Inaugurations

Finally came the glorious day when I was publicly joined as a member of the Royal Society of the scientific community. The event had held at their Somerset office in London. My father didn't come to the event. I never found out the reason for his absence. I was, of course, extremely disappointed because I was not prepared for that. Rather, I waited for Erasmus to cancel his arrival. I felt great pleasure as I thought of my big brother sitting bothered among the dignitaries watching me be ordained as a member of the community. Erasmus would get a princely lesson on its younghood bullying. This selection of me a was little strange. It would have been more natural if Henslow or Grant had been selected for the association. They had achieved brilliant scientific results in their careers. What would the members of this association say if they knew I hadn't studied at university for even one full semester? If someone had then told me that I would be ordained a member of the Royal Society in the future, I would have treated it as a great insult. I tried to shake, I think, those shameful memories of the past because they would never matter again. We arrived seriously with Grant at Carlton House Terrace, where the association's premises are located. Inside, I was surprised at how few people were there.

I was waiting for hundreds of people to come here. Grant said only a few men become members of this organization every decade. I should be really humble and grateful for this selection. A burst of joy flooded my heart as I saw Henslow with his wife coming to the scene. I didn't pay attention to Grant at all but ran to them to tell them about my future marriage. They were both sincerely happy for me. My brother arrived with his wife at the very last moment, just like protesting something. Erasmus was tired-looking, and Caroline clearly pretended to be happy for me. We walked from the entry hall directly to the ballroom, which was large and nicely decorated. The ceiling was high, and the white walls were lined with large portraits of prominent British men from past centuries. They had all been members of this community. There were about a dozen community members present. Royal Society President Joshua Compton handed me a Latin language certificate of my membership. I didn't understand a word about it. I was indeed the only man admitted this year. After the ceremony, we were offered a gala dinner in the cabinet. This time I was able to avoid drinking too much alcohol. The Henslow family seems to have a calming effect on me. Erasmus was really quiet throughout the event. He hardly talked to anyone, even though he knew Henslow for a longer period of time than I did.

Grant also treated Henslow as if he hadn't been. Their disgust seems to be mutual. In this icy atmosphere, I had to try to be the center of attention and keep the story going. It was as hopeless as igniting ice into flames. At the end of the event, we went to a nearby church to listen to the music of Johan Sebastian Bach. The devout atmosphere of Bach's music made me almost to tears of joy. As I listened to the organist playing Toccata Fugue, my thoughts galloped into the birth of the universe. The slow point of the composition seemed to tell us how wonderfully diverse nature is. Bach's music had a great educational effect on me. Even though I couldn't hum the simplest chord in my mind, this music still brought me great pleasure. In the early evening, the festivities was over, and we all set out in our own ways. On my home trip, I had in mind to still deviate to the pub for a couple, but I managed to restrain myself. Soon I would be leaving for Shrewsbury to spend another consecration. This time the journey from London to Birmingham folded nicely, for as a sign of the new modern age, a railway had been opened between these two cities. The train ran on coal, and the journey folded much faster than ever on a horse. By the time I left London, I was home in Shrewsbury in two days. Yes, indeed, technical progress is awesome! I can only imagine how these trains will develop in the future.

Perhaps such a rail network will be available to the entire British Isles as early as this century. To my surprise, my father had come to meet me at the train station. He was exceptionally friendly. From there, we continued towards my childhood home, from where we would continue to Maer Hall, where the wedding would be held. I only brought a black suit. I think that was enough for this event. My dad thinks I should have had a tailcoat. My siblings had come with their spouses earlier. When I superficially talked about all sorts of idle things with Erasmus, he seemed to have recovered well from my appointment as a member of the Royal Society, or at least he played his part well. I would have liked to have seen Henslow and Grant at my wedding as well, but they were blocked by their busy schedule. We left with the whole family towards my uncle's farm. There, everything was carefully arranged on top of the last one. Their large living room had been converted into a dining area with many different flowers brought in. The wedding guests came mainly from the Wedgwood side of the family and circle of acquaintances. I went to meet Emma. It was like I went to a clothing store, as I didn't experience any major outbursts of emotion due to our wedding. I went to Emma's room upstairs. There, her mother and friends had helped Emma wear a white wedding dress.

Emma's hair had been lifted up onto the bun, and her face had been make-up. She seemed quite pretty and submissive to her destiny. We briefly exchanged greetings. Emma's behaviour had changed since our last meeting. Now she showed respect for me. She didn't longer question what I said. She had packed all her clothes as I had been told to do. The ceremony would begin in a few hours. Nervous about this situation, I left for a nearby church. The rest of Emma's family's wedding guests were already at church when I arrived there. The women were already in a sensitive state of mind with handkerchiefs in their hands. I sat on the right side in the first row of benches next to my father. Emma's relatives were on the benches to the left of the corridor. The priest came precious slowly to the altar. He hinted at my brother and me. Emma waited at the front door of the church with her father. The cantor began to play a wedding march, at which point they set out slowly to walk toward the altar. I walked to them. We met each other in the middle of the church hallway. I nodded to Emma's father while grabbing Emma's right hand. Together we walked calmly towards the altar. The guests stood respectfully until we reached the altar. At the altar, under the priest's observing eyes, I felt myself very calmly. The priest gave a short, ridiculous speech.

My father had told him before the occasion that he should not read anything from the Bible. The ceremony could very well have been held at a police station where a judge would have handled the official part. My brother was the best man, and he gave me a ring. While at the altar, I realized I had not even kissed Emma before this, and now was no time to practice. Finally, the priest asked us both. "Do you want to live with each other as well as in adversity?" We both answered in turn in the affirmative. The priest told me to thread the ring I received from Erasmus into Emma's left-hand finger. After doing that, the priest told me to kiss Emma. I lifted the veil off her face and pressed my lips firmly to Emma's lips. Perhaps less intensity would have been enough, but that kiss must have seemed passionate to the wedding guests. Emma smiled happily at me. We turned to the guests. The cantor played the same wedding march again. Then we slowly walked toward the front door of the church. After the wedding ceremony, we went back to Emma's home and ate the wedding cake. In the travel trolley, Emma wiped the traces of lipstick off my face. Uncle Josh, who now became my father-in-law, had arranged a small orchestra in their home to play background music. When all the guests came, he welcomed them to our wedding celebration. Josh was moved by his own short speech.

In it, he said he always considered me a hardworking and decent man. After finishing his speech, he asked us to the middle of the living room floor. For a moment, I was already afraid of him asking us in his silly gust of emotion to tell us how we had met, but luckily he only asked us to cut the first piece of cake. We went around to the table in the middle of the living room. Together with Emma, we cut the first piece of cake hand in hand. The guests applauded us approvingly. Emma's father raised the toast for our happiness. Everyone drank glasses of champagne. The orchestra then played a short melody in our honor. Josh went to the orchestra conductor and, drunkenly, loudly told the orchestra to play the wedding waltz. Then he asked us to dance to it. I hadn't danced anything in my life, and now then, I had to survive trying to dance to a wedding waltz without booze. Well, at least I decided to give it a try. I grabbed Emma by the hand and put my right hand on her wide hips. At first, I started rotating counter-clockwise while Emma was moving naturally clockwise, so we collided with each other. She whispered in my ear that I should lead her. In a slight panic, I began to rotate in the opposite direction. Emma had danced in high heels before, so she followed me. I focused so closely on staying upright that I wasn't listening to music at all. I felt silly as I spun around at the wrong pace.

In that hassle, I inadvertently stepped on Emma's toes a few times. Suddenly in the middle of the dance, I had enough of that spinning and left Emma standing on the floor. I walked in frustration to sit on the bench. I wondered to myself, guess I don't have to do things at my own wedding that I don't like. A multitude of people began to irritate me, especially when most of them were completely unknown to me. My father saved the situation by continuing to dance with Emma. I decided to drink a glass of wine. The wedding guests went dancing. I quickly drank the wine while watching others spinning on the floor. The intoxicating effect of the wine reassured me. In it, as I watched the guests dance, I thought in my mind about the reasons people want to dance. What on earth makes people spin on the floor while the music is playing? Luckily, that violin tingle ended short, and I got to eat. We sat with Emma side by side in the middle of a long table. I whispered to Emma that we would be leaving right after the meal. I ate quickly without talking to anyone. It was a huge disappointment for the wedding guests when we left Shrewsbury right after the meal. I quickly told my father we were in a hurry to our new home in London. We left quickly after saying goodbye to our parents. It was already dark when we finally arrived at the inn.

When we checked in, the receptionist congratulated us on our wedding, and he kindly arranged for us a room of our choice with a large bed. I dragged Emma's suitcases to our room. I had no intention of performing any silly ancient ritual of carrying the bride over the threshold. Dear wife should walk after me. I was really stressed and tired. I just wanted to go to bed quickly. Our room was dark, cool, and damp. When I closed the door, I realized this was the night when our marriage would be fulfilled. How should I act here? After undressing my outerwear, I went under a blanket. Emma was standing in front of the bed in her wedding dress, urging me to help her take off her skirt. I told her to take off her skirt by herself. I wasn't going to perform any ancient silly romantic ritual. After a long trying, she finally successfully removed her cover skirt. Then I told her to turn off the oil lamp. She came to bed shy. In it, we lay quietly side by side on the same bed. Now that there was a moment when I could get make love right with permission, of course, I didn't want it at all. It's weird when there's a chance. Then you don't want to. How many times in my life had I dreamed of making love with a woman? Probably thousands of times, I guess nothing helped here but to dream about that baker-Emmy again. The thought of her always ignited me. I slowly turned to Emma and said in an uncertain voice that she was pretty today.

Emma stated that I was also manly, though I was perhaps a little tactless on the dance floor. I wanted to forward slowly by chatting to her something. Finally, I honestly told her I was completely inexperienced in situations like this. As you might guess, so was Emma too. In the dark, I kissed harshly on her lips. Emma pulled away, startled. She advised me to kiss her more gently. Emma touched my neck lightly while gently kissing my lips. I instinctively squeezed her breasts. As I moved, I oversight touch between her legs. I was startled to find that she was in a really aroused state. Instead, my penis showed no signs of life yet. Emma was embarrassed by my reaction. I crawled over the top of her. Inadvertently I had forgotten to take off my panties, so I had to spin back to my own side to take off my pants. After getting them off my feet, I told Emma to spread her legs. I got on top of her and started rubbing myself against her vagina. After a moment, as if unnoticed by itself, my half-stiffened dick slipped into Emma's vagina. At first, it didn't feel like anything at all. It was as if I had waved my cock in a big bucket of water full of warm water. Instinctively, I got up on my hands and began to move my hips back and forth at an accelerating pace. I thought of my former girlfriend, Fanny, so I immediately ejaculated into Emma's vagina. It felt really good, but the feeling of relief quickly passed.

I got up off the top of Emma's, twisting to the side of the bed. I didn't know what I should have done or said now. I am just only panting for my tiredness. I felt ashamed and weak. Emma was apparently also ashamed of this situation. She lay quietly on her back. As my breathing stabilized, my mind began to smoke tobacco, so I got out of bed to get dressed. I wanted to go out to smoke. I walked in the yard thinking about this day. How many revolutionary things have happened in my life today! While at sea, it could have been half a year that nothing happened. Today I got married and had sex with a woman for the first time, but it was pretty much nothing. But what can you expect when you go to bed with your cousin? It was hardly that our action lasted a few minutes longer. What did Emma think of our actions? We Britons are certainly not any of the best lovers in the world. It's probably because we focus on more honourable things in our lives, like warfare and doing science. At that point, I didn't think about the possible consequences of our actions. After smoking, I went back to our room. I watched Emma, who was already snoring in a deep sleep. I crawled next to her, and I fell asleep soon, satisfied with myself. I had fulfilled the masculine way of married duties with honour. We woke up early. We didn't discuss our last night's quick action but went downstairs to eat breakfast.

It was quite a hearty, traditional English breakfast. After we ate, Emma wanted to have a bath. She recommended the same to me too. Emma promised to take better care of my hygiene in the future. I replied to her that I had washed often enough, but this time I agreed to go to the bath after her. In the bath, I thought about our activities. It still felt really good despite all its clumsiness. I felt a great bitterness toward destiny because I had lack of this sexual pleasure in my youth. Now would be the time to take back those lost moments. I got out of the tub and got dressed. Emma had already packed our bags. She had also packed her wedding dress in a suitcase. She wore a plain black skirt. To my disappointment, I found it drastically changing Emma. Romanticism was gone, and it was replaced by ordinary practicality. When we traveled to London, Emma was quiet all the way. I thought she was angry, but she claimed everything was fine. She just had nothing to talk about with me. I looked at the landscapes while sinking into my own questions about this marriage. What kind of life should be with a wife? Where is it the much-talked-about romance? Why I can easily talk to totally stranger's women, but I don't have anything to say to my own wife? I arranged a ride from London station to our apartment. In the yard of our apartment, a driver helped me carry suitcases to our apartment.

Inside, Emma was pleasantly surprised by the size and location of our apartment. After a quick meal in the dim kitchen, we went to sleep. The next few days passed by arranging the apartment. Emma cleaned our home. She put the items in the places she thought were best, and I bought more of the items he found necessary. I followed Emma and made positive observations about her. She no longer nagged me. Instead, she had submitted it to me. Yes, Emma suggested different things to me as a good wife should do, but she still let me make the final decisions. I realized how handy the creation of a woman was. She realised things that didn't even occur to me. Emma knew how to decorate our apartment and create a cozy atmosphere there. She chose the curtains, dishes, furniture, and everything that made our apartment a home. Emma brilliantly complemented the shortcomings I had. I started to like her fussing. She also took care of my adequate food intake. Likewise, I gradually got used to her taking care of me. In the beginning, it offended me when she treated me like some helpless little brat. I told her I was an adult man who needed respect and less hassling around me. She understood my point of view, giving me more of my own space. Best of all, Emma was a great cook. She thought I was too skinny, so I had to eat more. Thanks to Emma's food, my weight started to rise rapidly.

Maybe this marriage of ours was just a good solution after all. I didn't like her at first because we are so similar in my self-annoying traits. We can both be described as aloof in characters, silent, phlegmatic, boring, analytical, and without a sense of humor. Our fathers guessed we were just the right people for each other. Emma remembered our birthdays, which I often forgot. She soon got used to the fact that I never remembered even our wedding day. As I learned to know Emma better and built up our common home, I was almost completely alienated from other people. I didn't think about our theory or anything else related to the work. I took a break from Grant and the other architects of our theories. I just wanted to get laze with Emma. When summer came, Emma told me she was happy to be pregnant, so that quick wrestling on our wedding night had immediately borne fruit. I guess I have some really tough stuff between my legs. At this point, I wasn't yet thinking about the responsibilities associated with paternity. I just earnestly hoped the child would be a boy. My brother had still not become a father, even though they had tried the child for many years, and no one really couldn't blame them for the lack of trying. At last, we went to visit my siblings. They had wondered why we had not invited them to visit.

Amused with Emma, we explained that the days were just going so fast that we hadn't remembered to pay any attention to them. We had all sorts of things to do, home remodelling and buying things. Besides, now that we live here permanently, we can regularly meet every week. Erasmus's wife Caroline was clearly envious of us when she heard Emma was pregnant. Erasmus let me understand that their problem was due to Caroline. Their family had infertility. Erasmus would last a life without children, but for Caroline, it seemed like a tough situation. It was certainly heavy for her to be beautiful but barren. Catherine had had her firstborn with her husband, Kevin. Their time was spent primarily with the Kevin family.

Chapter 23: Transmutations

Due to the circumstances, I had to plan our future in more detail than usual. Because of the addition of a family, I was forced to think about my career, or rather its absence. How would I support my family? I would have liked to be a researcher at a university, but I would have no chance of that. I also weighed the writer's career, but it seemed mentally too heavy. I ended up concluding that I would rather continue the baron lifestyle for a few more years since most of the dowries from the wedding were still in savings. After a long hiatus, Grant invited me to the university for a presentation of his new revolutionary theory. I thanked him for the invitation and promised to come, even though I had no passion for the event. Familiar faces were there again. From the back row, I looked at Edmond analytically. He was exceptionally important today. In a way, it is respectable to get excited about work as passionately as he did, but I think marriage was much more relaxing. Grant told us that he had visited Germany in several different cities, gaining a lot of support for his ideas, and he also had influenced by Germanism. He saw the future of the British Empire and the German Empire as allies. Besides, the husband of our new queen was also a German prince.

In his view, in the next century, these two brave nations would divide the world. In this matter, I had heard that he had turned his coat, for, in the past, he had a sceptical attitude about the Germans. Grant enthusiastically explained to us his theory of two new kinds of natural law, which he had invented together with his German colleagues. According to them, there were more individuals in each generation of each species than they were able to survive and reproduce because food would not be enough for everyone. As food dwindles, the strongest would survive, and the weakest would starve to death. Those individuals who best adapt to the prevailing conditions would survive as winners in the battle for life. This same law of nature also applies to humans. Individuals of different species that survived the battles of life had better heredity than those that clotted on the road of life. They were able to leave more offspring than less well-off individuals. As they multiply, the inherited traits would evolve even better. Thus, the species would evolve better and stronger all the time. This would ensure that poor traits are eliminated from the population over time. Grant called this law natural selection. It consists, according to him, of the constant change of organisms, the ability to reproduce, and the occasional inheritance of beneficial traits to offspring.

Thanks to natural selection, the best traits become more common among species. Among humans, natural selection is best seen when members of the white race take over the lands of the wild tribes, resulting in the enslavement of the natives or their extinction. The best example of this development was Australia. There is no morality in natural selection. Then Grant introduced their second theory, which was called transmutations. In short, with this transmutation theory, he claimed to be able to prove how elements in nature slowly transformed into other elements. This, in his view, would be a basic precondition for the transformation of animal species into more advanced species. My interest arose in this idea, so I decided to ask Grant a couple of questions.

"Do these two theories work together and simultaneously?"

"Good question, Charles. In principle, natural selection proves the transmutation to be true. In nature, we see the end result of what transmutation had developed perhaps for thousands of years before it appeared in nature."

"You said that elements become other elements. What are these elements? And why are they changing?"

"I do not yet know the answer to either of your questions."

"How, then, do we prove this transmutation and the necessary changes in the various animal species?" I continued with my sharp questions.

"By archeology. Scientific progress will move forward at a tremendous pace in this century. I am quite sure that in a few decades, there will be scientific evidence for these things." Grant said in an indignant voice.

Edmond was nervous every time I asked him difficult questions that he didn't know the answers to. As a result, his speech rhythm accelerated, and his voice rose higher. He did not tolerate objections.

Aware of that. However, I decided to continue my questions.

"Does this transmutation explain heredity? Such as inherited diseases?"

"We don't know that yet either, but the transmutation is partly the result of our own choices. If someone marries a close relative, for example, then it may weaken the heredity. On the other hand, transmutation takes place independently of us."

Grant explained, staring into my eyes at the same time. I realized from his hint that it was the right time to stop asking critical questions. As a result of the lecture, Grant concluded that human life is only the result of lucky coincidences. It was an inconsolably hopeless decision for this lecture.

As I walked home to home after the lecture, I wondered in amazement at Edmond's speech. His theories raised more questions than these were able to give to answer. It might seem to work when it comes to animals. Natural selection explained the extinction of the species over a long period of time, but it did not give any answers to how the species could turn into different species on their own without outside help. How could one simple species evolve into a more complex creature as a result of the extinction of other species? Did the beetle evolve into a lion? How had fish, birds, or insects evolved? And above all, from what animals had they evolved? How had sexual reproduction in mammals developed? In the history of mankind, this natural selection gives little to no explanation, for man is far too complex a creature to be explained by such a theory. Didn't that fact make any difference to what social class a person happened to be born in? I think a person's success in life is the result of many different factors, just as a birthplace is of tremendous importance to a person's success. If I had been born a hundred years ago, for example, as a son of a miner in Russia, then what options would I have had in my life, even if I had been smarter than now? In Russia, it is not possible for a miner to educate his child, and they can't help their kids to survive in life.

Grant was a familyless man himself, and yes, you could hear that from his speech. Above all, his understanding of the logic of a woman was really flawed. I had lived with Emma for some time, but I still couldn't say for sure I knew her. The world of thought of women is so absurd that it cannot be explained by transmutations. Luckily, woman does not decide on any important things in her life, cause her world of thought is a mystery. It is a great fortune that a woman's father chooses a husband for her. What would follow if women were allowed to decide independently with whom to marry? Surely it would cause a national emergency because they would be led astray by their simple pleasure-seeking minds and fall in love with lying drunkards. Had Grant left alone as a result of this natural selection or of his own free will? Did that make him a weak loser? In any case, Grant's enthusiasm was admirable. My enthusiasm for our cause was rather waning. Everything was fine in my life now. I didn't want to bother myself with difficult things. I had achieved all the important things in my life. I had a family and a home. I no longer felt any need to show anyone. In the future, I would just like to spend time in peace with my family. I lived the life of a serene adult man. At home, I told Emma about the lecture for some completely incomprehensible reason.

In her view, such a theory exuding the meaninglessness and hopelessness of human life sounded like the invention of the devil itself. Her answer was predictable. What other answer could her simple, religious woman's mind have offered? I didn't start arguing about it because Emma was in a delicate state of mind due to her pregnancy. Her stomach was already moderately large, so I helped her with all sorts of things. In addition, I had hired a part-time housekeeper for our apartment to help her. The child's calculated time was from the beginning of the year. Oh, I wish it was a boy. Emma and I waited happily for the birth of our firstborn. It was great to be alone in peace. My nerves rested when I didn't have to be my father's annoyance at my childhood home or fight with relatives. I had finally achieved some independence from my father's grip. We ate well, and I didn't drink alcohol almost at all. With Emma, I also got to know myself better. I began to realize I wasn't a drunkard. I drank too much alcohol only if I got into uncomfortable situations. I escaped social challenges into liquor because it was easier to be drunk with people.

On Christmas Eve, Emma received her first strong contractions. The time of childbirth began to approach. In the morning, I woke up when I heard Emma's hard contractions.

When I instinctively moved the blanket aside, I noticed the sheet was wet from amniotic fluid. The birth had started early and, of course, on Christmas. Where can I get a midwife at this time of year? All I could think was that I should go to Erasmus and ask him to help with the birth. I quickly told that to Emma. When I arrived there in the sweaty wet, I pounded my fists with all my might on the front door of their apartment. Finally, the sleepy Erasmus came to open the door. I told him I anxiety about Emma's situation and asked him to dress quickly. Then we ran lightning fast along the empty streets of London to our apartment as fast as we could our feet. When we arrived, Emma lay naked on our bed. She looked painful. I was startled by the view, but Erasmus was not perplexed at all. I brought water and towels to Erasmus at his command. Childbirth could begin at any time. Watching all this, I felt helpless and started to panic. Erasmus told me to calm down and go support Emma. I stagger to our bed. I took Emma by the hand, encouraging her. At the start of labor, the bleeding was greater than usual. Fortunately, I did not faint this time. Erasmus said the uterine opening phase was going on, which caused Emma to have painful contractions. The effort phase finally began. Emma's expression was really painful. It looked like she had torn it apart from her legs.

Erasmus roared fiercely, telling Emma to push the child out of her womb. I felt terrible. It was awful to be watching this struggle. I had no way I could have made Emma feel better. If Emma survives childbirth and the child is healthy, then I am forever grateful to my brother. As Emma screamed frighteningly voice, Erasmus roared almost at the same time, that now the child's head came into view. Once again, Emma pushed the last of her forces out of her burly body, causing the baby to slide out from the womb. The child immediately began to cry. It was a good sign as it proved the child was alive. Erasmus lifted the child up from his arms and said: "It's a boy!" I quickly got up next to Emma and peeked at the child. He was indeed a boy. After cutting the umbilical cord, Erasmus washed the child. Then he gave the child In Emma's arms. The child calmed down immediately as he got close to his mother. Emma cried, but she said she was happy. I went to Erasmus and hugged him with tears in his eyes.

"Thank you, dear big brother, for all your help. How could this ever have successfully without you? I am forever grateful to you for all this. Forgive me my envy."

My brother looked me straight in the eye and nodded at me with a smiling smile. He himself was in a moved state of mind too.

"Congratulations, my dear brother, about your son. I wish I could experience the same joy myself." Erasmus said in a wistful voice.

We went to the kitchen with Erasmus to eat yesterday's food leftovers. We watched Emma at the same time as she was breastfeeding the baby. I looked gratefully at Erasmus. He seemed to have gotten older a lot this year. I almost felt pity for him. What a great starting point he had in his life, but Erasmus did not complain about his fate. The more time I spent with him, the bigger person he seemed in my eyes. My brother checked on the condition of Emma and the baby and found that both were well under the circumstances. I told him at the front door to say warmest greetings to Caroline. After saying goodbye to Erasmus, I went back inside and looked at the bloody rags on the floor. I realized that I really couldn't have been a medical doctor. How great is the responsibility they must carry every day? In their hands is a human life, from babies to the elderly.

We decided to name the boy William Erasmus Darwin. By choosing a name, I wanted to honor my brother, who became the boy's godfather. Our son grew up fast. It looked like he was eating his own weight of food every day.

At night he woke us up regularly, but it didn't really bother me because, as unemployed, I was able to sleep even during the day. I eagerly followed the boy's growth, making observations about it in my notebook. Emma cared for the child with great love. The child was the most important thing in her life, and because of that, our relationship became a little distant. I felt slight jealousy for my son. I wondered how quickly a woman adjusts to life with a child. It seemed that nature had designed all the necessary procedures into the woman's mind. I didn't do quite as well because I got sick again. This time, my seizures were extremely severe. I vomited and had diarrhea in turn. I had to stay with a bucket in my hand around our apartment, so I wouldn't shit into my pants. My condition was also aggravated by migraine attacks and heart arrhythmias. I thought my head was exploding as I vomited in a terrible migraine attack. Compared to this, a hangover was a little thing. The most humiliating of this illness was the immense flatulence that I have suffered to this day. Sometimes foul-smelling fart seizures could take many minutes for a single time. We had to ventilate our apartment all the time because of this embarrassing disease. During these shamefully humiliating weeks, I inevitably came up with some unpleasant questions myself.

Could these ailments be due to the inbreeding marriages that have continued in our families for generations? At least I knew about my family that Erasmus suffered from severe mood swings at times. In his weak moments, he could sink into gloomy depression for days, closing himself in his own room, medicating himself with alcohol. How will these diseases affect our children? Do they inherit these same diseases? Or are they perhaps inheriting something even worse? I wanted to break this sick tradition of marriages between cousins. Under no circumstances would I force my children to do so. I wrote to my father and wanted him to examine me thoroughly as I no longer trusted other doctors. My illness made me a recluse. Because of my illness, I did not dare to move to public places. I couldn't write either because of a headache, so I decided to give my note to my wife for proofreading. She should make grammatical corrections to them. After writing about my ailments to my father, I received a letter from him asking me to come to Shrewsbury for an examination. Traveling in this condition was just as hell. I cursed in my mind all the doctors to the deepest hell. On arrival, I noticed how even my father's few hairs were almost completely grayed out. Due to his obesity, he moved with great difficulty, gasping. Apparently, he escaped his loneliness by overeating.

He congratulated me on becoming a father while reminding me of the great responsibility it brought. Due to the migraine, I barely said anything. When we got to my childhood home, I just wanted to eat lightly and go to bed. My father said he would examine me right in the morning. I asked the servant to darken my room completely. At night I saw frightening nightmares and shivered a few times awake due to severe cardiac arrhythmias. I woke up to a terrible feeling of hunger. I went to our kitchen, where the servants had already made us a tasty breakfast. I did not believe that my father could diagnose my illness either, as his medical knowledge was based on the teachings of the early 19th century. At the behest of my father, I stripped my upper body bare for examination. At first, he listened to my breathing, which seemed normal. I had no problems with my lungs. Next, he measured my heart rate. My heart rate was roughly normal, but my beating rhythm was irregular. There was nothing to be done about that. The rest of his methods mainly amuse me in this aftermath. The last treatment was to suck blood from my stomach with leeches. He made small wounds on my skin with a knife and placed suction cups on top of the wounds, as this procedure was supposed, in my father's opinion, to remove the pathogens from my blood.

He put leeches on my stomach to suck blood from my stomach environment and thus improve my digestion. I tried in vain to explain to him that there was nothing wrong with my digestion, but he held his head. It was disgusting to watch those little black worms suck blood from my body. They grew into dark red spheres before my father tore them off my skin. At the end of the cupping, he threw the worms into the blazing fire in the fireplace, where they cracked due to the heat. The physical examination ended here. After wiping the bloodstains from cupping my body, he told me to get dressed. At the end of the examinations, dad told me to eat raw vegetables every day. I meant to suggest a vegetable diet to him too, but luckily I got to restrain my tongue. Instead, I asked my father about the possibility that my illnesses were caused by the inbreeding in our family. That possibility was sharply ruled out by my father because if it had been the cause of my illness, then it should have been visible in my siblings as well. Because they were healthy, then it could not have been possible. He thinks my illnesses were due to a trip around the world. The latest and worst option was that these symptoms could be partly psychosomatic. Was I insane? In my father's opinion, I wasn't. Personally, I wasn't always nearly so sure, but we seemed to be incapable of deciding on that.

The end result, however, was that even my father could not diagnose my illnesses. During that time, I tried to eat vegetables on my father's advice and drink lots of water, but they made me feel even weaker. I also took hot baths in the big tub in our bathroom. During my illness, I did not drink alcohol at all. On my father's advice, even before returning to London, I headed to a nature care parlor in the countryside. He said my mother knew well a lady named Byrne who worked there. In their nature-themed spa, I was offered aroma baths. The purpose of the sower was to cure my illness with herbs and old British spells. After the massage, some natural healer hag came to read their spells while I had to lie in the bathtub. She was dressed in the outfit of an ancient druid. I watched with interest this slightly silly-looking aunt. This witch said my illness was due to my distorted energy field, which in turn was due to my guilt about things that happened in my life. She firmly told me in a loud voice to stop all kind of repentance and apologies. Cause I had no reason to regret anything, for I was full of love, tolerance, truth, and supernatural goodness. At her command, I began to imagine my spirit body gliding in the sky. I needed to see a golden ball that would represent my spiritual goodness. At the same time, she urged me to think about who was to guilty for my illnesses.

Next, I had to open my head in my thoughts to receive this golden goodness into me. I wondered a little bit if this could work, but on the other hand, I was so sick that I would receive help from anyone, even from Satan. At the end of the bath, she asked me to close my eyes and breathe deeply calmly. The woman finally said she was praying for an angelic introduction to my life. I thanked this druid woman for enlightening my thoughts and asked her to leave the room so I could dress in peace. After she left, I got up from the tub and took a towel from the bench. After drying myself, I got dressed and left for my room. Oddly, the symptoms eased in the following days. I think stress and environmental factors triggered my illness. I can't stand large crowds around me, and in London, that was hard to avoid. There was peace in the countryside here, so I didn't feel any stress. Should we move to the countryside somewhere near London? Emma might like that idea. In rural areas, raising children would also be easier. On my way home, I also wondered about the possibility of God's existence. If He was once good and loving, then why in the world did I get sick? Why had He even allowed these diseases to haunt me for years? What good did these diseases do for me or anyone? I couldn't find the answers to these questions and knowing it, I started to feel negative feelings about God.

Yes, I acknowledged the existence of God, but I did not felt in love with Him. When I arrived home, I suggested to Emma that we move to the countryside. She was extremely happy about it; she never even wanted to move to London. While I was in Shrewsbury, Emma had gotten some oddly idea in her head about the dangers of tobacco smoke. She had believed tobacco smoke could be dangerous for children. I laughed at her face and said that matter is exactly the opposite, tobacco smoke would open the alveoli to get better to oxygen. However, I didn't start arguing with her about it because arguing with women makes no sense. However, for the sake of our child, I will continue to smoke outside while exploring nature.

It was midsummer, and I felt good, so I decided to drink wine at home for a long time. In intoxicated, I offered to Emma, too, but she didn't even want to taste such devil's venom. Maybe good so because someone had to look after our son. As I sipped my wine, I looked out the window at London's cityscapes. I again enjoyed the feeling of hops, and I was happy. I started falling in love with Emma, and I told her about drunken intoxication. She didn't react to my romantic chatting but thought it was drunker nonsense. When I was drunk, I felt sexually attracted to Emma, so I told her to take our son to sleep.

After getting him to fall asleep, Emma came back to our living room. I felt the sexual obstructions on both of us disappear. I hugged Emma and, at the same time, stripped her. We made love on our couch as the rays of the evening sun coloured the wall with its yellowish rays. After we made love, we fell asleep on the couch. In the morning, we continued our lovemaking in our bedroom. In a small hangover, I coveted tremendously more sex than on ordinary weekday mornings. If Emma were to get pregnant, our baby would become our lovechild. In a sensitized state of mind, I almost hoped the child would be a girl. Emma occasionally went to feed our son and then came back to laze with me on our bed. She skipped church ceremonies from that weekend. I was more interesting company at that time. This is how our lovechild story had begun. I spent this warm summer my time with my family walking in the parks. I really enjoyed watching my son grow. I vividly remember the moment of those days when Emma hugged me on our bedroom bed, and at the same time, she whispered in my ear that she was pregnant.

Catherine helped Emma proofread my writings. They both were an invaluable help to me, for I have never learned to produce grammatically pure text. Just as I was finding my inspiration for my work, my sickness seizures returned. They were just as drastic as before.

This time I was in deep despair. Who would help me now that all possible doctors had already examined me to no avail? At home, I couldn't help Emma, so I had to re-hire the housekeeper I had already once fired. I admired Emma's loyalty to me. I wouldn't have blamed her even if she had left me. Fortunately, Emma's pregnancy progressed well. I was like another little baby to her, lying on the bed. Whenever I could, I read rewritings of Catherine from my texts. I added to it the insights I had received from Grant, thus again spending my time at home within the four walls. I couldn't visit anywhere. I thought I was going to die. John Henslow came to us to encourage me in the midst of my worst illnesses. He tried to comfort me by faith in my quick healing, saying that they had prayed for me. I was glad to see him, but I did not warm up to his words but told my cold opinions about the goodness of God. We also briefly discussed my research work. John presented me with his critical views on my conclusions. Before leaving, he gave me some homework to think about a few things, the first of which dealt with the birth mechanism of the bird's wing as a result of Grant's proposed natural selection. How and from where did the wings of the birds develop? Where were those intermediate forms of a wing? His second question concerned the property of matter. Where did it come from?

Did energy turn into matter in the early days of the universe? How could inanimate matter evolve on its own without outside guidance into plants, animals, and ultimately humans? At what point and how did the substance become aware of time, place, and itself? I had no idea where I would have found the evidence for him, good when I barely even understood John's questions. I had no choice but to ask these questions to Grant. Due to my illnesses, I was unable to attend the meetings of the Board of the Geological Society, so naturally, I was expelled from the Board. It didn't bother me at all. Honestly, I was disappointed with their activities. I still managed to remain a member of the club, even though I hadn't done any scientific research for them. At the time, I was much more interested in following the growing up of my son William. I felt great joy as William learned to walk. Our family doctor visited us weekly to examine the progress of Emma's pregnancy. Everything seemed good. This time we were better prepared for the upcoming birth. I had booked a midwife and a familiar doctor well in advance.

Chapter 24: My daughter Annie

Our second child was born earlier than expected. The baby was a delicate girl. Her birth was easy for Emma, unlike William's birth. I was naturally involved following the birth. After giving birth, the midwife unexpectedly gave the baby first into my arms. The baby stopped crying as soon as I laid her gently against my chest. When I gave her to Emma, the child started crying again. I stayed next to Emma to stroke my girl's thin hair, causing my little baby girl to stop crying. I fell in love with the newcomer immediately and was convinced the feeling was mutual. Grant sent a congratulatory letter in which he hoped the natural selection would produce a lot of healthy children for our daughter in the future. About Emma, such a wish sounded silly. Henslow wanted to attend our child's baptism, and John also wanted to be our child's godfather. That was exactly what I had secretly hoped in my heart, so I gladly agreed to his requests. That would be a great honor for our family. Our daughter's baptism was at a nearby church. I also invited my siblings and their families to the event. The priest who performed the delivery was familiar to Henslow. John visited with the priest to get to know us better. I liked this priest because he really seemed like a believing Christian man.

On the day of baptism, the sky was clear, and there was a little frost outside when we went to church. Emma and the baby girl were both dressed in white clothes. The priest welcomed us at the front door. He began the occasion with a prayer, one hymn was sung, and then John gave a short speech. Finally, he read the following passages from the Bible to the Book of Psalms:

> *"What is a human, and yet you remember him! What is a child of human, and yet you take care of him! Lord, you have created me. In my mother's womb, you have braided me. I am a miracle, a great miracle, and I thank you for it. Your works are wonderful. I know it. Your plans are good. How great those are."*

John's manly voice echoed beautifully from the stone walls of the church. The women were moved by the words John read. The priest asked us with the baby to the altar next to the baptismal font. As Emma held the baby in her arms, he asked us. "Did we want to baptize the child into the Christian faith?" Emma answered in the affirmative. Then he asked me the same, to which I answered in the same affirmative. As a sign of acceptance, the priest made a cross sign above the child, praying briefly. The priest then turned to us, saying our child had made a covenant with God today.

I wondered to myself how a little baby could credibly make a covenant with anyone, baby has no understanding of the world around her, let alone God. The priest continued the liturgy, asking Emma to be near the baptismal font, then he dropped water on the top of my daughter's head with her palm, naming her Annie Elizabeth Darwin. My wife had asked her father to arrange a small orchestra to perform after baptism. At the end of the event, they performed a touchingly beautiful instrumental composition from Johan Sebastian Bach's aria hunting cantata 208. We said goodbye to my siblings in the churchyard and continued with Henslow's to our home. We ate delicious cake baked by Emma. I presented to John the conclusions I had written about the evolution of nature and the birth of the world. He was a little amused by those, but he nevertheless read my writing carefully to the end. I told my fears that these writings could be used for atheistic purposes, to which John sarcastically stated that the problem would be solved by not publishing my thoughts. Embarrassed, I changed the subject by telling about I and Emma's different worldviews. As a result of our discussions, Emma had become afraid of me going to hell because of my research. Henslow explained to us the differences between customary religious culture and spiritual life based on Biblical Christianity.

Among other myths related to our customary culture, he crushed Emma's delusion about the Christian origins of Christmas. He warned Emma about outward piety. The values we lived by ultimately showed who we loved the most. John challenged Emma to think about what motivated her in a relationship with God. Why do you go to church? Do you read the Bible? Why are you reading? Do you try to earn something from God? Have you had to pay the price to follow Jesus? It will cost you everything at some point. It is not worth pretending to Him. You can't get to Heaven by running escape from hell. Finally, John reassured Emma, saying that no one would go to hell for it if he was sincerely searching for the truth.

From the beginning, I had more fun with Annie than with William, so Emma got to take care of our son more. We began to seriously consider moving to the country. I wrote a letter to my father explaining our decision. My father replied that he would agree to finance our move again. Emma and I explored a few potential destinations, but they didn't please us. Finally, as an introduction, I found a house of interest near Kent. It was a white two-story mansion with a living area of over fifteen hundred square feet. There I would find my own meditation room, and our children would also have their own playrooms.

There would also be room here for our housekeepers. The apartment was located in the middle of a beautiful forest. It had an extensive front yard and behind the house was a beautiful flat grass. The size of the plot was over ten acres, and the nearest houses were a few miles away. My dad bought it for us at a moderately affordable price. The house should have been renovated first, but I said I wanted to move there as soon as possible. Due to my haste, we moved our goods there quickly. During our relocation, poor beggars broke windows and stole public property on the streets of London. I wondered at their brazen ingratitude to our government. As we settled into our new home, I felt deep down in my heart that I had made the right decision. Here I would have my own peace, and yet I was close enough to London. I could build my own chemistry laboratory here, for example. This time it would be just the right lab and no playroom like the backyard of our childhood home. I congratulated myself as I watched my mansion. This wasn't bad at all for a man in his little thirties. The weeks after our move went by arranging our goods. I had commissioned the builders to make renovations to our apartment. There was quite a turmoil in our apartment when at the same time we were arranging the rest of our belongings and elsewhere, the renovators with their tools were trying to do their job.

Now I understood my father's concern for rapid moving. It would have been wiser to do the repairs first and, after then, move. Emma and her assistants also cooked food for the workers. I tried to get to know them, but it was hopeless. Couldn't talk to them sensibly. I let them do their work in peace. I saw myself as a manor lord, so I also had to behave like that. I realized I couldn't surrender or indulge in a conversation with any ordinary workers. I needed to myself my own levels of interlocutors. During the day, I toured our mansion back yards, making scientific observations. For a long time, I experienced again, in the midst of nature, the peace I have not been able to experience anywhere else. As I walked through the woods with my thoughts, I felt how my soul recovered from the busy rhythm of life in London. I sat for many hours on a fallen tree trunk, watching the scenery. In my thoughts, I took a distance from Grant's ideas and questioned the meaningfulness of my sailing trip. I didn't want to think about difficult things but let my brain rest. I felt moderately healthy again. When the renovation was completed, we were able to enjoy our new home in peace. I toured all the rooms in our mansion and was really pleased with the results of the renovation. The quality of the work was of a high standard, and the scent of fresh wood hovered in the rooms. I was proud of myself and happy with my life.

Now I was finally independent. I made the decision to be lazy for the next few months. I wanted to throw my brain into the cloakroom and just be idle. I also told Emma of my decision. For her, too, it was a good idea. I slept for a long every morning. We didn't have to bother me with household chores because I had hired more servants for our house for that. Emma gave them instructions on what they had to do. Emma invited her female friends to our home every Sunday evening for a visit, some of whom were familiar with the church. They locked themselves in one room to discuss their affairs. There was nothing for me on those occasions, and I would not have dared to spend my time with them, even at the risk of the death penalty. I jokingly called their gathering a gossip club. After lazing around for a while, I started looking at my sketches written cleanly by Catherine again. It contained less than a hundred pages of my recollections of my trip around the world and our conclusions about nature. I had serious doubts about how we could get this published. Who would want to buy a book on such a boring topic? Grant should come up with something more interesting in this book. Frustrated, I let my writings be and focused on playing with the kids. During the days, Emma played beautiful classical tunes on the grand piano as I played with the children on the floor of our living room.

Oh, how I loved my daughter Annie. I eagerly followed her faltering first steps. As Ann fell, I hurried to her, gently lifting her into my arms. After wrapping Annie in my arms, her crying stopped almost immediately. I felt loved by her. If only our children would stay healthy. It would be really intolerable if they were to suffer the consequences of our inbreeds that has continued for generations. They play a lot with each other while giving Emma and me their own time. In the evenings, I covered Annie to bed and read her an evening tale. In the midst of our happy manor life, Emma received a letter from her home. It was told briefly that her father had died. This was the natural cycle that no one couldn't avoid. We attended the funeral with the whole family. Josh was buried in Maer Hall Cemetery. The blessing was in the same church where we were married. The event adhered strictly to tradition. Emma thought her father was a believer, but based on the conversations we had, I couldn't say anything for sure. At the end of the event, the priest read an excerpt from the Bible, the Book of Psalms.

> *In vain, he assembles property; he does not know in whose hands it will fall.*

This passage from the Bible remained in my mind. I looked sideways at my father sitting in front of me, who was even more, getting older.

He sat quietly, hunched next to my brother. I also had in mind the possible imminent death of my own father. It would bring more wealth to me. Josh had secretly made his will years ago. After the funeral, the division of the estate was made, which turned out to be quite favourable for us. He had bequeathed his farm to his son, but he transferred most of his money to Emma. It eased our financial situation, and it was through this money alone that I was able to continue the carefree days of the Baron for many years. At home, I decided to focus on working again. I completed the classification of animal species I started on my sailing trip. I ended up in five different categories. The first were fossils, the second mammals, the third group I decided to put birds, the fourth fish, and lastly, I placed reptiles. I wrote to Grant about my achievement. At the end of the letter, I added that I would come to visit there as soon as it suited him. I don't know if this sorting was good enough for Grant, but this one is better than nothing. If I were to die soon, I have ordered Emma to give all my writings to Grant. He can use them in developing his theory as he sees fit. However, despite all my ailments, I was more concerned about my daughter Annie, as her growth was clearly slower than normal, and she was quite thin. Nevertheless, we celebrated Annie's birthday in a happy mood. Emma had baked a big cake for our daughter.

Catherine's children were with us to celebrate birthdays. Annie was wearing a pink dress knitted by her mother, which she presented to me, flirting around me. Her long hair was braided into two braids. After she had spun a few times around me, Annie sat on my lap. Together we blew the cake candles out. As the candles went out, Annie turned happily, giggling at me, looking straight into my eyes with her beautiful eyes. It's as if we've been alone in the world. I held my daughter's hand as we cut pieces from the cake together. I gave Annie the gifts I bought. Excited, she opened the gift wrappers with her little fingers. Oh, the joy when she found two new dolls in the package. I am sure that those dolls had similar angelic faces to Annie. Nothing in this world overcomes the sense of happiness I experience as I receive a grateful hug from my daughter. She put her little cheek on my bearded cheek. Emma played happy songs on the grand piano, singing to the children. During that day, our home was like messed up. It was happy evidence of life in our home. On sunny summer days, Annie and I flew a kite in the backyard of our house. Many times, we took our snacks with us and went on foot to explore the nearby forest. There I taught Annie the names of different plants and animals. At the same time, we followed the nesting trees of the birds and fed the squirrels. When we hungered, we sat down to eat our snacks.

In all the questions that preoccupied her mind, she came to ask me for advice. Annie worshiped me, and I loved that feeling of irreplaceability. With Annie, I completely lost my sense of time. Many times, we came home when the evening was already dark. We ate an evening meal made by Emma, continuing to be together by the fireplace in the living room. When we spent the evening in our home, the heat of the fireplace often made Annie fall asleep in my arms. Annie liked to play the most, where I took her in my arms, flying her like a bird. Our educational principles were often put to a severe test when Annie received a negative response from her mother to something she asked for. She soon learned that it was useless to ask her mother for anything because she could always ask the same thing directly from me, and I often didn't want to deny anything good to my beloved daughter. Although my wife was often nervous about Annie's pampering, Annie still obeyed me when I asked her to do so. The most embarrassing incident happened one Saturday morning when Emma and I were in bed performing our marital duties. We had carelessly forgotten to close the door to our bedroom. Unnoticed, Annie walked into the room to look at our intimacy. Luckily, as if by chance, I glanced to my left, and at the same time, I saw Annie standing in her pyjamas on the edge of our bed.

There was a shocked look on her face. I was frightened badly and, in my shame, moved away from on Emma with lightning speed while pulling the blanket over us. Annie's expression was contemptuous. As if she had surprised me from the adultery. She asked in a crying, angry voice, "What did you do?" At the same time, Emma lost her temper completely. She got up naked from the bed and grabbed Annie by the arm, dragging her daughter out of our bedroom.

"It doesn't belong to you at all of what we did! You have no reason to come to Dad and Mom's bedroom without knocking." Emma shouted in the hallway.

I lay in our bed with my right arm on my forehead. I was startled by Emma's reaction. I had never seen her react to anything with such rage. How did this happen here? Oh hell, what a shame. I told Emma to come back to bed and let the girl be at ease. She came, but not very gently mind. She told me to act like a man and stop spoiling Annie. I had reportedly completely forgotten about our other children. What I could do, that I love to spend my time with Annie. I didn't get along very well with our other kids. Especially at the beginning of our marriage, I often felt that William was disturbing our relationship. I couldn't forget it. William had some of the same unpleasant character traits as me. He was becoming an attention-grabbing, sassy, and flatterer.

I loved Annie more than the others combined. Annie was jealous of me, and I was about her. How do I behave when he gets married? I don't think there will be any problems as long as I can choose a decent man for her.

Chapter 25: The crazy year

Erasmus came to visit us for a long time. They still lived in their small apartment in central London, and it clearly annoyed my brother. He had visited our father. Erasmus said our father is already in really bad shape, so death could come at any moment. He stared at me in my eyes, urging me to prepare for the worst. I was a little annoyed by my brother's distressing way of announcing our father's well-being. I had lived a happy time, was relatively healthy, and had not bothered my head with the illnesses of others. I left home from the peace of the countryside with my brother on the same ride towards London. I did not visit Erasmus's home at all so I could avoid meeting his wife. I wanted to meet Grant. He received me cheerfully because he had received good news from Europe. Revolutionary events were taking place in several European countries. Grant recounted excitedly how the old power was overthrown in the way of new ideologies. Finally, the Christian churches would lose their power, and nationalism would replace it. For once, the French had accomplished something good. Grant prophesied that if a German-speaking unified nation-state were to form in Central Europe, Britain should immediately ally with it against France.

However, we must keep our carefulness for possible new competing ideologies. Industrial progress may give rise to political movements that will require a new kind of income distribution. It can lead to a leveling out of class differences, and the demands for all kinds of equality can increase. These things could threaten our social status. This movement is not necessarily limited to Europe alone but may spread to British colonies as well. Such demonstrations must be end with rapid violence. In the end, Grant described this development as positive for our ideology, as this will certainly promote science-based rational thinking. At home I had received a telegram from my brother that would change our relationship for the rest of our lives. Erasmus wrote briefly that our father was dead. He had found our father dead In his bed. Erasmus was already in Shrewsbury taking care of the funeral arrangements. He asked me to arrive with Catherine as soon as possible. A bunch of questions came to my mind, to which I desperately wanted answers. Why had Erasmus been visiting our childhood home? When and how had our father died? I didn't take my family with me to the funeral. A snowstorm greeted us late in the evening when we arrived in our childhood hometown. Erasmus was waiting for us.

He announced in a nervously, nearly hysterical state of mind that the funeral would be held at our father's request in our home in a non-Christian manner. My brother refused to talk to me and didn't answer my questions. He said he was tired of everything that happened and wanted to go to bed quickly. We could discuss what happened later after the funeral. My doubts arose about Erasmus. I was reminded of an episode of our youth when Erasmus had finished his chemistry studies before graduating. He had arrived home and had fought in the living room with our father. After the fight, our father threatened to deny Erasmus his inheritance. I had never seen my father so disappointed. No wonder because Erasmus was his favourite child. I wondered very much why my brother had finished university so close to graduation. I have never received an honest answer from Erasmus. Back then, as a young, destitute man, I could not resist the tempting idea of how much my share of the inheritance would increase if our father really denied Erasmus his inheritance. It was as if my father had guessed my future thoughts then, and he would quickly roar to me in a loud voice. "Boy, don't just think that your share of the inheritance is growing! I'll come up with a better use for that money!" I was startled at his shouting down to my heart roots.

As I recalled that of our family quarrel, I felt how shameful blushing rose to my face from the power of those discouraging words. I shook myself to this moment from those ugly memories of my youth, as our horse's carriage arrived at the front yard. Inside, I noticed the living room door was locked. When I asked why my big brother replied that our father's body was there. I settled for the answer and went to the kitchen. There, I ate quickly and then I went to sleep. Erasmus came to wake me up early in the morning. We went to the kitchen, where Catherine was already eating. We wished good morning to each other's, but we didn't say anything else. The atmosphere was oppressive. After getting off the table, Erasmus said the funeral ceremony would start at nine. He wanted to go back to his home as soon as possible after the inheritance was divided. The first guests arrived soon. Most of them were men unknown to me. Erasmus opened the living room door. I followed guests into the living room. Guests sat on benches talking quietly to each other. Most of the benches were left empty. I watched in embarrassment before, so such a life-filled large living room. Now it was like some kind of interrogation room. The furniture, tables, and plants had been moved away and were replaced individual chairs. At the front of the living room was a long table transversely with a large, sealed porcelain vase on top.

There were a bunch of letters on the table from those who were unable to attend the event. I quickly scrolled through them, noticing the letter that was from Professor Grant. The relationship between them seemed to have remained warm until the end. I glanced at the room, looking for my brother, but I didn't see him anywhere. Just as I was leaving to pick up Erasmus, he came into the room with Catherine. We sat in the front seats. The atmosphere was oppressively quiet.

"Where's the coffin?" I asked, whispering to my brother.

"That's where it stands on the table in front of your beak." He replied with a sarcastic smile.

"Do you mean over that cheap Chinese porcelain vase?"

"Yes, that's right." Erasmus responded by gritting his teeth.

"Have you cremated his body?"

"Yes."

"Why?" I asked in wonder.

"Because that was his last wish." He snapped to me.

"Did they make our father autopsied?"

"No, of course not. Why should have? He died naturally. Only victims of crime will have an autopsy." Erasmus snorted in a growled voice.

I was shocked. I would have liked to see my father's face one last time. Now all that was left was a pile of ashes in a cheap porcelain vase.

I would never know if it really was our father's ashes. I didn't know what I would have answered my brother. Nervously, I pressed my fingers to my fist. Catherine sat next to me and cried. She was apparently too shocked to comprehend this situation. At last, our father's old humanist acquaintance arrived to open this ceremony. He had a syrupy but fortunately short speech about our father. He praised our father from the earth to heaven, telling how dear he had been to the members of his community. Our father's morally exemplary behaviour had been an example to all of England for decades. Critical questions about them came to mind. If our father was once so dear to them, then why did he died alone? The ceremony was quickly over. There weren't read the Bible or mentioned anything related to Christianity. At the end of the ceremony, the guests expressed their condolences and quickly left for their homes. After they left, I talked to the housekeeper about my father's death. She said Erasmus found our father dead in his bed. Erasmus had previously given the housekeeper five days of paid leave. The cause of death was never determined by anyone outside. My brother had said that while studying medicine, he immediately realized that the death was due to a heart attack. He had taken the body for immediate cremation to a local crematorium.

How in the world had Erasmus managed to drag our father's body downstairs? Our father probably weighed over 280 pounds. An executor came to lead a review of the will. He was a formal, mathematical, analytical, quiet older grey-haired gentleman. He first introduced himself and then opened the will. Our father had drafted his will in the full force of soul and body years ago under the guidance of his personal lawyer. The signature had taken place in the presence of several persons, so it was legally valid. I sat with my brother face to face and watched his expressions as the trustee began to read our father's will. The further the reading progressed, the more disappointed, furious, and bittered face of Erasmus became. He began to realize that he could not buy the manor he wanted from the countryside with this heritage. The vast majority of our father's wealth passed to me according to the will. When the trustee finished reading, Erasmus stood up briskly and kicked his chair back. He lost his temper completely when he roared at me with a full voice, accusing me of incredible accusations. I had reportedly poisoned our father's mind and falsified the will. Erasmus claimed I was indebted to him for everything in my life. Without him, I wouldn't have accomplished anything else than a dead baby son, if even that. During his flood of accusations, he stared at me angrily, pointing his finger at me.

Erasmus knew how to throw himself into a melodramatic martyr role when it was needed. I realized that if his gaze could have killed me, I would have died immediately. I tried to interrupt him, but it was in useless. I would have been willing to make some sort of compromise with him, but he didn't want to hear my explanations. In the end, he added that he never wanted to have anything to do with me again, and if I took any action against him, he would kill me. After shouting his threat, he left the room. The trustee listened calmly to my brother's shouting while he arranged his papers. He calmly said such situations were more the rule for him than the exception. Before leaving, he handed over the documents to me, so I could find out where our father's wealth came from. Before he left our home, he finally said that this country needs the law to guarantee fair treatment for all heirs. Catherine cried softly to herself, repeating hysterically, wanting to go home to Kevin. As a woman, Catherine was content with her part. She received approximately the same amount as Erasmus. With her share, she was able to be financially independent of her husband for years. This situation was really embarrassing for me. I wouldn't have wanted to pay such a hard price for an easy life as a baron. My siblings left for London the same day. I rested for another day, remembering our childhood here.

While packing my luggage in the evening, I flipped through the documents superficially before carefully putting them in the side pocket of my suitcase. I noticed father had holdings in a few large companies. I would study them carefully in London.

Chapter 26: The secret of heritage

At home, I told Emma what had happened at the funeral. I let her know that we would no longer have anything to do with my brother's family. She was saddened by the rupture relationship between Erasmus and I. Finally, I told my dear wife the good news about the amount of the inheritance. Emma was extremely pleased with the size of the heritage I assessed. It would guarantee us enjoyable conditions for the rest of our lives, and I would no longer have to worry about going to work but could focus fully on my own stuff. Deep in my heart I admitted that I rather wanted a larger share of our father's inheritance than friendship with Erasmus. Ungrateful envy or not, I think he got what he deserved. When Annie heard I had come home, she ran up to me, jumping on my lap. I hugged and kissed her as the other children watched next to us. After I lowered Annie down, she spun around me, asking if I had bought her any gifts. Well, I hadn't bought it. In that funeral hassle, I had totally forgotten everything I had promised to buy for my family. That distressing funeral had suck all my energy from me. I told Annie that I was going back to London and sacredly promised her to buy whatever she wanted as a gift from there. As you might have guessed, she screamed excitedly, wanting a pony for herself.

I tried to explain to her that we didn't have a stable where the pony could have been kept, but to that, he replied with her cute little voice that the pony wanted to live in her room. I didn't start arguing with my beloved daughter about the living space required by the pony, but I took my daughter back in my arms, hugging and said playfully, promising to consider it. I went to my office to calmly read the papers I had received from the executor of my will. I poured myself a glass full of cognac to make those papers easier to read. The documentary told exactly what my heritage consisted of. Everything else was relatively clear except the gains from the sale of shares in the two companies. In addition, our father had received about half a million pounds in compensation from the state. I desperately wanted to find out what for about an enormous amount of money had been paid to him. I contacted the man in charge of managing my father's wealth, and we arranged an appointment for next week.

In London, I checked into the suite of the best hotel in town and ordered dinner there. I planned to drink red wine with the food and at least a couple of glasses of champagne to accompany the dessert. Life began to taste real life when I no longer had to think about where shack I would spend my night.

Now that I have the money, I'm going to let it show up, too. The treasurer arrived at my room just in time for dinner, so I offered dinner to him as well. After we ate, I brought up the documents. It was better to get to know these few problem areas with sober minds, as I could celebrate my heritage once all the problem areas had been cleared up. I showed him the three points I didn't understand. He said the first company ran a logistics business. When I asked him to specify what that company had transported, he replied in a laconic cool voice that it had handled the transport of the slaves from colonial countries to Britain. Because Parliament had not enacted a law on the transportation of slaves, they could be transported in extremely poor conditions to maximize profits. It didn't matter how many slaves died during the transports because the material was available almost indefinitely. Another company was responsible for accommodating the slaves. The state paid a certain lump sum under an agreement to accommodation for imported slaves. Again, the law did not define any standard by which the accommodation should have been met, so it meant miserable conditions for slaves. Thus, most of the money received from the state and the buyers of the slaves slipped into the pockets of the owners of the company.

After Parliament banned slavery, the government paid compensation to those who lost their livelihoods with the enactment of the law. My father was a medical doctor, but because he owned significant stakes in those companies, he also received proportionate compensation for them. That almost a million pounds were just that money. My father was one of the thousands of Britons who had benefited princely from slavery. The executor said he did not want to moralize anyone because money does not stink. It doesn't matter where and how you get the money, as long as you have enough. Companies and limited corporations cannot have a moral responsibility in society. It belongs to the churches. The role of companies is only to generate maximum profit for shareholders. According to him, no one will ever have any legal right to come to demand my money or sue me. To my shame, I listened to his narration. I felt uncomfortable and didn't know what I would have said. I wanted to escape this reality, so I poured my glass full of cognac. The treasurer was absolutist, so he settled for a glass of water. That, too, still had to stand. How much longer do I have to listen to that glowing-eyed, emotionally disabled psychopath? To make me easier to listen to this, I wanted to feel the cognacs in my throat. At last, I asked: "Was surely everything being in this?"

He said to me that if I had no other questions, he would leave for home. I said everything was clear as water. Having said that, he said goodbye to me coolly and then left the room. This treasurer was a traditional financial economist. His speech was only strictly with the facts. The things we dealt with were just numbers and company names for him. I sat alone in a dim hotel room with an empty cognac glass in my hand. I had thrown a tie on the floor and opened the top buttons on my shirt. So, such was the truth about my heritage. What are the other secrets about our family yet to be revealed? It was quite clear that this money was blood money. At the same time that I was touring South America, hypocritically horrifying the treatment of slaves, companies owned by my father delivered slaves from Africa to Britain. My father must have been fully aware of the treatment of slaves. I felt myself the worst kind of Pharisee. Suddenly, the heritage had lost its significance. This money started to make me sick. I didn't want to admit to myself that such a fortune couldn't be made by honest means. I'm not telling Emma anything about this. I must write a book about the abomination of slavery and all its inhumanity. That's the only way I could get my conscience calmed down. I desperately wanted peace with myself.

Chapter 27: "Laudate Dominum"

I bought a lot of different toys as gifts for my children from London. When I got home, Emma immediately noticed that everything had not gone as it should. However, I did not tell her the whole truth. I decided to start writing a book about the horrors of slavery, but I didn't get beyond the first page. It was easier to escape my internal emptiness to buying goods. I wasted my money on all sorts of things without any kind of guilty. I told Emma to decorate our house and buy new furniture for our home. I ordered a large patio with a stone floor in our backyard. A local carpenter made tables and chairs for our patio according to the dimensions I gave. For weekend afternoons, I often rented an orchestra to play music for us while dining. Usually, they continued to play accompanied by Emma until the evening. While they were playing, I was sipping my wines from Italy. My sweet life was again reflected in the abundant use of alcohol. The heritage was to guarantee me financial and scientific independence. I had to have a lot of time for research, but things went quite the opposite. I was aloof from almost all research on our theory. I didn't want to bother myself with such burdensome things, especially when all the evidence seemed to be against us. I avoided both Grant's demands and Henslow's critical questions.

My laziness came to a bitter end after Annie got seriously ill. At first, we thought it was just a little flu. She had a fever and a malignant dry cough. The fever passed, but then began the same symptoms that had bothered me as well. I was frightened. Would Annie have to suffer from the same ailments as I did at such a young age? In my mind, I blamed God and my father for this hellish situation. I commissioned several different doctors to our home to examine Annie but to no avail. Their diagnoses differed so much from each other that I began to doubt their professionalism. On the advice of the doctors, we tried to feed Annie vegetarian food, but she did not like at all, and she threw it up. Again, I felt completely helpless in this situation. One of these clowns told me to give Annie ice-cold baths, so I arranged a big barrel in our bathroom. I cooled the water outside. I immediately decided to test this doctor's advice. Annie screamed in horror as I tried to push her into the wooden barrel into the icy water. Outraged by the situation, I told her to calm down. I forcibly pushed her shoulders into the water. I kept her in the water for several minutes. Annie cried and screamed about coldness. She looked at me with pleading eyes, on cold-bluish lips, and with a vibrating voice, my daughter asking me to lift her out of the barrel, but I coldly turned my gaze away while shouting this was in her best interest.

After these icy baths, I took her to bed and told her to drink hot herbal tea. Annie began to be scared about me. Every time I tried to approach her, she thought I was pushing her into that wooden barrel in the middle of the ice cubes. Annie screamed in fear at her mother: "Why is Dad forcing me into cold water? Does Dad no longer love me?" Those cries echoed in my mind as I tried in vain to explain to her all this was in her best interest. Perhaps it was precise because of the baths that her fever worsened into pneumonia. The next doctor suggested tuberculosis. That diagnosis was of no use because he did not know a cure for the disease. Frustrated, I shouted to the doctors: "Don't you damn scammers know how to heal anyone! What for am I paying for you!?" I sat desperately next to Annie's bed, watching her struggle. I looked at her fading body. I watched whole nights next to Annie's bed as she sweated and coughed up bloody snot. During those days, those terrible memories of my beloved daughter revolved in my mind. At night I had nightmares of Annie's painful face as she cried time after time again to ask me to heal her. I explained desperately that I couldn't heal her then she realized that I was not an almighty but an ordinary man. I saw deep disappointment on her withered face. Joy and fun had disappeared from our home.

Desperate, I prayed for a long time to the angel Israfil to help Annie in this situation. It was of no help. As a final treatment, I tried witchcraft to heal my daughter, but I still didn't notice a change in her condition for the better. For the first time, the possibility occurred to me that Annie would not survive this disease.

On a cold spring night, lying in bed without sleep, I felt death move in our house. It wanted its prey. I got up to sit on the edge of the bed and lit an oil lamp.

"What evil have I done to you? Take anyone else, but please don't take Annie." I muttered to myself in horror. Emma woke up, and she looked at me in fright. Emma said the children were afraid of me. Emma herself no longer knew me.

"Charles, what's happening to you?"

"I don't give a damn what's happening to me. Look what's happening to our daughter!"

"Charles, for what do you believe?"

"What do you mean? I no longer know what I believe in!" I shouted in a pained voice.

"What's really going on in your family?" Emma asked in a hysterical voice.

"What do you mean?"

"Are your family members Christian?

"We weren't, as you well know. I have participated in all kinds of rituals. Why are you asking me such stupid questions? What does it have to do with Annie getting sick?!"

"Oh my God! You have cursed your own family with your tricks, and your daughter will have to pay for it!"

"You superstitious fool! Do you blame me for Annie's illness? I've spent hundreds of pounds on doctors and all sorts of treatments to heal my daughter!" I shouted in frustration. Emma burst into tears and began to pray aloud to God for forgiveness. I told her to go to another room, mumbling, so I could sleep in peace. I spend that night alone in my bed without getting any sleep.

In the morning, I stated that Annie would be best taken to the hospital. I wrapped her in warm blankets, and I carried with scared my slender daughter to the horse carriages. Annie lay in my arms all the way to London. On our way to the hospital, I looked out for how nature came to life after the winter. The sun shone brightly from the cloudless sky. At the same time, my loved daughter was dying in my arms. Annie shivered in my lap. This journey never felt as long as it felt that day. In the hospital yard, I crunched Annie in my arms and carried her in great distress inside to hospital.

I shouted at the woman at the front desk, telling her to pick up their best doctor right away. I panicked and behaved accordingly. Soon she returned with some young doctor. He looked like a recent graduate. At first, I asked the man if he was qualified. After he responded in a calm tone of voice to me in the affirmative, I quickly told Annie's symptoms. The doctor told me to carry Annie to a room where there were other patients as well. I told him I was a rich man and would pay anything to get our own room for her. After a moment of looking me in the eyes, he told me to follow to the second floor, where an empty room was found. I carefully put Annie to bed. I sat on the edge of the bed and looked at her in worry. After covering her under a thick blanket, I dragged the bench next to the bed. The doctor immediately began examining Annie. At first, he estimated my daughter had a high fever. He then listened to her breath and measured her heart rate, which was already weak. He tried to ask Annie things, but she did not respond to the questions. I really started to fear the worst. The doctor could not say with certainty what was bothering my daughter, but he assumed she had a post-tuberculosis disease. He told Annie to drink juice made from berries. Lastly, he told my daughter to just rest. I asked if nothing else could be done. He just stated that she could always try to eat.

Having said that, he hurried to the other patients. I sat tiredly on the stool next to my painful daughter's bed. Now I only realized I hadn't eaten anything all day. I told the nurse to bring me something to eat. I stayed up all night by Annie's bed. There was no significant change in her condition over the next day. I went to the hospital manager to tell them who I was and told them about my wealth. I urged them to put in one doctor and nurse around the clock to take care of my daughter. For starters, I gave him £200, which I knew was roughly his monthly earnings. Now they took me seriously. The hospital manager arranged the things I asked for my daughter. I went to Annie's room. I ended up exhausted and fell asleep on an empty bed. I woke up early in the morning to the medical staff noise down the hall. When I got up, I immediately glanced at my daughter. Annie's condition was the same. During the day, the fever subsided, so she could drink warm juice. Fortunately, the juice remained inside her. She was even able to talk a little. I burst into joy, crying. I wrapped Annie's tender embrace and told my daughter that I loved her more than anything else in this world. She didn't smile, but simply stated laconically that she was a necessary sacrifice for the new world. I asked, horrified, what you mean, my dear daughter, but she didn't spoke to me anymore.

As the evening approached, the fever rose rapidly again, causing Annie to lose consciousness. I got a doctor on the scene, but he couldn't do anything at all. The nurse put a cold towel on Annie's forehead, and that's it. Did she expect a cold towel to heal my daughter? I was left alone, powerless, with Annie on the edge of her bed. Annie's breathing was intermittent and superficial. She had a high heart rate. She no longer responded to speech or touch. I was tired, scared, and totally frustrated.

It was night. I was still sitting on the stool next side of Annie's bed by candles light. I was dead tired. I tried to keep myself awake, but I fell to sleep. I woke up by dropping from a chair to the floor. I didn't know how long I had slept. I went watching my lovely daughter. She lay on the bed with her eyes closed and mouth slightly open. Annie was somehow too calm. I tried her chest, but I didn't feel her heartbeat at all. In anxiety, I put my hand in front of her mouth to see if she was breathing, and at the same time, I also tried to listen to the sound of her breath. Realizing that she was not breathing, I began to shout in a trembling voice nurse to the scene. The nurse quickly came from the next room. She told me to get a doctor from downstairs. When we came to the room with the doctor, the nurse tried to revive Annie by blowing oxygen into her lungs.

The doctor quickly examined Annie, finding her dead. He turned sadly to me, expressing his condolences. After his complaints, the doctor coolly told the nurse to wash Annie's body and put her in transport condition for the morning. Having said that, he left the room. In shock, I told the nurse to leave the room because now I wanted to be alone. She could do her miserable job in the morning. When the nurse left, I threw myself on the bed and cried bitterly. My mind was empty. I couldn't ask or think anything. I just cried inconsolably out loud. I was sad, bitter, angry, exhausted, and completely disappointed in life. I saw nothing beautiful anymore in this world and nothing worth living. When I got up to sit, I looked at Annie's lifeless body and cried bitterly to God. Why did Annie have to die!? What evil had she done!? Within majestic silence, I trudged in grief to the bed next to my daughter and, crying gently, tried to shake my little girl awake. I called her by different nicknames. I hugged her. I stroked her hair, but nothing helped. She was dead. My feelings ranged from grief, frustrated rage, and despair. I could no longer sleep, but sitting and hysterically walking at the time, I waited for a scary morning. I shuddered from the bench into the cold reality as the nurse came into the room in the morning. She took Annie's body downstairs for washing. Soon she announced the body was ready to be taken home.

I carried a light coffin on board the horse-drawn carriage with the hospital janitor. No one comforted or said goodbye to me. I set off in a gloomy mood towards home. The situation seemed unreal, as if out of a nightmare. This can't be true. This must not be true! I wished I woke up soon from this state of being. I didn't wake up because this was the truest truth. How could I bring Annie to life? The driver was aware of my condition, and judging by his face, he was afraid of me getting insanity. I couldn't speak to him about anything. As we went home at the same time, the birds were singing to each other. The situation was horribly paradoxical. In the evening, we arrived at the home yard. Emma came to me dressed in a black dress, seriously hugging me firmly. As a result, I burst into tears. She hugged even harder, saying In the same quiet voice that she loved me. We walked slowly inside our house. Emma said she had already arranged everything. The funeral is tomorrow. Our servant brought Annie's coffin to our house with the horse driver. I told them to put the coffin on the floor of our guest room. I was hungry. The housekeeper brought me food. I ate it urgently. I felt tired. I told Emma that I would sleep in tonight's guest room next to Annie's coffin. Emma's face had a surprised look, but she agreed to my wish. I walked slowly to the guest room. I moved Annie's coffin next to the bed.

I thought about the possibility of sleeping next to Annie one last time but gave up on the idea. I stroked the lid of the coffin and wished Annie a good journey into eternity. As dead tired, I fell asleep soon. I had a wonderful dream where Israfil was my wife and Annie was our daughter. I woke up uncomfortably as Emma poked me in the shoulder, telling me the funeral director had come to pick up the coffin. At the same time, I realized this was the most horrible day of my life. I went with a funeral contractor to church. My opinion was that Annie should have just had a memorial service at home, but Emma wanted a Christian funeral in the church. When we arrived at the church, I went to the sacristy next door to look for a priest. He was already there, dressed in a black priest's robe. He expressed his condolences for what had happened, trying to comfort me with his usual clichés. I asked him to stop complaining and tell me where we would take the coffin. The priest was frightened my straightforwardness, quickly coming to his senses. In the courtyard of the church, he asked us to take the coffin to the altar. After opening the church door, I was surprised by the finished flower arrangements in the hallway. Inside the church hall, I was even more surprised when I saw a string orchestra, choir, and soprano rehearsing on the altar. Emma apparently was going to make the occasion memorable.

We laid the coffin in front of the altar. Everything seemed so unreal. The choir members stood on their altars in beautiful white costumes. The musicians were in black suits. They ignored us all as if we had been invisible to them. I watched Annie's coffin cover while feeling my throat constrict as tears wet my eyes. This is going to be crushingly final. After this day, I would never see Annie again. I couldn't stay in this gloomy stone church but went out alone for a walk. It rained outside, drizzling, the sky covered with a thick grey cloud cover. Confused by my thoughts, I wandered backyard of the church. Inside of me, I felt like someone dragged me to the cemetery. I was standing there in my grief. I had gone past this church several times without paying any attention to the cemetery, but now I looked at the area more closely. It looked like an execution site. The leafless trees standing here and there reached out with their skeletal black branches in every direction like possessed demons. It was as if the souls of the dead had tried to reach for heaven through these. I froze at those footsteps after seeing a few pre-excavated tombs further away. To one of those tombs, Annie would soon be buried forever. The thought of it bothered me immensely. Bitter cry in my throat, I hoped Israfil would come back to comfort me. Will I ever meet her again? Without receiving an answer, I walked anxiously to the front of the church.

At the same time, my family arrived in the yard on another horse carriage. Emma got out of the carriages calmly. I saw no sorrow in her at all. She helped the children down one by one from the carriages. I walked slowly to them. Our children seemed blissfully ignorant of this situation. Not even our eldest child, William, seemed to care about the finality of the matter. Without saying a word, we walked inside the church and sat down in the front row of benches. Before the funeral began, Emma spoke briefly with the priest. As the priest had his speech, I only recalled our moments together with Annie. Our common nature walks, games, plays, birthdays, and songs which she sang for me. What could she have achieved in this life if she had only been allowed to live? After the speech, the orchestra and choir came to perform W.A. Mozart's heart-breaking, beautiful song "Laudate Dominum." As I listened to it, I suddenly experienced, in the midst of deep grief, how this song opened up to me. I broke into tears completely. The soprano looked at me touchingly as if Annie had been her own child. I listened to the show, watching the coffin, face wet with tears. It was as if I had been alone in church, even though my family was sitting next to me. As the singer finished the song, the priest dropped sand on the deck of the coffin and uttered inconsolable words:

"From the land thou art come, and into the land thou shalt come again."

When I heard that, I wanted to cry out to God in heaven, demanding that He cancel Annie's death. At the end of the event, Emma put the flowers on top of the coffin. I carried the coffin out with the Church staff. We put the coffin on top of the four-wheeled carts and set out to push the carts in the drizzle, following the priest toward the cemetery behind the church, with the others followed us. The priest stopped in front of the ultimate pit. We slowly lowered the coffin to the pit. My heart pounded fiercely, and at times, it beat so loudly that I thought it would come out of my chest. At the same time, I was weakened and felt dizzy. I felt the horrifying cold sweat running down my back. I tried to focus on this moment, as this would be the last time I would see Annie's coffin. When the coffin was lowered to the bottom of the pit, the priest read a short passage from the Bible:

> *"Jesus said: I am the resurrection and the life. Who that believeth on me, though they were dead, yet shall they live and whosoever lived and believeth in me shall never die. Verily they that heareth my word and believeth on him that sent me, hath everlasting life.*

Then men began shovelling soil over the coffin. Emma came next to me with the children. She grabbed my hand. We watched the pit fill up, forming a small, beautiful mound on the tomb. As we lowered the flowers on the tomb, we went home.

After the funeral, I think alone at home about everything that had happened during the week. I couldn't sleep but sat alone, depressed in my dim office. Why did this tragedy happen to me? How had I gotten into this situation? Who was guilty? Who is responsible for all this shit which happening in the world? Just as I was about to burst into tears, I heard a lovely feminine, soft voice longingly calling me by my name.
"Charles."
Was that Israfil's voice? I was confused, but at the same time, I felt an immense sense of joy in my chest. Even after years, I remembered her voice. How wonderful her voice sounded. It must be Israfil!

Excited, I bounced up from the chair.

"Israfil, is that you? Where are you!? Please, could I see you?" I shouted fiercely with my voice trembling.

"Turn around. I'm behind you." The nymph said in a charmingly soft voice.

I spun around quickly, and there she stood. At the same time, Israfil began to radiate brightness illuminating the entire room. She was as beautiful as she was last time. Israfil's long blond straight hair descended on both sides of the face, arousingly over the plush breasts, always reaching to the curve of her hips. She had worn on white linen clothes that seemed to move slowly over her body, as if by themselves. Enchanted, I looked at her. Time, place, and reality disappeared in my mind. That enchanting smile removed all the pain and sadness in my heart. I didn't even remember Annie anymore, let alone my family. I was again completely mesmerisation by Israfil. She cut off my admiration with her questions.

"Are you happier now? Did my reappearance comfort you?" She asked sincerely.

"Ye...ye....yes." I stammered in my enchanted.

"Have you missed me?"

"Yes, I am! I just couldn't imagine meeting you again! I didn't even know if you really existed or if I had just had a dream." I explained excitedly.

"Yes, I really do exist. Charles, I saw you today at your daughter's funeral. You were so broken by grief that, for a moment, I thought you would be unable to complete your future mission. After hearing you sighing, I came to tell you the truth about who is to blame for your daughter's death."

"I don't want to talk about anything sad with you!"

"Maybe it's better not to see me so you can focus on my message." She said with an alluring smile.

"Please! Do not leave me. I want to look at you. I promise to listen to you. What do you want to tell me?" I yelled in panic.

Israfil walked smoothly in front of me, looking straight into my soul with her dark eyes adorned with thick eyelashes. I was incomprehensibly in a sexually excited state of mind. I wanted to touch Israfil, but I didn't dare. I would have desperately just wanted to make love with her. She knew my feelings and raised her right hand in front of my mouth with a smile. Israfil asked me to listen very carefully to what she had to say. Then Israfil told her message with a serious face.

"I know your grief, and I want to encourage you. You must understand who is guilty of Annie's death. Please, understand why Annie died."

"Yes, I do, but not yet. Please, I just want to enjoy your presence. Tell me later." I asked pleadingly.

"Charles, we have to talk about this now. I want to motivate you for the mission. You must not give up now. Otherwise, everything has been in vain." Israfil said firmly.

"Let's talk then if you want. Where is Annie now? Does she have good to be?"

"She's in the same place where I'll be back soon."

"Could you bring Annie here?"

"No, I can't bring her here." Israfil replied coolly.

"Israfil, please, kill me and take me with you!"

"Charles, you know you can't follow me yet. You must first complete your mission here on earth. After you die, you will surely get to the same place where we are." Israfil promised with a smile.

"Do you know why God didn't heal Annie?"

"I know Him from eternity. I know His character and purpose. He is not loving, fair or merciful as you have been lied to. He himself is guilty of all evil by allowing death to haunt humanity. Charles dear, would you believe me?"

"Yes, I believe, but I don't want to think about it now. Your presence makes me forget all my worries. I feel so free, immortal, strong, and completely independent of everything. With you, all my pain will go away. Don't leave me alone in this cruel world!"

"Charles, I can't stay here. You must harden your soul. Trust me." Israfil said grimly.

"When will I see you again?" I asked deeply, longingly.

"I can't tell you. I am leaving now, but I will return to you at the latest at the end of your life. I have power over you. I chose you. You are mine." Israfil said, smiling viciously from under her beautiful eyebrows.

"I ask you, dear Israfil. Please, stay here even a moment." I prayed on my knees in front of her.

"The sun will soon appear, and before that, I will have to leave. Remember what I told you and stay loyal to me!" She said at final.

Having said that, she just simply disappeared. Darkness took over the room again. I sat on the bench thinking about our recent meeting. There was already time from the last time, but Israfil had not gotten older at all. Now I remember our first encounter like yesterday. Oh, how enchantingly beautiful she is. After I die, I have a chance to spend an eternity with her. I felt a great longing for death. When I got up to stand, I felt strong. Loneliness no longer bothered me. I realized Israfil was right about everything. God was guilty. He could have healed my daughter, but He didn't. God was to blame for all the difficulties in my life. He had deprived me of my youth, the wife of my dreams, my academic career, and in the end, my beloved daughter.

I realized how my mind began to tear apart. I acknowledged the existence of God, yet at the same time, in my madness, I wanted to fight against the Almighty by questioning His existence. I hated His will because it always seemed to contradict my will. I could not understand who benefited from this situation. My grief turned into bitterness, blame, resentment, and hatred of everything about of Christianity. I found justification for my hatred of God.

After a time of grief, I wanted to catch up with my daily rhythm as quickly as possible. First, I consecrated Annie's life to Israfil and made the decision to dedicate my own life to Grant's theory. Enthusiastic about my decisions, I gained new strength to begin to examine my notes. I received a letter from Henslow in which he expressed his deepest condolences over the death of Annie. John was going to come to visit us over the weekend if that suits us. I responded to his letter welcoming him to our home. John arrived at our home with the gift he had given Emma. Then we had dinner. At the dinner, we mainly discussed his work matters. I envy John's work. He had a challenging and interesting job. I had already drunk some wine in the afternoon, and I continued to sip while we ate. I told John that I wanted to talk openly with him this evening about all possible things. It suited him.

In my thoughts, I wanted to challenge his religious views. I guessed John anticipated the topics of conversation. After dining, we went to my office. I offered John cognac, but he politely refused. Instead, I took a sip of my glass and opened our conversation.

"John, I really appreciate you as a friend. We are grateful to you as you remember us in this moment of great sorrow. I don't want to offend you, but I have to ask you a few difficult questions related to religious matters. I ask these questions for you because you are a professing Christian."

"Thank you for the invitation and the courtesy words. I also greatly appreciate our friendship and will be happy to help you with things related to understanding Christianity." John replied almost too kindly.

"To avoid useless chatting, I will say straight away that I lost faith in the loving, healing, and merciful God with the death of Annie."

"Understand well your disappointments and sorrows. I am not judging your feelings, but those are not evidence of atheism against God. Your feelings are just a human and healthy reaction to Annie's unfortunate death."

"John, where was God when Annie died?"

"Closer to Annie than you think."

"Then why He didn't heal Annie!?"

"In order for you to credibly blame anyone for anything, then you must first admit the existence of that creature. Otherwise, you can blame, for example, some druid for the death of your daughter. Or it was just an accidental appear illness. Do you believe in the existence of the God of the Bible?"

"Yes, I somehow believe in some higher power."

"Christians do not believe in any mystical superior higher power, but we believe in a personal God who has revealed himself in the Bible and in creation. Did you pray to God for Annie's healing?"

"I didn't pray. I never even thought to pray."

"Then how can you accuse Him of inaction?"

"Does not God realise to heal my child without my prayers?" I replied, frustrated.

"Of course, He does, but prayer is a sign of your faith in Him. We live in Faith, not yet seeing. Our prayers are also a sign for evil spirits who oppose God. He has reasons why evil things happen in this world. I still want to comfort you with the fact that God does not heal everyone, no matter how we pray for them. Do you understand that humanity is plagued by personal evil? Why don't you blame Satan? It is the real culprit."

"I do not know. I've never been to think about that." I replied anxiously.

I remembered my meeting with Israfil, but I did not dare to mention anything about it. John could have thought I was completely insane. Instead, I decided to ask a philosophical follow-up question.

"Why didn't God immediately kill Lucifer when he rebelled against God?"

"Would it have been fair? What evidence would God have had against Lucifer in that situation? What kind of image would it have left of God to other angels? He allows the devil, with its fallen angels, to tempt people up to sin within a certain limit in order to obtain evidence against evil."

"Why does God need evidence?"

"So that He can rightly prove by the Last Judgment that the devil was wrong in starting a rebellion against God. He will then destroy the demons in hell forever time. God is merciful to His own and just and incomprehensibly patient to all. He will not destroy anyone without strong evidence. This whole creation is at war against God, as a result of which there is so much evil here. It is difficult for people to understand this because we only look at it from the perspective of our own short lives. God, on the other hand, views this problem of evil from the perspective of eternity."

"For whom does God need evidence?"

"God allows evil to rule this world with limits so that we can learn to hate sin and its consequences. Second, like our parents, our Heavenly Father raises and disciplines His own children because believers are heirs of God's kingdom. In eternity, at the latest, we understand that He is good. I have understood from history that this world will never become a paradise without God."

"What a heavy speech. I have to take a sip of cognac to stay in sane. Don't you really want one drink?"

"No thanks. I don't need it. I want to keep my mind clear, especially when we talk about spiritual things."

"That's clear. Let's continue the debate."

"Charles, sorry for my curiosity, but how much alcohol do you drink?"

"How much alcohol do I drink? How does it relate to what we are discussing?"

"Well, not directly in any way, but you're my friend, and I'm a little worried about your drinking. It takes anybody to the wrong roads fast. Do you work at all?"

"At the end of this period of mourning, I thought again of examining my notes. Can you promise Annie access to heaven?"

"No, because I'm not an omniscient God. Second, I don't know how Annie's life would have gone if she had lived until old age. Therefore, only God, who is omniscient, can decide the eternal destiny of everybody.

I know from life and the Bible that we are all born into this world contaminated with original sin. It is impossible for everybody to save themself by their own actions. Charles, I understand your disappointment and sorrow. I am not judging your feelings, but to be just to God, you need to study what the Bible tells us about evilness. God Himself, in Jesus Christ on the cross of Calvary, has paid the most precious price of us all. He has also suffered in this world. He knows what it is like to be a suffering person. Charles, think about this. What good is it to you even if Annie enters the kingdom of God unless you yourself will be there?" John asked graciously, looking into my eyes.

I didn't answer anything because I knew exactly John was right, but I didn't want to humble myself in front of God's will. I wanted to maintain my stubbornness.

"Then why are you taking care of Annie's fate? You can no longer influence it in any way. Stop those childish accusations and focus on your family. If Annie gets into eternity, then you will only meet her there if you yourself die in Faith in Jesus."

"Does God want to humiliate us?"

"No, but to break so that He can make us new people for His use. We do not naturally want to serve God, but our own selfish character."

"Can I decide when to become a believer?"

"You cannot. Faith does not come according to your own mind, but God gives you Faith by grace. You can get to faith only when God calls, not when you want. God determines the time of conversion and the terms of the covenant. We can only either accept or reject His call."

"I see. Why doesn't God give clearer evidence of His existence?"

"The whole world is full of evidence of creation! Everything is in a fine-tuned order, and nature with its animals seems planned. We also live in a moral world where our actions have consequences. Even children know that hurting others is wrong. If you saw the Holy God face to face in disbelief, you would die immediately."

"I died? Shouldn't God have been just that good giver of life?"

"He is that too, but He is also perfect justice, truth, and love. When you can't stand even my speech sober, how could you stand to endure the Almighty Holy God? Could you demand that kind of thing on the Queen of England? Hardly, and she is just only a human being, so how can you demand such a brazen thing from the Creator of the universe? Respect Him, Charles! We are just dust and ashes in front of Him! God reveals Himself to those with broken minds and shattered hearts. Proud people, He sends away with in empty-handed.

Charles, I want to tell you one more thing, I am sure that God mourned the death of Annie far more than you can imagine."

"Where do you deduce that?"

"Because He has created everything, and He knows Annie infinitely much better than either of you. You're not the only one whose child is perished. There are a lot of families in England whose children will die before the age of ten. Why can't you see this as a call from God to you?"

"An invitation to me!? How could Annie's death be God's call to me? If God imagines that I will be interested in Him because He allows my lovely daughter to die, then He is mistaken badly!"

"He must have been aware of your reaction. God has chosen His own ways to approach us, and we must be content with that. He often approaches us in our lives through crises."

"Why?"

"So that our Faith is not based on our own feelings or selfish self-interesting pursuit. When you follow Jesus unconditionally without any benefit for you, it will be more credible. The credibility of your faith is further enhanced if you are persecuted for following Jesus. There is a price to be paid for following Him."

"That sounds logical. When I was on that sailing trip, I met a couple of missionaries in South America who said the same way. I had a bad crisis in my life then. They told me that I had an invitation time, and God called me for the first time then. They tried to convert me into a believer, but I did not bow to their persuasion. The older of them said God would call people a couple of times in their lives. The second time would reportedly be much tougher than the first."

"So, what did I tell you? What did you do after you rejected God's call?"

"I took part in a witchcraft ritual organized by the Indians in Tierra del Fuego Island." I said, a piece in my throat.

"Why did you attend?" John asked in amazement.

"When I participated, I didn't know it was witchcraft. I went there out of sheer curiosity when the Indians asked."

"What happened in it?"

"It's hard to say because such terrible things happened in it. I was drunk, so I don't remember everything very closely. However, I remember that the old man who performed the ritual drank the blood of a murdered baby girl." I explained what had happened in my shame. I poured myself more cognac.

Henslow looked shocked.

"That is also a serious warning to me about what happens to a person when he rejects God's call. He leaves humans to the power of his own lusts. You have acted really foolishly. Now I understand why God has allowed evil things to happen to you."

"I have been involved in all sorts of witchcraft ever since." I confessed with a laugh.

"Why on earth?! Didn't you learn anything from the first time?"

"I don't know. Maybe the tension in it attracts me. My parents also did all sorts of witchcraft things. I didn't consider it such an evil thing."

"You may didn't think that way, but God does! How dare you, all of that, still blame God for the death of your child!?" John asked, his eyes flaring with anger.

I couldn't answer John anything. Fleeing shame, I tipped the cognac glass empty. I immediately poured my glass full again, as I didn't want to yet feel a longing mood in the landing hops. I escaped this situation by shifting the conversation about my mistakes to my father's set of values. I explained to John that my father did not believe in the God of Christians and that he also taught us children. He had found his own values from Freemasonry, to which he had belonged since he was a young man. Throughout his adult life, he regularly attended their secret meetings.

When I was an adult, my father told me how he had gone through an occult rite when he joined the Masons. There was a hanging rope around his neck, after which his upper body was stripped bare. My father had been put on his back, lying on a big table. While he was lying on the table with his eyes covered in a bandage, the leader of the Masons had read some foreign language spell, and at the same time, my father felt how a wound was made on his chest with some sharp object. After the ritual, they removed the bandage from my father's eyes. My father looked at his chest in amazement, as there was no even scratch on it, even though he had felt pain during the incision, and no signs of bleeding were found. When the event was over, my father still had to swear an oath of allegiance to the organization that he would never reveal any secrets to anyone or else he would have to pay for his crime with his life. My father called himself a humanist. In his opinion, human is themself masters of their own happiness. John replied that I could not blame my parents for my own sins. He said nothing about my father but stared distracted out the window. It was already late at night, so I suggested to John that we continue our conversation sometime later. He just nodded without saying a word. Before leaving, John apologized for his anger, and he told me to stay away from all kinds of the occult. I promised it to him.

After saying goodbye to him, I went to sleep.

The following week, I humbly went to the University of London to meet Grant. As usual, he was late for work in his room. Grant asked about my accomplishments in an interrogative style. I told the harsh facts about my laziness. He began to share his new ideas in support of our theory. I assured and sword to Grant now of my full commitment to supporting our ideology with all available funds. Having said that, I changed the subject and talked about the end of my grieving time. I told him that my daughter had died a while ago. Annie's death didn't seem to move him in any way. Grant only succinctly stated this to show well how cruel and indifferent the Christian God was. This, he said, was to show me clearly that either the Bible was a fairy tale book, or their God was incapable and unwilling to help anyone. I spoke briefly about my conversations with Henslow, but Grant interrupted me, saying firmly that there was not the slightest interest in Henslow's nonsense because nature explains everything. "Charles, now that you have come to your senses, we can really begin to develop our theory. It is now your job to finally write the book that deals with this theory. You put in it all your notes about your trip and our observations about the evolution of the animals. Forget Henslow's nonsense about a loving God and focus on the essentials.

The Bible is full of mistakes! Have you ever read the Old Testament? It's just a brutal book. There is no loving God invented by Christians!"

"I've looked at it from a couple of points, and I agree with you. By the way, do you remember when I told you Henslow had given me counter-questions about our theory? Have you already obtained evidence for his questions?" I asked in a fearful voice.

"I couldn't be less interested in his delusional palavers! As I said, I don't have anything to do with him. Time is on our side! When we do excavations around the world, there will be found evidence. Then we shut up their mouth forever. Just focus on writing that book. That is your only job."

"I've already written it for almost two hundred pages."

"Good! I will give you my writings so you can add them to them as a follow-up. I've had a long day today, so I'm leaving home. Can you come tomorrow at seven o'clock PM to pick up my notes from my home?"

"Yes, I can. I book a room at the hotel for the night."

We left, walking from the university on a dark evening. The moon flickered from the dark sky between fast-moving clouds as we walked the empty streets of London. A strong wind blew in the twigs of the trees, moving the leaves of the trees, and waving our coats. Grant was also in a furious mood.

Swearing, he blamed us all for cowardice and laziness. Grant feared we would lose our leader position in developing the theory. He said we had already wasted valuable years. I picked up his notes and returned to the countryside. On the way back, I wondered about Grant's attitude to the scientific factual questions raised by Henslow. Was it the case that he had no answers to the criticism made by Henslow? If, on the other hand, Grant was right, then Annie was just an unfortunate victim of the laws of nature who had no right to survive because she lost her fight for the right to live.

At home, things began to recover to normal. In our family, Emma took responsibility for parenting. In that, she was an invaluable help to me. I had somehow lost touch with our other children as Annie took all the attention. Now again, in support of our theory, writing a book takes all my energy. However, out of new enthusiasm for our theory and the resulting revenge for God, I wanted to meet Henslow again. I wrote him a letter asking him to visit us because I was anxious to continue our discussions about where we were last time. I promised to be sober all the time. John came to our home again with his wife. I didn't tell John about my meeting with Grant. After we finished light evening snack, our wives left gossiping in the kitchen.

Instead, we went to my office to discuss intellectual and scientific issues. For starters, I told John I had been sober for some time. John thought that moderate alcohol consumption was quite acceptable. Instead, binge drinking is a danger to the body. His opinion is when someone is drunk, a human only humiliating it selves. I felt again the irresistible temptation to challenge John's Christian values in life and wanted him to testify to me that the God of the Bible existed. I immediately decided to throw at John the hardest possible question I had come up with.

"The last time we talked, you said that there are signs of design everywhere in nature. On the surface, it seems, at least in part, but when you look deeper than the surface, you come across a lot of things that seem to contradict the good design of the Creator." I threw confidently to Henslow.

"Like what?"

"Well, for example, all kinds of parasites."

"Yes, it's embarrassing that there exist. Personally, however, I see these, and all other nasty things being caused by the Fall. In this rebellious state, God allows parasites to exist. In eternity, they certainly do not exist."

"Isn't that a little too easy an explanatory model now?"

"Maybe, but that's the best explanation for all the evil I see around me.

Do you have any better explanation for the parasites you mentioned? Or let's turn your question upside down. Why would the evolution proposed by Grant have developed parasites?"

"I have no explanation for that either. I desperately want to get waterproof evidence from you of Biblical God's existence."

"I can't give them. You must find out for yourself and pray to Him in sincere faith. Ask God for answers, and He will give them to you for sure. The answers may not please you, but they will at least prove His existence. I'm not going to prove anything to you because that's not my job." John said firmly.

I was thinking about what John suggested, but I didn't want to take that risk, so I suddenly decided to change the subject.

"Why are there so many contradictions in the Bible?"

"You are absolutely right. There are many things in the Bible that we do not understand. Some things humankind will find out later or only in the kingdom of God. Could you still tell me what contradictions you mean in particular?"

"For example, the God of Yahweh in the Old Testament seems quite cruel compared to Jesus in the New Testament."

"Do you have any examples?"

"I have heard that in the books of Moses, God commands the Jews to exterminate all those tribes that inhabited the Promised Land before them."

"That's right, but there was also a justification reason for that order. God had given those tribes hundreds of years to repent of their sins, but they did not want to do so. What do you think of people who sexually exploit children?"

"They should be hanged in public or at least castrated. Did these tribes then do that?"

"Yes, and many other serious sins such as murder, cannibalism, and incest. They engaged in sexual intercourse with animals and even sacrificed their own children to idols."

"What weird things make people behave in such a sick way?"

"According to the Bible, sin occurs in all of us in some way. There are several passages in the Old Testament that show God's great love for mankind. Charles, why do you want to be an atheist? Are there so many nasty secrets in your life that you don't want to account for them to anyone? For what sins do you seek justification? What scientific evidence do you have to support your atheism?"

"I don't consider myself an atheist but rather an agnostic.

I would like to believe God, but I just don't see enough evidence."

I didn't even want to think about John's rest of the questions, as they would completely disarm me if I had tried to answer them, then my answers would have only revealed my openly pathetic cowardice.

"What evidence do you want to see?"

"Some biblical miracles if they have even happened." I replied in a sceptical contemptuous voice.

"I believe miracles have happened just as the Bible says. Why would the apostles have lied about those? What benefit would it have given them?"

"I do not know. I haven't thought about it that far."

"The fact that there are supernatural events in the Bible is a basic condition for it to be of Divine origin. It would be problematic for the Bible if there were no miracles in it because then anyone could say that I can do that too. You don't have to be the Son of God to share bread. Charles, what price are you willing to pay to see a miracle? Or do you think it won't cost you anything? You won't continue your life as before if you are genuinely sincere, but you start to follow Jesus and testify of Him, whatever it costs you. It cost everything to the apostles. Are you ready for that?"

I didn't answer John anything. I had too much to lose, and I was afraid of people's reactions.

"Then, you should not challenge God if you are not willing to do your part and pay the price. However, miracles do not create living Faith. The Bible is full of examples of how people soon forgot the miracles God performed. Even the resurrection of the dead did not make them believe. But on the contrary, it aroused in them even more envy. If you don't want to believe, then no miracles or evidence will ever be enough for you. Remember that conscious belief in the existence of God will not save you. Christianity is not just about admitting that some creature created the world. Even evil spirits acknowledge the existence of God but being aware of that fact will not save them because they are rebelling against His will. I have met a lot of people who criticize God for not doing anything. Then, when God is clearly interfering in things, these same people criticize Him for that too. So, whether God did this or that, they think it's always wrong. Do you understand what I mean?"

"Maybe. "

"Most people are aware of God's existence, but they do not want to love Him. They simply do not want God's will to be accomplished in their own lives or in anything in this world. In their arrogant pride, they imagine that they know things better than God. As if they were omniscient!

I have discussed these matters many times with atheists, and I have sadly found that they are not motivated by the truth. They cannot admit that they are only seeking justification for their own evilness. There is not even such a concept in their world of values as truth, but everything seems to be relative to them. As if they were independent even of the laws of nature!"

"Could God take all people to heaven?"

"Even those who don't want to get there?"

"Then doesn't everyone want to get heaven?"

"If everyone wants to get to heaven, then why do so few people want to follow God's representing values here on earth here and now?"

"What values?"

"For example, honesty, truth, mercy, forgiveness and justice. What do you imagine you to be in eternity? Do you expect the same lie, pretense, gossip, and evil to continue there as here on earth? It is the kingdom of God precisely because the will of God is fulfilled there. If all people got to heaven, would that be true mercy? Living Faith must continue until the end of life."

Again I didn't know what I would have answered. Deep down in my heart, I knew he was right, so I decided to be quiet.

"Let's go back to nature. Charles, think about this. What is the point of studying nature if its origin is not rational?

How can you rely on your own brain observations if the origin of your brain is not rational? If everything in this world is just a pointless coincidence, then why study it? There could be no extremely precise, fine-tuned orderliness in nature and life born by chance, yet when we study nature, we see how everything works exactly in a certain way."

"Yes, those arguments seem logical."

"Could you tell me even one thing, an inanimate or animate, that arose by itself out of nothingness? Even this teaspoon has not appeared here by itself. So, how can you believe that the Earth with all the animals and plants was born by chance?"

"I don't know."

"Finally, I want to tell you, Charles, if you want to know God's will unconditionally, then read the Bible in a humble spirit of prayer."

"You often urge me to read that book. Isn't it a bit old-fashioned already?" I challenged John.

"What's old-fashioned about it?"

"I suddenly did not know how to mention anything special, but I think the biblical image of man is negative. I believe in enlightenment and human wisdom. When people have more education and civilization, then wars and crimes will end."

"I do not believe in such a theory, but tell me, in what way the biblical image of man is negative?"

"It claims that all people are morally evil."

"Isn't that true then? It's not the fault of the writers of the Bible if they tell the truth as they saw it. Besides, you said to yourself that you saw a lot of evil on your trip around the world. I have often heard that accusation against the Bible, so I will answer you as well as others. On the day when all wars in this world end and no being suffers because of human evil, the enslavement of people will end, and people will remain healthy and not die, then the Bible will be old-fashioned. Do you see such a future in front of humanity? I cannot see. It has a few arguments for you in favour of the biblical image of man and the image of the world."

"I haven't thought about this from that angle at all. Maybe I'll get to have time to get acquainted with it someday. It's just such a very obscure book." I explained in embarrassment.

"Let's talk about it another night. We must leave for home." John said.

So, we left my office room for the living room where the wives were talking about our children. As we walked downstairs, I thought of John's intense speech. What motivates him in our conversation? Love? And what made me throw myself into this conversation?

Only Annie's sudden death? I would have liked to have continued the conversations with John, but apparently, he didn't think our conversation was going anywhere anymore.

Chapter 28: "The preservation of favoured human races in the struggle for life"

I started little by little putting together the material I had collected for my book, and that's why I had to read through Grant's material as well. After that, both works had to be written as one book. The most challenging would be to fit Grant's texts unnoticed into my own observations. I made a plan to write for a few hours on weekdays. For years, my daily schedule had been similar. I slept long but still tried to get out of bed before ten. I ate breakfast prepared by the servants in complete peace, either in the kitchen or in my study. After breakfast, I usually went for a walk in the nearby forest. On those trips, I always had my notepad with me, as I usually got some new ideas while walking alone in the woods. In the afternoon, I was lounging on the couch at home as Emma read the letters I received to me or some interesting novel. After that was time to eat a well-deserved lunch with the whole family. Usually, Emma told the servants to prepare two different dishes. When eating, we naturally used cutlery made by silver. In the summer, we had lunch on the patio in our backyard. Then I took about an hour nap, during which I usually got more good ideas for our book. I've noticed the best ideas come to my mind as I laze.

After naps, I flashed through the newspapers of the day where I was most interested in disaster and war news. In the early evening, I finally wrote only as much as it felt good. If I didn't have fun writing, then I drank a couple of glasses of wine. We ate dinner at six in the evening. In the later days, at Emma's request, it was only replaced with a hearty evening snacks, as Emma didn't want to gain weight too much. Before going to bed, I played board games with Emma and tasted more wines. I was careful not to strain myself too much, so Emma was allowed to help me again in this writing job. So that my wife would not have to work too much, I hired a couple of housekeepers to help Emma take care of our children. As I thought about the additional topics in my book, I found my old collections of beetles from the outdoor warehouse. I watched those wistfully. In my youth, I imagined these bugs to have some scientific significance, I thought museums would take these out of my hands, but they didn't. Now they mostly amused me. Perhaps I could come up with some examples from these of the transformation of species into other species. It was really hard to start this book writing. We had no scientific evidence to support our claims. Where would I get the motivation to write? I admitted this was the best way to avenge the death of Annie to God.

In fact, the idea that we could take away the glory of God from creating the world motivates me the most. I decided to start by reading through Grant's notes. It was a harder task than I could have imagined. Grant's handwriting was so vague that I didn't get anything clear about it. It looked as if the magpies were running on Grant's papers. I didn't dare mention anything to Grant about it, but with Emma's use, I tried to guess what each letter could mean. After much deliberation and experimentation, we were able to translate one, even at some level, rational sentence. From it, we picked out the letters used by Grant, from which we translated the rest of the letters he used into comprehensible ones. This is how I learned to read his text. Grant's writings were more of speculation and wishful thinking than proven science. Intermediate comments with exclamation marks were like from some kind of political declaration. With the pictures he drew, he tried to clarify his text, but those were poorly drawn pictures of skulls that were meant to depict differences between different races. As a model, he had presumably used the skulls I had dug from Tasmania. Grant sought support for his claims of racial inequality through differences between societies. After reading through his writing, I noticed they were totally different from mine. My own notes focused mainly on the observations we made in nature on a sailing trip.

Grant, on the other hand, focused on analyzing different human races. Soon, however, I got enough of reading and writing. Next, I wanted to focus solely on studying different insects. I dug earthworms from a nearby forest to study if they could be some precursor to insects. I cut the worms into pieces and looked at them with my microscope. I would have needed a more powerful microscope, but one was not available. Anyway, I got some new insights from the worms into my story. This was a good variation on boring writing. After intensively studying insects, beetles, and worms, I came to the conclusion that they all had anatomical similarities. Probably they had all evolved from some simple animals. The more I developed our theory. The more questions came to my mind that I had no answers to. One problem was how all the plants and animals had migrated to different continents. When had the plants appeared on the earth at all? Can seeds remain viable if they travel in the sea with the waves? According to the second option, they could have moved to different continents inside of the birds. I received regular letters from Grant inquiring about my progress. He rushed me in his letters, writing that our matter was in a hurry. He sent me more material for my book. Those were the thoughts of his new friend Herbert Spencer. Due to my research work, my relationship with Henslow cooled.

He claimed I wasted my life researching a theory that could never be proven to be true. I didn't care about his comments. I focused all my energy on writing. After I added the texts of Grant and Spencer on top of the paper stack I wrote, I was horrified to see how thick the book could become. Perhaps the biggest problem would be that this book doesn't just become too massive. As a first topic, I dealt with livestock and crop modification. I soon realized that the boundaries of animal breeding is very narrow. The horse did not become a cow or vice versa. Even cats and dogs did not reproduce with each other. Animals could be breeding within their own species, but they always remained the same species. For example, how would we prove the evolution of a horse? I had the jawbone of an ancient horse, but it's not enough. I came to the conclusion that despite the lack of evidence, I have to write this book. I repeated to myself Grant's mantra again and again: *"Time is on our side, and the evidence will be found in some time, as long as we do enough soil excavations around the world."*

Proving the birth of different cereals did not seem any easier. Where did wheat and barley come from? How have the fruits evolved? Why do those taste good? How have the human senses developed? What is the role of insects in fruit production? How can bees found to its nest and cooperate with thousands of other bees?

I began to become desperate for my book. Again, I wrote to Grant anxiously, openly expressing my doubts about our theory. I wanted to get more tips from him on where to get evidence for our claims. I also listed my questions to which I had not found the answers. He soon replied to me with an encouragingly powerful letter. Grant told me to forget the critical questions and focus only on writing. He advised adding a lot of assumptions and clever theories to the book, the truth of which no one would bother to study. He ended the letter with a defiant call to stop toing and froing because preciouses years had already been wasted far too much. However, contrary to Grant's advice, I took a break from writing because I found such a hectic work rhythm distressing. I was lazy at home for a while, reading novels and drinking Italian wines. I was already losing my motivation, but as a drunk, I got a great idea to get to know Spencer's thoughts. I read his text with great interest. He had a marvellous idea to transfer our theory from the struggles which happens in nature to human communities. I immediately realized I was getting more interesting material on this for my book. According to Spencer, nations and humans also had a similar struggle of survival with each other as animals in nature. I put the title of the chapter as a struggle for existence.

I also added my own observations of South America, and to the end, I predicted, according to Grant's instructions, how the white race would displace other races from the planet in the next century. Now I felt I had gotten to the point. This book becomes, to the greatest extent possible, a work of social policy. I finally began to understand Grant's thoughts. I continued the text, broadening the perspective on who would be worthy to survive. To this section, I attached Grant's theory of the natural selection between nations. At the end of the paragraph, I put the criteria for who would be entitled to reproduce and what the reproductive criteria would be. In my writings, I criticized a lot of savage's people lifestyles, but in one thing, they had to be praised. Namely, they quickly weed out individuals with weak minds or bodies. We civilized instead do our best to prevent that extremely necessary elimination process. In the future, this kind of stupidity can lead to weak members of society starting to defend themselves. It must be very detrimental to the evolution of humanity. As I wrote, I came to the conclusion that only in countries occupied by Christian culture do societies allow the weak to live and even multiply. What a madness waste! I was excited to read the text to Emma, but she was shocked to hear it. In her view, the text was contrary to Christian principles. I should have guessed her reaction!

Women have some strange need to appear as morally good people. I didn't care about my wife's comments. I kept working. Deep down, I felt we were on the right track. Next, I wanted to address the birth of life. In this chapter, we put God out of office. Based on Lyell, Grant, and my own observations, everything has emerged all by itself from scratch in some mud pond, without supernatural help. All of our findings suggested that the Earth is millions of years old, and that man appeared to be just one species of animal among other animals. The visible matter is all that exists, and everything else is a mere product of the imagination. I also wanted to deal with the transmutation invented by Grant, on the basis of which the species did indeed become other species. It also gave rise to completely new species. I also began to think about the origin of man. I knew this was a sensitive issue, but sometimes this issue also needs to be raised to light. If we do not dare to get to grips with this topic, then someone anyway will. Why give credit to someone else? I remembered when Grant presented us in London with a pile of bones, which he claimed to be the remains of a human ancestor, at that time rebelling against such a perception. Now I see things differently, and I am mature to accept the notion that through transmutations, man would have evolved from some ape-like ancestor tens of thousands of years ago.

But where has this evolution taken place? We need to show that evolution had happened on all continents at the same time. Otherwise, some gentle-minded healer of the world could claim that all of humanity is distantly related among. That, in turn, would eat the bottom of our race theories. When I compared wildlife and man-made societies, I realized that nature transmutations force all animals to evolve, whereas, in human communities, intelligence dictates the direction of evolution. In the midst of hard work, I received a letter from Catherine. She wrote that Erasmus's wife Caroline had died. She had committed suicide. The funeral had already been organised. Apparently, infertility had been too heavy for her. I sent a letter of grief to Erasmus. I never got an answer to that. He probably still bore resentment about smaller part of inheritance. I quickly wipe the case out of my mind to concentrate on my work again. Grant wanted us to meet soon in London. The purpose was to see what stage my writing work was at. He told me to take all my notes with me. In addition to him, there was a high-ranking officer from the army, Lyell and Spencer. I met Spencer for the first time. I liked his outspoken writing style. After our presentation, I quickly showed them my accomplishments. Grant said there was already enough material. Now I just had to condense the text a little bit, after which it had to be written clean.

Others were also satisfied with my work. I thanked them for their great help. Without their great material help, I would never have been able to write just about anything. Grant gave us instructions on how to present our theory to decision-makers. He forbade us to talk about ideology anymore because it referred to politics. The word theory was also not allowed to be used because it again referred to some vague utopia that could never be scientifically proven. He had invented a new term. Its name was the doctrine of evolution. It sounded smart, scientific, and modern. From now on, it was the only term that could be used in publications and speeches. Finally, Grant briefly went through what had happened in the world. He began by saying that he had received a report from a general of an uprising in India. It had surprisingly started with a superstitious rumour that had spread at the rate of an explosion among that primitive population. Rumour spreaders claimed the British had used cows' fat in the goods we sold to them. The Indians are mostly Hindus, and for them, the cow is a sacred animal. According to Grant, this too showed well how intellectually low level a religious person lives. The real cause of the uprising was irrelevant, but its consequences showed well how poorly prepared we were for such situations. First, these black rogues managed to surprise our soldiers completely.

Second, the suppression of the uprising took place far too slowly and gently. According to Grant, this once again proved well how the Christian worldview had weakened our army. Britain must learn from this event. The combat skills of our army will deteriorate if it does not get to war at regular intervals. As a result, we may have nasty surprises in the future if this situation continues like this. To prevent this from happening, we need to make some colonies a kind of military training ground where our army can train in real combat situations. The most likely option could be some country in Africa. Our case will help if there is already a serious conflict in the region that, by feeding, we are keeping the country in a constant state of war. Our soldiers would be free to kill the rebels of that country while practicing their military skills. It would keep our army alert and capable of striking. From such a conflict, we would constantly gain valuable experiences in how the armaments of our army should be developed. We need to learn from the Spaniards about how the inhabitants of the conquered countries should be treated. Grant went on to say that he did not generally value Spaniards as human beings, but the way they handled the Indian problem a couple of hundred years ago was exemplary of him. The Spaniards had also invented modern racism. They had expelled the Jews from Spain hundreds of years ago.

Grant recounted how industrial progress had demonstrated the cunning of the Jews. They had spread widely to the leadership of the world of money. It could soon happen that some important financial institutions for Britain would be transferred to Jewish ownership. That would be a national disaster. After concluding his encouraging speech, Grant closed the meeting. I went on to the city with him. I asked Grant as we walked for additional evidence on the point of human origin, but he didn't have it. He said excavations were carried out in India, Africa, and England, but no intermediate forms between the monkey and man had been found. Again, I received a familiar instruction not to focus on the missing evidence. Grant swore to me that he would even put his head as a pledge to find intermediate forms. He was so sure of it that he dared to say that the doctrine of evolution would fail if they could not be found. Now the most important thing was to publish my book as soon as possible. The evidence will then be found later. Instead of doubting, Grant urged me to write down the things that proved our race theory correct. I told Grant about a conversation I had with Henslow. I told him Henslow claimed that Europe's scientific lead was due to the Christian world of values. Before I had a chance to go any further, Grant completely knocked out Henslow's argument.

According to Grant, also in this matter, the human race explains everything. The white race is superior in intelligence to compare the black race. Therefore, in his view, the Christian world of values had nothing to do with technical or scientific progress.

Emma gave me a letter from Catherine, telling her that Erasmus was probably seriously depressed for his wife's death and the fired he had received. She had written to, but Erasmus had not responded to her letters. Catherine feared he had become an alcoholic. I quickly forgot the letter because my writing work took away all my interest. I added Grant's writings to a section where I dealt with racial differences. Intellectual differences manifested between different races in the evolution and culture of societies. At the end of the paragraph, I added a section warning about the dangers of mixing different human races. It would be dangerous to mix people of different races, as it would inevitably lead to racial, physical, and intellectual destruction of the entire nation. Surely I got enough clear evidence for this conclusion and justification from my experiences of an expedition. Even though I had accurate notes of my trip, I still should have travelled again. Cause now, I understand life much better than I did when I was a boy. However, my weak health prevented me from all longer trips.

Even visits to London were strenuous. At the end of the book, I added about the against the laws of nature traits, which occur in humans, which are homosexuality and love of neighbour. What mental health illness makes a person covet their same gender? From our point of view, homosexuality is a big problem. Since the purpose of life is reproduction, so why has evolution developed such a character trait in mankind? Homosexuality does not sustain life, nor does it produce new life, so why hasn't natural selection pruned it away from humanity? Likewise, the love of neighbours and charity are also a big problem. Why does a person unselfishly help a completely unfamiliar person who may not be of any use to himself? I cannot understand why altruism is needed in evolution. Anyway, a person has a lot of tendencies where, at first glance, it makes no sense, such as different art forms. Yes, I accept classical visual art, but why in the world does a person compose and play music? Let's think, for example, of a bagpipe instrument favoured by the Scots. Could there be a more annoying sound than the sound of a bagpipe? What are the benefits of music for the growth and survival of mankind? Or why do people dance? I wrote about these issues only briefly to arouse readers 'interest in these topics. I guess I'll get a lot of objections to the topics in my book, but I'll leave them unaddressed.

Basically, the book was now complete. I felt relieved and happy. I felt I deserved a short vacation. I wouldn't travel anywhere; I would just laze around at home. The older I got, the faster time seemed to pass. The memory of Annie remained very fresh in my heart. I own this book for Annie. I told Grant that I didn't know what name I would give the book. Grant said he had already come up with a name. It was The survival of nature-favoured races in the struggle for existence. I thought it sounded too long and aggressive, so I suggested a shorter name for Grant. I think the name should describe more animals than humans, and that's why I suggested the title of the book as a short, concise Origin of Species. Grant admitted it was a more politically correct and selling name, but still, he believed the word natural selection had to somehow appear in the name. We could not reach an agreement, so we let the publisher resolve the matter. Lyell had already arranged a publisher for the book through his acquaintances. We went to the publisher with the script. The publisher said the book would become too thick. The subject was also odd for his mind. Grant demonstrated his ability as an agitator, explaining that no one had dared to write a single line on this subject. This book is going to blow up the whole science world. Grant promised that the book would sell more than 2,000 copies of this book a month.

At that point, I was almost to come to my pants, but at the last moment, I managed to restrain myself. The publisher admitted that the book would sell those two thousand copies in a year but didn't believe it could happen in a month. I had almost run out of faith in our cause, so in a panic, I promised with my funds to contribute to the publishing of the book. I had spent years writing this book, so I wanted to get it into stores at any cost. The main thing was that the book would be published. Now, all we had to do was come up with a name that would sell it. The publisher felt that the title of the book should combine the suggestions of both of us. We adopted it, so the title of the book became: "*On the Origin of Species by Means of Natural Selection, or the Preservation of Favoured Races in the Struggle for Life.*" Quite a name monster. Amused, I wondered who would remember that name when they went to buy my book. On the other hand, based on the title of the book, people might think I'm intelligent. The publisher promised to take a batch of just over a thousand copies from the first edition.

At last, came the day our book was published. I was home then, and Grant represented me in London. Indeed, many mistakenly thought he had written the book. A week later, I received a letter from Grant asking me to come to London quickly.

I went straight to Grant's apartment, where he kindly received me.

"Charles! Try to guess how many books were bought on the first day?!"

"I have no idea, hopefully even a few." I answered uncertainly.

"All of it! The entire edition sold out on the first day!" Grant shouted excitedly.

"Are you serious? Are you just kidding me?" I asked sceptically.

Grant walked in front of me, grabbing my shoulders.

"Charles, I'm telling the truth. The entire edition sold out in one day. I told you we would succeed! This is what people have been waiting for decades. I am so happy about this success of ours. Now we must do articles about you for magazines and start lecturing on our topic." Edmond said, full of enthusiasm.

"Where?"

"All over Britain, of course! Now this doctrine of evolution must be brought to everyone's attention. I will be visiting Germany soon, and I am going to have the book published there too!"

"My health does not allow long trips, good when I can even travel to London." I explained in fright.

"That's the problem of that time. Don't worry about it now. We must celebrate this achievement of ours."

Grant said, full of boyish joy.

We left Grant's apartment for a nearby restaurant. As I ate, I asked Grant, curious about possible critical comments on my book. He didn't think it should be cared for, as it was part of the matter. All great things have always been loudly opposed at first until they are later accepted for granted, and so it will be our case too. I told him I wasn't any type of debater, and I didn't want to sacrifice my life to fight for this cause. According to Grant, there was no longer an alternative. He said he had already taken a new edition of my book. This time the edition will be three thousand copies. Grant said he would use his influence to advance our cause, and he said he would soon meet a familiar count to whom he was going to suggest that the Count speaks to the Queen in favour of my nobility. That would be a tremendous honour, but it probably also included responsibilities. I just wanted to spend a quiet country life at home. Grant told me to calm down. No one will be nobility on frivolous grounds, and our opponents do their best to prevent it. The next few days were the most interesting of my life. I had read all the possible newspapers looking for reviews of them from my book. Grant's claims soon came true and critical writings began to emerge. They came first written by representatives of the Church. That didn't surprise me.

Those didn't matter at all, as they didn't even understand what they were criticizing. Instead, the writings of university professors were distressing. One of them wrote:

"Most of the findings Darwin found on his expedition are lies. The rest of the things he presents in his book have been known to all scientists in the field for decades. Darwin does not mention his sources in his book, although one of them is his own grandfather. The idea of the transformation of species into other species is a direct quote from the theory introduced by the French Lamarck as early as the last century. Darwin has not dealt mathematically with the analyzes he presents in his book. Instead, he uses sayings like a relatively large number or a moderately small number. Such attributes do not meet the requirements for scientific research. This book also makes no mention of the origin of the species. The book is full of mere assumptions and speculation. Darwin really can't be said to be a profound thinker, let alone a genius."

Critics found my book a boring, confusing bungle full of mere conjecture without evidence. Henslow had also written one article. In it, he did not criticize me as a person but focused on criticizing our methods. Henslow believes such an immoral worldview would destroy the Christian value base of our society.

He naturally stated his opposition to us. More annoying were the cartoons they had made. They attacked my appearance. I know very well that I am not a handsome man, but I do not look like a monkey anyway. Those pictures really hurt my pride. My wife Emma was my invaluable comforter in times of harsh criticism. It wasn't until later that I realized how much pressure Grant was under at the time. He was constantly involved in debates in London. Grant, with his "bulldogs" (as his companions were called), wrote articles in the magazines in support of me. The younger generation of scholars showed their support for us, just as Grant had prophesied. They were open-minded, wanting a radical change in the values of our country. In them, we have a future.

Chapter 29: Other side of the medal

To my great surprise, I received a letter from the Royal Society telling me about the medal awarded to me for my book. The award ceremony will be at the association's headquarters in London. I was bursting with pride. Now I have been recognized as a prominent scientist at the highest possible level. This book seems to be a much bigger thing than I could have imagined. I wrote to Grant and asked him to join the medal ceremony. The medal would belong to him. I was just a secretary who just wrote things down. We went with a familiar group to receive my award. In addition to me, there were Lyell and Grant with their "bulldogs," they followed Grant like a shark on a ship. They treated me like a religious leader. I liked this flattering situation immensely. At last, I was in a position where other people admired me. At the ceremony, I listened with pleasure to the speech of the president of the association about how my book opened a whole new unwritten page in the history of making science. With my book, we would be freed from the worldview that limits science. At the end of his talk, he used my last name as a synonym for this doctrine of evolution. How good it felt when I heard the phrase, "Darwinism is the future." We, as a nation, were heading towards glorious times.

I felt really proud to get the medal on my chest. If only my mother had seen this day. Somehow, Erasmus should also be informed about this. At the end of the event, I was so in my thoughts that I didn't notice the orchestra playing our national anthem. Grant clung to the collar of my jacket, rose me up to my feet. As I stood there, I pondered Grant's prophecies about our theory. He seems to be right. There seems to be a social demand for this doctrine of evolution. Emma had arranged a party for our home in honour of receiving the medal. I just wanted my own family to attend this party. I sat in my recliner eating a cake with a silver spoon from a porcelain plate, at the same time watching our youngest children's activities. I had lost touch with them years ago. They were overshadowed by Annie. Why don't children ever become what we hope for? They always have some unpleasant traits that are quite immensely annoying. Do I live through my children? Do I want to realize my own dreams by them and usually still against their own will? Despite that, Emma and her assistants had raised them decent young people. I rejoiced when I was moderately healthy, so I wanted to celebrate this event. I no longer dared to drink heavily for several days, like when I was younger, but I could drink a couple of glasses of wine every now and then. In the evening, Emma played beautiful songs on the grand piano until night.

At lunchtime on Sunday, Catherine came with her husband to visit us. She was in angry looking state of mind. Her husband Kevin followed, cheeks red and his forehead wet with sweat. He looked embarrassed. I greet them with a kind hug. Catherine did not answer my hug but told me to keep my bloody fingers away from her.

"What makes a mature aged lady like you, get so angry?" I asked in surprise.

"Don't start commenting on my age in any way. Where can we talk alone, the two of us?" She said in a cool voice, staring sharply into my eyes.

"Let's go to my workroom." I said in a surprised voice.

I told the others to continue eating. Then I went with Catherine to my room. I closed the door behind me.

"Please have a seat, dear sister. What is the matter?"

"I have no worries. Have you been in contact with Erasmus since Caroline's death?" Catherine snapped to me with a tense voice.

"I'm not because he forbade me to contact him." I answered to defend myself.

"Now, you don't have to keep in touch with Erasmus either. He is dead too."

"Dead? When had he died? Where was he found?"

"We found him yesterday hanged himself from his apartment with Kevin. He did not respond to our letters, so we understood that something was wrong.

We went to the apartment with the landlord and the police."

"That's terrible." I complained to Catherine

"Oh, do you feel so too?"

"What do you mean there? I didn't cut relations with him! He himself did not want to see me anymore. What can I do if he was envious of me for the inheritance I received from our father? Are you blaming me for his suicide? Am I guilty of it if he didn't make it in his life? Life is a constant struggle for the best places." I shouted at her in indignation.

"Exactly! "Life is a struggle!" That is what your group is shouting for everywhere nowadays. What do you pampered old man know about fighting? You haven't done any work for a single day! Don't you start preaching that devil's gospel to me! What would happen to you if you had to work long days in the mines in that condition? You would have already certainly lost your battle for your existence!"

I was shocked by Catherine's furious words, not least because she was absolutely right. I was constantly sick so much that we would have starved to death without the plush inheritance. I tried to put myself together to continue the conversation.

"Did he leave any message behind?" I asked calmly.

"Yes. It was a bitter letter about the injustice of life. He accused our Father and you of conspiring against him." Catherine said, looking tightly into my eyes.

"I see. When is the funeral held?" I asked distractedly, looking at the walls of my office.

"In next a week. He is blessed and buried in St. James's Church in West London."

"I can pay all the costs involved."

I escorted them to the yard, where I said goodbye. As I walked back inside, I wondered why Erasmus was buried in a Christian tradition in the church-blessed cemetery, even though he had said he was an atheist. Had he been scared at the last moment, or what had happened? That and much more would be revealed later.

In London, I checked into the same hotel where I had already been countless times. I didn't want to go to Catherine's apartment, especially when I hadn't long time any financial compulsion to do so. Probably I wasn't welcome even there anymore. After this ceremony, I will take a little break from her relationship as well, especially if she doesn't start to show respect for me. For what do I need her anymore? I arrived alone at the church where the blessing was held. In the yard, the priest directed me to the adjoining chapel, where the cinerary urn of Erasmus was on the table.

The unsophisticated ceremony was quickly over. After that, I asked the priest why he held the Christian funeral openly for the atheist man. The priest said he served all members of the Church regardless of belief. I think that was the stupidest hypocrisy that I had ever heard. If a person has not believed in God in this life, then what miraculous benefit was it for him to read the sacraments of the Church? Do the sacraments save anyone? I continued a challenging of priest, but I didn't get answers to the rest of my questions. As a childless, Erasmus had bequeathed his remaining small fortune to Catherine. I left to my home in relief. If I stay even reasonably healthy, I will devote all my resources to advancing my career.

Chapter 30: X - Club

Lyell and his partners set up a newspaper to publish propaganda in support of our evolution theory. Officially, the name of the magazine was a scientific nature journal, but its articles were purely ideological, intended to shape people's minds in favour of evolution. Lyell's artist friend had made a spectacular drawing for the first issue of the magazine about how a monkey had evolved into a human through transmutations. He had drawn the pictures using his lively imagination and the instructions he had received from Lyell. Lyell thought the simple working-class population was the best target group with which we could test the popularity of our theory. I alienated the idea of taking our theory to such a group for testing. How could they understand anything about evolution when they couldn't even read properly? Why throw pearls to pigs? In any way, Grant's "bulldogs" began to preach the gospel of evolution at trade union events. There, they shared for free travelogue, which I wrote. They claimed to be able to prove how the Church had oppressed the working population for centuries, and now they had the opportunity to avenge the injustices they had experienced. One of these "bulldogs" proposed a bill to repeal the state status of the Anglican Church.

They received a joyful reaction to their speeches from the leadership of the working population. The labour thought that believing in the doctrine of evolution was more masculine than singing hymns in the church. Our claim of the kinship between man and ape sank into them like a knife into butter. Lyell said that it was amazing how easily the working-class population believed us. In his view, it only showed the fact that they were indeed meant to work to death in mines.

Grant arrived from Germany, where he had visited to present my book. He had received a warm welcome there and an agreement to publish the book in German. He had met there a young man named Ernst Haeckel, an avid supporter of our evolution theory. Haeckel had already read the English version and considered it his own Bible. Haeckel had promised to spread the doctrine of evolution throughout Germany. They said they went to listen to an opera by a German composer named Richard Wagner. Grant was completely enchanted by Wagner's music. In his view, such music best described the music of the next century. It was new, pagan, powerful, and nationalist. During the opera, they had got the idea of setting up a secret club that would promote knowledge of evolution theory among government officials. The name of the club became X - club.

I, too, received an invitation to the founding meeting of the association, which was held at the university. Grant chaired the event. I watched with envy at Grant's energy. He told with fanatic enthusiasm about the things he had experienced in Germany. Then he introduced Ernst Haeckel to the rest of us. Haeckel looked handsome, a defiant young man. She had blonde, thick hair. His face looked as firm as a marble sculpture. Haeckel watched us with his icy blueish eyes from deep under his gloomy corners like an eagle. The narrow face was completed by a straight, narrow nose. He was wearing a black suit jacket and tight light-colored pants. The well-groomed look was completed by Prussian, long black boots. Haeckel told how the nationalistic emotions raised its head strongly in Germany. There were many political movements that wanted one state under which all the German-speaking peoples would be gathered. That state would be united by a strong belief in the doctrine of evolution. He added to the end that such a state would in no way be a threat to Britain but rather an ally because we are like brotherhood nations. When Ernst finished his presentation, Grant began the founding meeting of the association. In addition to me, the following men were admitted to the association: Grant, Lyell, Spencer, George Busk, Edward Frankland, Thomas Archer Hirst, Joseph Dalton Hooker, Thomas Henry Huxley,

John Lubbock, John Tyndall, a couple of business representatives and Colonel Mosley of the army staff were joined as members of the association. Our goal was to meet once a month. Four main issues were to be discussed at the association's events:

1. Measures to promote evolution education in every area of our society.

2. From scientific observations that are completely free of the views represented by the Church.

3. Come up with more ways to crush our opponents.

4. Develop ways to strengthen the British Empire.

Chapter 31: Henslow's Swan Song

During intense work, I received a letter from my old friend, Professor John Henslow. The handwriting of the letter was filled with pain. Even after all these years of separation, he was still a dear person to me. Reading the letter made me very upset.

> *Dear Charles,*
>
> *It has been a pleasure to know you all these years, although, in recent years, our paths have been different. I hope you are not resentful that I am not supporting your theory of the birth and evolution of life. A year ago, I was diagnosed with cancer that has spread widely throughout my body. It cannot be improved. So, I invite you, my friends, to watch how a Christian dies.*
>
> *Dearest farewell, John*

I read the letter many times. I felt a piece in my throat as tears filled came my eyes. In anxiety, I walked in a circle in my room, and I crushed the letter into my pocket. I felt anxious about John's letter, but at the same time, I was angry with myself for not keeping in touch with him.

I couldn't just acknowledge John's death as a cold law of nature, so with a sad mind, I left for a final visit. Arriving, John's adult son George came to open the front door. He took me to their living room, which had been converted into John's last battlefield. Next to John's bed was his wife Elizabeth and on the other side of the bed was their family pastor. John, who had lost weight violently, lay on the bed in great pain. His withered face reflected a passionate desire to get out of this realm of death. Elizabeth said John refused painkillers because he wanted to keep his mind clear until the end, though hardly any of them would have been helpful anymore. I walked slowly to the side of the bed. I felt sad and powerless. I would have liked to ask John something, but I was so touched I couldn't dear ask anything. I wanted to apologize for the relationship break of years, but I couldn't say that either. I just stood next to the bed, watching his withered body. John searched at me with his gaze. Recognizing me, he smiled painfully. He grabbed my hand with strongly, pulling me close to him, and then he hinted at me as if to say something. Fearfully, I bowed over him as John uttered the last hopeful words into my ear: *"I know that my Redeemer lives, and He will be the last to stand on the Earth."*

Having said that, John breathed for the last time, breaking away from this wicked world.

I squeezed his hand, whispering his name, but John no longer answered. Elizabeth and George rushed to the side of the bed. I was shocked, and I pulled away from the bedside, giving them space. Elizabeth slumped over John, crying against her husband's chest. George tried in vain to comfort his mother, but nothing could be done anymore. The respected man, professor, friend, and Father John Henslow was dead. I walked sadness into the next room. I no longer tried to fight the tears but let my grief erupt. After a while, I came back into the living room, and then I hugged Elizabeth and George, trying to comfort them. They thanked me for my visit and asked me to come to the funeral. I promised to come. I apologized for the situation but told them I wanted to leave my home now. On the way home, I remembered our conversations in the past with Henslow in Cambridge. When I began studies in theology at Christ College, John gave us a series of lectures on intelligent design occurring in nature. It was a compulsory part of our first year of study. It dealt with the evidence of creation that can be seen in nature. In those days, I couldn't imagine how important a person he became to me in my life. I immediately liked Henslow's way of teaching us in a living way about the diversity of nature. End of the lectures, I encouraged him to ask to discuss with me topics related to nature and creation.

I was surprised at how approachable a person he was. Henslow was friendly, intelligent, embarrassingly outspoken, and deeply religious. He asked at first about my school's success. I responded honestly that I waded through elementary school with mediocre grades. I tried to lighten the mood by throwing jokes about my school success was so miserable that I had no fear of a statue being erected there for me. I was particularly interested in the Bible creation story, even though it was short compared to the importance of the event. I wasn't bothered by it, even though our elementary school teacher didn't believe the Bible's creation story. He said the Bible is not a scientific book but only deals with Jewish philosophy. According to Henslow, the elementary school teacher's claim could not stand in the light of historical and archaeological evidence. According to John, Faith in the God of the Bible and science are not mutually exclusive. Once, Henslow even attracted me to charity work. I was startled by the suggestion because even the thought of it irritated me. I was appalled by the idea of serving people who were socially below me. I had been allowed to live a safe and secure life. I was blissfully indifferent to the everyday problems of ordinary people. I later learned that he often gave food and old clothes to his poor parishioners, as well as various charities were close to his heart.

I didn't longer mourn John's death, but subconsciously I feared my own future destiny.

At the funeral, I met John's acquaintances from the ward in the churchyard. I felt like an outsider there. The guests shared their fond memories of John. For my part, I remembered about John only inside my own head. From him, I received the best teaching in life about how important it is to listen to people who know a lot about things you don't understand anything about. John encouraged me in my deacon studies and tried to courage my low self-esteem. Only now do I begin to understand his views on moral philosophy. As I ate soup in the downstairs hall of the church, the embarrassing question of Henslow popped into my mind: "Why would a person live by Christian ethics if he did not believe in the existence of God?" I replied wittily that it might be beneficial. Now I laughed in my mind at the naive enthusiasm of youth. John did not remain silent but asked a counter-question about the benefit of it. Before I had time to say anything, he uploaded me with an answer, to which I still know of no honest objection to this day. According to Henslow, adherence to Christian morality is difficult because it requires from man to refuse. We all always want more or less a reward for our refusals in the future.

When does man receive a reward for his rivalry, and from whom if God does not exist? Who wants to pay the price for nothing? I remember totally dropping off the conversation, and I didn't know what I could have answered him then, so I was quiet. That silence was the wisest deed in my life. Even today, I really had to think seriously about human's motivation to act morally right, even if they don't believe in God. Why would I pay my taxes or be loyal to my spouse? Apparently, the fear of punishment imposed by society keeps people, even to some degree, law-abiding. Or is it that what we consider to be morally right is just a customary culture invented by our own imagination? In that case, moral patterns of behaviour will be changeable over future by generations, as Grant argued. Sure, they will change to some extent, but would those changes benefit societies? Henslow often repeated man to be an intelligent but utterly immoral being. At the time, I did not understand his argument. In that respect, my eyes opened to the facts on a trip around the world. After eating, I left the church for my hotel where I met Grant quickly, as he had something new to tell me again. I told him I was at Henslow's funeral, but it didn't seem to interest him at all. Instead, Grant had gotten the idea of updating the book before it was reprinted.

I told him my new discoveries were mere logical reasoning devoid of real evidence. We still lacked all the answers to the big questions. The worst shortcoming is the transmutation that would prove that a human descendant from a monkey. In any case, Grant felt that the book needed to be updated in some way. After finishing his speech, Grant sat down in his chair, looking worried. I asked him cause for concern. He said he had heard the United States of America plunged into a civil war. There was nothing new in the war itself, but the reasons that led to the war made Grant think the Americans had gone mad. The real reason for the war was the slavery of the Negroes, but he thought the background was still about economic power. In any case, the federal government wanted to end slavery, while the southern states would have wanted to maintain slavery. Grant thought it was utterly incomprehensible that whites were killing each other because of negroes. This showed that democracy is destructive to the human mind. The best form of government would be a nationalist dictatorship. He was sure of the break-up of the United States after the war into several small states. In that case, Britain will have to take over parts of the northern states of the United States and annex them to the provinces of Canada.

Canada was already largely under British rule, with the exception of the French-speaking territories. It is likely that France will also try to get to parts of the U.S.A carcass. That, in turn, will force us to ally with Germany at some point, as it would reduce France's influence in Europe. After Grant finished his summary, I told him I had received a letter from a German social theorist. He had read my book, and his groups were currently developing a new revolutionary society ideology based on my book. This theorist wants to meet me tomorrow at the British Museum. I asked Grant to attend a meeting. He promised to come to the scene. As I walked around the city, I thought about Grant's account of the situation in the United States. Once again, I remembered my conversations with Henslow in my youth about the legitimacy of war. Then John asked me, on whose side was God in our war against another seemingly Christian nation? Was He on our British side or on the Spanish side, for example? Both peoples asked the Victory from the same God. Henslow claimed that He was not on either side. As justification, he said the immorality of the war, its duration, and the price it required. If in such equally strong armies, God were on the other side, then the war would last only a few hours, and on the victorious side, no more than a few men would die. They, too, would fall only because of their unbelief.

God had fought only on the side of the Israelites in the Old Testament, then the Jewish people were always clearly weaker than their adversaries but still won if they obeyed their God. Henslow concluded his philosophy by stating that the success of the British in the war was solely our own merit or fault. Those conversations were difficult for me when I was young. Usually, when I think about serious things like this, I get a horrible headache, maybe drinking liquor and shooting with a shotgun has been more of my business than deep thinking.

Chapter 32: An anarchist society theorist

Grant and I were at the museum well in advance to discuss the challenges ahead, and for a moment, I thought our guest wouldn't show up. Finally, half an hour late, a bearded, untidy, agitated obese man came to ask for my name. In the letter, which I received, the social theorist had described himself. It had been severely overestimated in relation to this person.

"Are you Charles Darwin?" He asked, gasping air.

"Yes, I am." I replied in embarrassment.

"I'm Karl Marx. I wrote you a letter a couple of months ago. I have read your book "The Origin of Species," and I think it is a masterpiece. It gives us the legitimacy to change societies in a radical way. Thank you for coming." He explained, wiping same time his forehead from sweat. I looked at this Marx In dismay. I was shocked by his outward appearance. Judging by the smell, he hadn't washed for weeks. Wearing an old pair of numbers too small a suit, which naturally sat badly on him. Dirty black hair was uncut, and a long fluffy beard untreated. In addition, his breath smelled of old liquor. This Marx seemed to live in poverty. I looked around, embarrassed as I was ashamed to show up in a public place with a person like Marx. In his armpit, he had a briefcase in which he kept his weird writings.

I glanced sideways at Grant; he was like a sign of a storm. I guess he wouldn't share Marx's world of values. However, I wanted to hear what this guy had in mind. I tried to treat this Marx matter-of-factly, even though he seemed somehow demonized. I asked him to sit with us. "What do you have in mind?" I asked Marx.

"I have all sorts of revolutionary in my mind. I am writing a book introducing a new economic model. It will displace these existing repressive systems in the future. I want to dedicate this book of mine to you, Mr Darwin." He said, staring at me anxiously.

"That sounds great, but could you tell us this great ideology first?" I answered correctly.

"After a long and in-depth reflection, I have come to the conclusion that Christianity is the cause of all social problems, as it gives those in power the right to deprive workers and the poor."

"Can you tell me in what way?" I asked in embarrassment.

"Religion prevents people from seeking a violent solution to their problems. Priests promise people bliss in the afterlife, making them content with these miserable conditions in this life. Workers do not even try to solve their current problems by violently but flee in their cowardice into the illusion created by religion.

I claim that rulers invented religion with priests, and that's how they then controlled poor, uneducated people. After reading a bit about the Bible, I have found it to be full of lies. The people who wrote the Bible have been somehow mentally disturbed." Marx explained hysterically.

"If that is the case, who invented Jesus? His mother Mary or the apostles? What benefits was it to the apostles and prophets to write the Bible?"

"I have not thought about such things, but as long as ordinary people obey the priests, they will not dare to face a real problem, which is a depriving economic system. Your magnificent book has given me the right to openly attack the churches. I go to a church almost every Sunday to shout and laugh at priestly speeches." Marx foamed.

"I did not write that book that it would be used against Christianity. My idea was originally to study nature, not to make politics. What kind of social system do you want then?"

"One where no one owns anything, but everything is common. That society is going to be atheistic." Marx rumbled.

"I have quite a lot of wealth. Do you suggest I should give away my property?"

"Absolutely, yes. The government should confiscate your property." Marx replied with bright eyes.

"That's completely absurd. Why then would people work if they can never own anything?" I asked indignantly.

"At this point, your theory of evolution comes into the picture. It will prove people are evolving to be morally better all the time. As humanity refines mentally, they learn to give up money for the benefit of others. They want to work for everyone for free." Marx explained hopefully.

"What good is it for them to make a revolution if they do not own more than they do now?"

"In that society, no one is hungry, and everyone has a job. Wars will also end because no one has any reason to go to war anymore because there are no more nation-states. Every border of different states will be removed. Also, hospitals will be useless, and those can be closed because people will be healthy. The police can also be disbanded because people no longer commit crimes."

"You must be a really naive man." I said in a contemptuous voice.

"How did you end up to that conclusion?" Marx asked with a stunned look on his face.

"How will such a society have established?"

"It will only be achieved through a violent revolution! The oppressors must be killed!"

"Who will carry out this revolution?"

"Workers and the poor."

"Where do they get guns for it?"

"They can be found when the time is right. The most important thing is to make people aware of their social situation. When people are atheists, then they understand the uniqueness of their lives."

"How is morality in this ideal society?"

"It's not a problem because people are morally good."

"However, you want a violent revolution. How can morally good people make a violent revolution?"

"Morality needs to be redefined. We must reject what the Church teaches about it."

"Who then defines this new morality?"

"It can only be decided by the working-class people." Marx yelled with his hairy chin upright.

"A pretty wide range of decision-makers. The things you are telling me are purely negative to me. They are of no use to me. Why are you telling me these things?" I asked, annoyed.

"I do not know. I hope to get to own my book for you. May I own my book for you?"

"I don't promise anything yet. I want to read it first."

"That's fine with me. My book will revolutionize the world and, with it, the evolution of humanity.

After reading my book, I am absolutely certain of your desire to be involved in this forthcoming process of creating new societies."

"It'll be seen. We need to continue our journey, so write to me when you have completed your book. Goodbye."

"Thank you for your time, Mr Darwin. I promise to write to you. Goodbye." Marx shouted after us.

Grant had sat throughout our conversation quietly with his hands tightly in a gust on his chest. We set off for a walk downtown. On that journey, we analyze Marx.

"What do you think of this Marx?" I asked Grant carefully.

"I don't want to waste my time talking about that brainless idiot, but in short, this Marx is a dangerous maniac who should be eliminated immediately. I first heard about that moron over 15 years ago, but I had blissfully forgotten about him. He is an anarchist Jew who has been deported from several European countries over the years. It is an immense shame to allow such a villain to live in England. It is really unfortunate that the doctrine of evolution we have created is supported by such fools. We must somehow take advantage of this Marx. He must be deported from England, for example, to France, where he will be allowed to cause social problems. Marx is alienated from reality, a fool, which will hopefully be forgotten soon. His image of man is so pathetically naive that he must be a very lonely man.

The society that he envisioned could not work anywhere in the world. Such a society would be truly destructive to the people in our position." Grant analyzes.

As we walked, I came to the conclusion that I didn't want to have anything to do with that criminal Marx. His ideology would be extremely harmful to me. I warmly recalled the spiritful conversations I had with John Henslow. Fortunately, I asked Marx those questions that questioned atheism. Yes, I accept rational atheism, but this Marx was totally lost with his own ideology. If atheism is based on that kind of argument in the future, then it has no future. Where were all the warm-hearted, wise people? I missed John Henslow.

From now on, I will focus on caring for our garden. Little by little, I began to understand the mechanism of flower reproduction, in which bees played a crucial role in their role as pollinators of inflorescences. In addition to my research work, I received many letters of encouragement from all over Britain, often with tips to support the theory of evolution. Some even sent me plant and animal samples. Emma kept the best letters in a large box in my office. I gathered the thinnest letters in one stack next to the living room fireplace. As I stared at the fire in the evenings, I threw those letters directly unopened into the flames.

Among these, one nicely decorated letter caught my attention. It was sent by the wife of Admiral Robert FitzRoy. That old fox had got the Admiral rank was my first thought. I hadn't seen him anymore after that sailing trip. Those distressing years in the same cabin room had been enough for both of us. I opened the letter and was surprised to read it. Admiral and creator of modern meteorology Robert FitzRoy was dead. I also received a letter from Grant on the same subject, who said directly that FitzRoy had killed himself by slitting his throat open. What had driven him to such a final solution? He acted in a radical way all his life. By character, FitzRoy was a charismatic, personal, innate leadership character that easily got the crew excited. He had a strong sense of duty. When work has to be done, then it will be done. The same formula is also applied to relaxation and drinking.

Like lightning from a clear sky, Ernst Haeckel announced that he was coming to visit my home. He had been in England for some time to become acquainted with veterinary medicine. He arrived proudly with Spencer and Grant at our home one weekend. I was a little surprised because I didn't really know the man at all. I had once seen him, and that's it. Haeckel came to our house like an old acquaintance. Grant and Spencer followed him.

Ernst came straight to me looking serious, thanking me for the honour of visiting our home. There was a strong German accent in the pronunciation of his English that sounded comical. In addition, he talked about things that happened in the wrong time format. Grant had studied German in recent years, so he turned Ernst's speeches to me. Ernst also wanted to introduce himself to my wife, Emma. He marched in front of her, tapping his heels militarily together, introducing himself in an audible voice. After his presentation, Ernst shook hands and bowed to Emma while kissing her outstretched hand. Emma was a little bit scared but cool of Haeckel's greeting. After the introduction, we went to our living room, where the servant had put us tea with fresh pastries. As we enjoyed the delicacies of the table, Ernst spoke in an audible voice about himself. He began by announcing his appointment to the University of Jena as a Professor of Zoology. He had also married his cousin. Ernst thought it made sense to marry a cousin because then there would be no danger of race mixing. Haeckel planned to publish books on heredity, human origin, and racial diversity. According to his own stuff, he seemed like a hard-working man. At least he was diligent in talking about himself.

Haeckel had the ability to speak things in plain style and was meant to popularize the doctrine of evolution so that it would be understood by even the simplest worker. He was currently organizing an atheist religious movement based on naturalistic monism for German-speaking areas. That knowledge made me feel critical feelings about him. With these tricks, our doctrine of evolution acquired traits that I would never have wanted to connect to it. I told Ernst slowly, clearly articulating, that my intention has always been just to study nature, not to make politics or to establish a new religion. At this point, Grant intervened in the debate, defending Haeckel, saying evolution science always has an ideological side as well, even if we don't actively bring it up. Ernst continued his speech by recounting a concept called the superhuman by philosophers launched in Germany. The best point in our discussion was when Haeckel announced that he was one of those superhumans. Amused, I listened to his sincere-sounding arguments. He obviously believed in his theory. In support of his argument, Ernst presented to us the "tree" he had drawn into which he had grouped the various human races on a scale of values. According to it, all of us in the room were Indo-Germanicus. I looked at his "tree" with great interest.

Spencer added that he had come up with more slogans for the doctrine of evolution that we could use when we need justification for some of the necessary measures. These were: Kill or be killed, reproduction of the fittest, and the survival of the fittest. Grant, for his part, said he heard Arabic music. That "music" was a mad screaming for him, devoid of any beauty. There was only one instrument, and its sounds lacked all the versatility, intelligence, depth, and beauty characteristic of classical music. From that experience, he received further confirmation of his theory of the superiority of the white race, also in the field of culture. The Beethoven Symphonies and the Wagner Operas proved our race to be by far the best in the world. Within these mind-uplifting moods, we ended our meeting this time. After saying goodbye to them, I looked at the drawings submitted by Haeckel. They were of an artistically high standard, but were the claims made in them scientiflcally verifiable? Maybe it was good to marry a cousin. At least I know that children don't become any mixed breeds. As I thought about these things, Emma came to my working room.

"I hope you never call that German shouter back into our home."

"What was so annoying about him? Well, he's a little loud, but I don't think it's so awful."

"That man is proud, boastful, selfish, and rude, and he has an evil spirit in him. Every sentence I heard him say started with the word me, I, and myself. That's his unholy trinity based on his selfishness!" Emma snorted.

"Well, he's so excited about our theory. Ernst is still so young. He is an intelligent man who does valuable work in the German-speaking area in front of us. How are you so nervous now? I must have neglected you. We should probably go on a short vacation, say to a spa. What do you say about that?"

"Sounds good. Let's just leave."

So, we spent the next few days at the spa, where I got treatments for my ailments. In the gentle heat of the sauna, I was able to forget all my troubles. While vacationing at the spa, I realized how amazingly happily it was to spend a peaceful country life financially independent from other people. I had enough money and got to do my own stuff in my own home. I had set my own schedules myself. It was mentally important to me because I hated tight schedules. When we returned home, I became acquainted with the letters I received, which started to come steadily throughout Europe, regardless of the season. Some were written in such poor English that I made no sense of them. Among those, I noticed a letter of invitation. It had come from Karl Marx. I had almost forgotten that insane visionary.

He wrote that he had completed his book presenting a new theory of society. The name of the book became known as "Capital." It was an invitation to come to London for the book launch. Is he trying to get free publicity for his book with my help? Isn't it an idiot realizing that, for me, is no use to his ideology? The letter was accompanied by a few pages of text extracted from the book, in which he demanded equal status for sexual minorities. After, I glanced through them quickly, and then I threw them into the fireplace. I really wasn't going to go meet this Marx. I replied to him briefly that...

> *... A rich "bloodthirsty capitalist" like me is no use to support your ideology. I urge you to get to know people better so that you learn to understand their true motives. We, humans, are, in reality, selfish. We all work to get something of our own for ourselves and our families. The system you have developed is absurd and cannot work anywhere in the world. I urge you, Karl Marx, to tolerate Christianity, for its repression has frightening consequences. Read in the history books what happened in France after the revolution, when Christian moral authority was broken.*

Immediately I realized that I was responsible for warning people about populist instigators like Marx. I immediately began writing letters that I sent to representatives of various organizations in our society. I wrote the first letter to the leaders of the trade unions. At the beginning of the letter, I urged them to maintain their humanity in these tough times and thanked them for their valuable contribution to the progress of our society. I warned them directly about scammers like Marx, who have lost their sense of reality and are only trying to get to power with the help of the working class. Once in power, they would be worse than those who have in power today. They themselves have never done real, honest work with their hands, but instead, in reality, they despise those who do manual labour. Irresponsible anarchists like Marx only cause disorder in our society. They are of no use to anyone. They are not really interested in peace; they are deliberately causing a civil war. The ideology that these cheaters represent will not work in any country. I added to the end as a warning to avoid allying with atheists. An alliance like that would be the worst mistake of the labour movement. Even today, I still don't understand why I warned them about this very thing. It just felt right. I wrote the following letters to the bishops and archbishop of the Anglican Church.

At the beginning of the letter, I apologized to them for the resentment I had caused because of the theory of evolution we had invented. I did not develop our theory for the purpose of harm but had come to those conclusions as a result of years of sincere research. I thanked them for their extensive enlightenment and charity work among our people. I urged them to stop politicking in their churches and to accept the working population as equal members of the church. I do not think that the Christian churches should take part in wars, but I think the role of the church is to support social peace through its impartial activities. I warned them of the atheistic agitators who would cause anti-Christian riots among the working population. At the end of the last paragraph, I added: "If churches had shown justice and equality in your actions, the Communists would never have stolen those words for their own propaganda. Now, they get support for their speeches about the mistakes and greed made by the Church."

I concluded my letter with a warning: The Anglican church should not fall into the same mistakes as the Roman Catholic Church in the Middle Ages. I sent the third and final letter to the employers' representatives. I thanked them for their invaluable services to our society.

> *"You have put all your power for years to keep Britain the world's leading country.*

All of you should be careful when you succeed, for greed lurks right behind you. Distribute your profits fairly to the workers, too, because they do the hard work. All of you now have the chance of your lives to stop the revolutionary movements provoked by criminals right from the beginning in this country. It only happens when you treat the working-class population fairly. Pay them a reasonable wage, treat them with respect, and train them to work to avoid accidents. Yes, they know how to appreciate such a gesture of goodwill. If you do not improve their living conditions, there is a danger that all sorts of instigators will fool them against Britain. It can mean widespread strikes, the disruption of social peace, and, at worst, even civil war. This extreme material calls itself communists. They use any criminal means to gain power in Britain."

I posted my letters without ever receiving a response from anyone. Apparently, the mistrust was so great on both sides. Employers think workers are ungrateful and only take advantage of their helpfulness.

The working-class population, on the other hand, mistakenly thinks the communists are really pursuing their interests. The Church counts its own position under the protection of the state last forever. The church's tax revenue will run as long as it remains loyal to the state. For bishops, church office has become a mere job, not a calling from God. When will they realize that the less the church has worldly power, the more it has spiritual power? We are living in interesting times around the world. Now we are dealing with the play cards that nations need to play with. Woe to those nations who are late for this game. They will never catch up with the rest of us, and we will not let them reach our standard of living. About that time, we got the good news we had been waiting for some time. We had become grandparents. Our eldest son William had had his first child with his wife. The child was a boy. This information made our happiness complete. This felt almost even better than the birth of my own children. It felt moving to realize my family was growing on. Judging from my illnesses, I hardly have many years of life left, and the best blade of my life inevitably began to disappear. Just when life starts to be good, it ends. I wondered how fast those years had gone. What had I accomplished in my life? When I compare myself to other people, mostly the working population,

I have lived a moderately stimulating life. I have sailed around the world, written scientific articles and even a book that is said to revolutionize the whole Western way of thinking. I wish I had had chance to live health. I could have given for that good, even half of my wealth to the poor. Speaking of the poor, how pathetic their lives are. I wonder if they even realize the uniqueness of their own lives. They live like animals, as most of their lives are spent on satisfying only basic needs. I received a letter from Grant that was written in even more unclear text than usual and was clearly partly written by someone else. In it, he asked me to arrive in London soon. There will be a meeting on the basis of our theory, where he promised to tell important historical news. All the architects of our theory of evolution come to the scene. At the end of the event, there will be a gala concert for the evening, which will last just over an hour. After retiring from the position of professor, Grant rented a study from the university for his own use. I also wrote to my son William I would come to visit them at the same time to see our first grandchild. In London I first went for lunch, after which I went to see William's family. They lived almost downtown in a comfortable apartment. After knocking on the front door, my son's wife Sophie came to open the door. When I got inside, she helped me take off my jacket as well.

She was an obese easy-going woman. Sophie said William would be coming from work soon. We drank cups of tea as Sophie introduced her new offspring. The boy rested in his mother's arms with a restful look on his face. It was touching to watch this little boy. What does the world look like when our grandchildren are my age? Surely technological advances have made people's lives much easier. As I thought about it, I felt jealous of future generations. At the same time door, there was the rattle of a key as William entered. I went to receive him and congratulated him on having a child. I tried to be as kind to him as possible, even though we didn't like much of each other. As William grew older, our relationship improved a bit. We no longer argued openly, but we both realized we were completely different in our characters. I spent that evening with them discussing William's work. I had initially planned to go to a familiar hotel for the night, but Sophie couldn't even imagine that possibility. Typically for women, in a neurotic way, she hysterically demanded me to stay with them for the night. I bowed to persuading Sophie and slept poorly that night on the couch in their living room. I woke up early to the loud crying caused by the baby's hunger. When Sophie breastfed the baby, she made us a tasty basic British breakfast, and then I went for a walk-in town.

After receiving a ride from Trafalgar, I told the driver to drive straight to the address provided by Grant. I was alone in the carriage, and due to short dreams, I started to fall asleep. I snoozed on the bench halfway between sleep and wakefulness. We arrived at the front of the high-iron gate. I got off the ride and walked over to the guards standing at the gate. One of them asked my name, and after telling me, he let me inside. There was already another ride waiting inside the iron gate. When I got up there, we set off immediately. As I looked out the window of the wagon, I saw a huge stone building. It was typically a large, old castle-style mansion amidst beautiful nature. There was staff in the yard to receive incoming guests. I was directed with others inside into the mansion. I made the mistake of thinking this was just a quick meeting somewhere in the usual place. This seemed like a well-organized event. After the butler took my jacket, I asked him about Grant at the same time. He sent a service boy to pick up Grant. In the meantime, I was looking around in the great lobby. There were already some men with their wives here. These couples were unfamiliar to me and looked at me respectfully. They were probably some of Grant's acquaintances. Finally, Grant came accompanied by a servant. Edmond has gotten older since our last appointment.

He noticed the surprise on my face, but in his familiar way, he turned the situation to his advantage with ironic humour.

"Good afternoon, Charles. Am I obsolete, or why were you so frightened?"

"Good afternoon, Edmond. And nice to meet you for a long time. I am sure we're both obsolete since the last meeting."

"Come on, let's go to our meeting room to have tea and eat."

"There are a lot of people here that I haven't met. Have you called them?"

"Yes, I had. They represent a wide range of science and business. They were actively making the theory of evolution known throughout Britain. This is no longer a game for a small group." Grant explained defiantly.

"I'm obviously a little secluded in our home in Down House. I am not quite aware of what has happened recently." I said in a surprised voice.

We walked towards the big hall. The servant supported Edmond from the forearm on the stairs. Grant's walk was already sluggish, but as usual, he didn't complain about his ailments. The servant directed us to a large hall where hundreds of people were already present. At the back of the ballroom were tables where beautiful young waitresses served tea, pastries, savoury snacks, and alcoholic beverages. I looked around and was shocked to see Lyell. His hair was also greyed out. This time, I controlled myself better as we formally exchanged affiliations. I was horrified at the passage of time and our ageing. The only people I knew from here besides Edmond were Lyell, Spencer, Haeckel, and Grant's disciples. I went to greet them as well. For others, things seemed to be fine, except Haeckel was somehow strangely restrained. I watched enviously at his golden yellow wavy hair that stretched all the way to his shoulders. He stood in a typical accentuated manner, like a statue. He drank tea but also whiskey from the big glass. I took a cup of tea and a couple of delicious-looking pastries. Hopefully, my stomach wouldn't start causing trouble in the middle of the event. Grant went to the podium, opening the festivities with his short speech. He warmly welcomed us all to this meeting. The beginning of Grant's speech dealt with a "disciplinary action operation" in India, in which millions of Indians had been deliberately starved, which he said was a necessary prelude to the global "reorganization" of the nations in the next century. At the end of his speech, he literally radiated joy as he told of the birth of a new European superpower. He invited Haeckel to the stage next to him as he told about this awesome news. What new country were they going to talk about?

After Haeckel leapt onto the stage, Grant began the rest of his speech.

"Ladies and gentlemen, it is a pleasure and an honour for me to conclude my speech about the new empire which, after long and painful stages, has been established in Central Europe. The man standing next to me represents the future values of this new empire. His name is Ernst Haeckel. The State whose birth I will tell you next is Imperial Germany. Almost all the nations that speak German as their native language are united under it. At last, scattered forces of the great nation have been united. And in what way were these connected? Of course, with war and iron! Once again, we saw that nothing valuable could be achieved without bloodshed. It has been shown countless times in history. This time, the parasite of Europe, France, imagined that it could strengthen its fading power at the expense of the Germanic peoples, starting a war against Prussia, but that war was quickly over, ending in German victory. As a result of this important event, a united German imperial was born. The fact that they fought victoriously against France is a huge advantage for us British, as it further weakened our rival France. Today we will build a foundation from the steel which is cast for the future success of the UK.

We may no longer be able to survive alone in the next century, and we probably need an ally equal to ourselves militarily and racially. The new Germany also needs a strong ally, and it cannot be France or Russia, so what could be a better option for both of us than the union of Great Britain and Great Germany? It is a law of nature when we see these two linguistically, culturally, and racially similar peoples uniting their forces. In the next century, these two great nations will create a new world order based on the laws of evolution. We both nations united by a strong belief in the doctrine of evolution and strong nationalism. Now we move on to dinner, after which a ride to central London has been arranged. There we will attend a gala concert to be held at the Royal Opera House in Covent Garden. The opera house is reserved only for us, and most of our guests only arrive there. Now I humbly thank you all for your presence."

We ate according to a long formula. The food was delicious, and I sat at the same table with the core crew. Who actually funded and organized these events? Grant claimed to be in charge of things, but I didn't think such an old man would be able to handle such complex things as this anymore. With a small group, we were able to talk about things more freely, so Haeckel began to explain his new ideas at the end of our meal.

In his opinion, the concept of evolution had to be extended to all aspects of society, such as the evolution of intelligence, justice, love, war, music, religions, languages and etc. In this way, the doctrine of evolution becomes an integral part of the lives of all people, including those who dare to criticize us. That's exactly what I had been afraid of all these last years. Our theory began to take on features that I would never have wanted to be connected to it. The evolution of love. Ha, hopefully, no one is so idiotic as to embark on writing a book on such a stupid feminine subject. I strongly disagreed with Ernst and decided to say that immediately.

"Thank you for your suggestion, Ernst. However, I completely disagree with you. Those things you mentioned have nothing to do with transmutations. After all, these do not in any way prove the transformation of animal species into other species. Those things you mention do not represent science in any way. I think even the idea of some evolution of love is completely absurd. How can we study love? It is from such "studies" that our opponents get more water into their mills." I told in excitement. Grant intervened in our conversation, defending Haeckel.

"Charles, I understand your indignation, but this issue needs to be looked at from a broader perspective.

We need to bring the doctrine of evolution into the consciousness of all people, and therefore our theory needs to be popularized. Because the majority of people are infinitely stupid, they are not interested in the scientific side of evolution because they do not understand anything about it. Therefore, the doctrine of evolution must also include those aspects of life that touch the daily lives of ordinary people. The people do not have time to get to know our subject in depth, and it is a great opportunity for us. We can, in a monopolistic way, define what the doctrine of evolution is and, if necessary, defeat any criticism against it. However, for the future of evolution education, it is extremely important to get it to affect all members of our society. We are forced to incorporate the doctrine of evolution into the lives of all people. Otherwise, we will remain a mere insignificant marginal movement. In that case, we will not be able to challenge the Christian worldview. With those things, we can also seek justification for differences between different races. For example, with the evolution of music, we can prove that classical music composed by whites is superior to compare the blaring of decay black human races. With the evolution of religions, we can claim that humans invented gods and religions.

With the evolution of working life, we can justify those workers compete against each other's in the workplace, and thus we get out more benefits from the workers. Gradually, we infiltrate the lives of every human being in much the same way as the church." Grant prophesied.

"I see. Do we also need to build temples to support the doctrine of evolution?" I asked, disappointed.

"No need. We already have universities, and society is building them for us." Grant said with a laugh.

"What evidence do we have to support those claims?"

"What arguments do you mean?" Grant asked in surprise.

"Such as the evolution of religions?" I asked in wonder.

"Nothing. Not at least at the moment, but perhaps archaeological finds will prove that the Bible is a storybook." Grant explained hopefully.

After the meal, Ernst came to me with a glass of wine in his hand to discuss our disagreement. He already seemed to be drunk.

"Charles, can I disturb you for a second?" He asked with a tingling look in his eyes.

"Sure, please."

"I want to say to you that I deeply respect the work you have done for evolution studies. I admire you as a man, and under no circumstances would I ever want to quarrel with you. Do you believe me?"

Haeckel asked with an innocent look on his face.

"Yes, I believe. I wasn't meant to argue with you either, but I just don't understand the reason why evolution should be brought to the whole nation. I see no need for it. Science has always been the prerogative of a small group of people."

"I agree with you, but you have to understand that the theory of evolution is not only a science. It is also a philosophy of life and a worldview."

"I've heard Grant say the same thing. I, on the other hand, have never thought of it as anything other than natural science." I said in good faith.

Grant and his disciples came to interrupt our conversation, telling us that the ride was already waiting in the yard, so we would start a solemn to toward Covent Garden. In mild ascent hops, I felt great pride in myself for being able to belong to this privileged people group. We watched the people walk down the street. When they noticed us, they stopped and took off their hat to show their respect for us, and some even bowed to us. Oh, how I enjoy this sense of power. This was even better than the feeling of rising hops. We were there in good time. On arrival, I noticed several groups in front of the building. As we went inside the house, we drank glasses of champagne. We were directed to sit in the front rows of the concert hall, as we were the guests of honor for the evening. As people flooded in, the hall filled. Grant sat with Haeckel on the first row, and I sat on the second row diagonally to the right behind them. I got Grant's disciples by my side. They were always loyal like lap dogs, and it also made them an extremely boring company. Now I realize that this object of admiration also had its downsides. There is nothing duller than around a herd of brainless flatterers. I browsed the program to pass the time. The conductor was some Edward Elgar. The program included a solo song, music by Beethoven and Wagner, and finally, a couple of surprise numbers. I glanced over my shoulder, noticing the hall was full. Finally, the host of the evening came to introduce the concert conductor and orchestra. The orchestra seemed experienced, but the conductor was a young man. The concert almost passed me as I thought about my own things. I was reminded of a time spent studying in Cambridge when we sometimes went to churches to listen to Bach's organ music. My fellow students often joked about my non-musicality because I couldn't distinguish false chords from even the simplest compositions. They often asked me how I could enjoy the music if I didn't even know if it was played correctly. I replied to them being basically a naturalist, not a musician. Now I had proved that to the whole of Britain.

During the concert, I noticed Grant and Haeckel having a heated conversation with each other. During that conversation, they drank whiskey from their small bottles. Apparently, they were going to make the most of this gala concert. Before the encore, Grant went on stage to present the evening's surprise numbers. The first to be played was the national anthem of the new Imperial Germany. During that time, Grant asked us all to stand up. The orchestra began to play the national anthem in silence. I seriously focused on listening to this song. It sounded incredibly beautiful, pompous music. I looked at Haeckel in front of me. He moved to tears from the national anthem of his country. After the orchestra finished its performance, we sat down. Finally, conductor Elgar presented the last program number of the evening. It was a march composed by himself, dedicated to Britain. That march started really furiously. There was something of such majestic grandeur here that it could have been immediately consecrated as the British national anthem. The march exuded immense glory and hope for a better Britain. Drunken Grant empathized with every cell of this music, waving his fists in the air to the beat of the music. In the slow, sublime part, which included the final stage, Grant bounced upright to stand. He raised his right hand straight, halfway oblique to the up. It was reminiscent of an ancient Roman greeting.

What the hell did he really mean? Haeckel followed his example, making a similar greeting. They both stood posture in this military position. Soon crowds of people began to rise beside me, and they all raised their right hands to a similar greeting. Was this part of the program, or was this a spontaneous outburst? I glanced behind me and noticed everyone but me standing up with right hand outstretched. The women waved their hands, weeping with joy. The hysterical atmosphere was like from some political occasion. At the end of the march, the audience burst into a wild cry. As Grant got on stage, he raised Elgar's right hand. Grant interrupted the audience's shouting, giving a short speech. He thanked Elgar for a brilliant composition that perfectly described the British national character. In summary, he said Britain was reborn tonight. He concluded his speech with a prophecy of the eternal covenant between two warrior nations, which our grandchildren will enjoy in the next century. At the end of the concert, most people went their separate ways. I stayed with the core crew to spend the evening in the big room reserved for us. We smoked cigars there, discussed our theory, and drank a variety of alcoholic beverages. I warned Grant about drinking, to which he just growled angrily to know his own limits. Haeckel came to me with tears in his eyes to express his feelings. He was clearly already on the side of the landing hops.

I noticed in his reddened eyes and melancholy crying look. Ernst explained in a melodramatic way with his hands vigorously gesturing the significance of tonight. He said this was a new beginning for all of us. I couldn't help but laugh as I listened to his narration, for as he got drunk, his German accent, filled with grammatical errors, became even more pronounced; thus, Ernst's voice rose to a comically high level. He was offended by my laughter but reconciled soon after telling him that I was not laughing at his speech but at his comic accent. After accepting my explanation, Ernst asked my opinion on the German national anthem. I said in a politically correct way that I was not an expert on music, but it sounded like a grandiose song. When I asked about the lyrics of the national anthem, Ernst replied distractedly, watching walls, that the words of the song told of the peaceful character of the Germans and the coming time of eternal world peace. I think that was a great thing, Europe had already seen enough bloodshed. Ernst put his hand around my neck, saying he had experienced a tragic loss from which he would never recover.

"I see. What had happened?"

"Charles, my dear wife died while ago." Ernst snapped at me in a crying voice.

"I'm really sorry for your loss, Ernst. Is there anything on how I can help you?"

"Thank you for your participation. I knew you would understand me in the midst of this great sorrow of mine. I just have to go on with my life. I am going to stay faithful to her, and I won't married again. In the future, I will focus only on disseminating the doctrine of evolution. I have already worked 15-hour days and slept a maximum of five hours a night. Due to the death of my wife, I have become completely immune to all criticism. As proof of my diligence, I took a few drawings that I have composed through human evolution by transmutations over tens of thousands of years. Do you want to see them?"

"Of course, I like to see." I replied enthusiastically.

"Wait here, I'll get my portfolio."

I was thinking about it while I waited for Haeckel's drawings. Had he received evidence of kinship between man and ape, or what drawings was he speaking about? Soon Ernst returned excitedly with a small briefcase in his armpit. After opening it, he dug a pile of folded sheets of paper from there, spreading them on the table.

"Here is my first draw that tells about the evolution of the fetal stages of different animals. When you look from the top down, you can see how different species evolve into their own species. The first series of images shows the evolution stages of a porcine fetus. The second image shows the evolution stages of the sheep, the third is the chicken, and the fourth series of images shows the different stages of growth in the human uterus. As you can see, all of these species go through the same stages of evolutionary history. In the first picture, all of these are in the fish stage, when they all have gills and a long tail as a memory of the time when life evolved in the ocean. In the second stage of evolution, we are in the frog stage. Only in the fourth point does the human fetus differ from other species. See Charles, how the pig and human fetuses are almost identical at the sixth month of pregnancy." Ernst explained excitedly.

"Well-drawn pictures. Have you done all these by yourself?" I asked in a sceptical tone.

"Yes!" Haeckel exclaimed sincerely.

"How do you know what a pig or human fetus looks like when it is four months old? Did you open the uterus of a pregnant pig or?"

"I have been researching this issue for a long time, and I have come to these results in several tests. Want to see yet another picture that tells the stages of evolution of different breeds, from monkeys to humans?"

"Well, show." I replied with a cynical voice.

Just as I was looking at the picture, the drunken Grant grabbed it from my hand, and in a loud voice, he started to praise Haeckel's drawing skills.

I asked Edmond, which was more important, the beauty of the drawings or their scientific truth value? Grant didn't even want to hear my question; instead, told Ernst to tell us what the picture showed.

"This picture shows the evolution of different breeds from monkeys to humans. As you can see, below are pictures of the lowest breeds. Take a special look at how small the difference between the negro and gorilla is. They are almost the same species. The top row contains a series of images of the Anglo-Saxon Germanic race. As I said, we belong to that race. Notice the large differences in the shapes of the skulls of the different races. The lower the race, the lower the forehead. Take a look at the side profiles of the negro breeds in particular. As seen from the side, their skulls are sloping, making their mouth further than their nose. It is the surest evidence of their close kinship with monkeys."

"Great, Ernst! These images must be available immediately to all universities and museums. This must begin to be taught as scientific truths to our youth. Ernst, you need to come in the future to lecture at the University of London on this topic."

"Thank you for the invitation, Edmond. That would be a great honor for me." Ernst replied, bowing in the direction of Grant.

"I'm getting really tired. I'm going to sleep. Edmond, thank you for this awesome concert." I said, yawning.

"Please, Charles. Anyway, this room is reserved for us until the morning, but if we all want to leave already that's fine. Thank you all for participating in this celebration." Edmond said in a friendly voice.

Grant went to tell the waiters about our departure. He asked me if I could take him home. It suited me very well because I also wanted to have a conversation with him. After saying goodbye to the others, I left with Grant on the same ride toward his apartment. On the way, I thought about the future of our evolution theory. Arriving at his apartment, I sat on the living room couch without asking permission. I decided to open the discussion with a direct question.

"In which direction is evolution theory to be developed?" I asked, looking Grant in the eye.

"We're both old men, especially me. I have discussed things with the younger scientists, and we are currently developing a new direction. There must even be some evidence of the kinship between man and ape. I have already asked Ernst to focus on that research."

"How about that philosophical side? I hope it won't become the main trend in the theory of evolution."

"Hardly, but it can't be left out. Charles, I have chest pains."

"In my opinion, we should, until the end, avoid incorporating philosophies and different ideologies into the doctrine of evolution. We need to focus only on the evidence found in nature!"

"That's what we have done all the time! It is nature that proves us to be right in everything that we claim. Things related to different races will forever be an integral part of the doctrine of evolution!"

As I listened to Grant's passionate sermon, I realized we had only created a new, aggressive, and intolerant religion. When I asked this to Grant, he jumped up from his chair and shouted, his voice hoarse with his fists upright.

"Yes! We have created a new religion, a philosophy, a political ideology, and everything what we need to lead nations! In the next century, everything will be defined through the doctrine of evolution, and we will be lifted among the great geniuses of mankind!"

As I watched Edmond in my fears, a memory of youth popped into my mind when I found a painting in my father's study with a group of other young people painted in addition to my father. In a tired state of mind, I decided to ask Grant about it.

"Have you seen an occult painting dedicated to my father, in which he poses in an ancient British druid outfit with other young people?"

"Of course, I've seen. What does it matter about?"

"How can you remember that?" I asked in amazement.

"Because I'm one of those young men! In that ritual, we dedicated our lives with your mother and father to the ancient Wotan. It was the most important decision of my life. It all started that evening."

I didn't get a word out of my mouth. I thought he was joking, but judging by his look, it wasn't about that. Suddenly Grant dropped to his knees, holding his chest. At the same time, his breath seemed to stop. His eyes almost bulged out of his pits, and his mouth was left open. He fell to the floor and stayed lying on his left side. The colour of his face turned red. Edmond tried to say something, but I didn't get anything clear about it. After that, he didn't move anymore. Edmond must have had a severe heart attack. Everything went so fast that I didn't have time to do anything. After surviving the startle, I grabbed Edmond's hand, trying to shake him awake, but he didn't respond to my questions. I turned him on his back, stripped him of the tie, and opened the shirt buttons. I tried the pulse but couldn't find it. As I limped in panic out of the house toward a nearby police station, I saw a full moon shining in the dark sky. I punched the police station door with my fists while shouting at them to open the door. At last, two constables came to the door.

At first, they meant to arrest me, but after explaining the situation to them, they set me free. I told Grant's address and asked them to come with me. They ran ahead of me to Grant's apartment, and I dragged myself slowly behind them. Edmond lay on the floor motionless in the position I had left him in. The older constable declared Edmond dead, and the younger set out to seek a doctor who could confirm the death. While we were waiting for them, I thought quietly about what had happened. The man who had made the most impact on my life was dead, and it didn't feel like anything. Was I too tired or in shock, as I didn't realize the seriousness of the situation? The doctor soon arrived with the police. The doctor noted everything quickly. Then we went to the police station to give an official statement. When I left there, the police took me to the yard of a nearby hotel, where I checked in. Due to drunkenness and hunger, I felt weak as I opened the hotel room door. In my dim room, I took off my clothes, tired, and then sat on my bed looking around. In my thirst, I slowly nodded my head, exclaiming in a rough, dry voice: What a day! I drank a glass of water and went to lay down on the bed. In a dark room, I recalled a painting I mentioned to Grant where my father was a young man with his five friends. Where was that painting now? What did that picture represent to them?

They had been painted in some large, dark room where they stood around a round table. There was a big black runic on the back wall with some text written in white that I didn't get clear at the time. There was a large transparent glass cup on the table with a big dice inside. My father was dressed in an old pagan British druid outfit and had a viciously arrogant look on his face. When he was alive, I never saw him look like that. Others were also in weird masquerade-style outfits. One of them was dressed as a vampire, and the young woman was dressed as a witch. She wore a purple velvet cloak and a sharp-tipped black hat on her head that shaded her face, so I didn't recognize her as a kid. Now I realized she was my dear mother. Above them was a pentagonal pattern painted in blood red with the face of a beautiful blond woman inside. They looked too confident. I banished these memories from my mind, trying to fall asleep. I was tired, but I just couldn't fall asleep. In my heart, I felt a great longing next to Emma. I felt old and weak. Oh, how I would have liked to spend right next night with Emma. I would no longer travel anywhere without her.

Chapter 33: Imperial concert

After a poorly slept night, I went to visit Grant's disciples to tell them what had happened last night. They reacted with great sorrow to the death of their master. After surviving the shock, they promised to hold a funeral. I also visited Haeckel, who was lying in his hotel room with a cold-soaked towel on his face. He was already in a delicate state of mind due to the gruesome hangover. After telling Ernst the sad news, he burst into a pathetically hysterical feminine cry. I tried to comfort him, but it didn't help. I left for my hotel when Ernst started to cure his grief with cognac. In my room, I also wrote letters to other core members of our group. As I checked out of the hotel, I dropped letters in the mailbox. Then I headed home. There I first hugged Emma. I thanked her for all the help I had received during our marriage. Emma wondered about my outburst of emotion. I briefly told her about the events of the last few days. My dear wife comforted me by saying I couldn't have done more for Edmond. I walked into my study, wondering how quiet our big mansion was nowadays when all the kids had already flown out from the nest. Emma and I attended Grant's memorial service. Edmond had no close relatives, so his faithful disciples organized the event at the University of London.

We gathered in the room to reminisce about him. On the table was a stern-looking middle-aged photograph of Edmond, with next to it his earthly remains in a black box. Edmond's last will was for his ashes to be spread after the memorial service on the lawn in the university backyard. The occasion was surprisingly relaxed, and the atmosphere was eased. All of Edmond's suffering was over, and the fruits of his work would live forever. It should come as no surprise that there was nothing Christian about the occasion. At the end of the funeral, one of Grant's friends took a bowl which has of Edmond's ashes. We watched seriously in the yard as he spread the ashes around the lawn. It felt horrible to watch the disappearance of a long-time comrade that way forever. The simultaneous summer sunshine with the bird's twitter created a great contrast to the event. Watching it, I decided quietly in my mind that at least I wouldn't be cremated after I died but wanted to be buried modestly in the backyard of our home. After the memorial service, Grant's companions told me that Edmond had suggested to the City of London a statue to be erected for me in the city center. At first, the idea bothered me a bit, but Emma thought it was an awesome idea. They reassured me by saying that a statue would probably not be erected in my lifetime. Before leaving for home, we paid a quick visit to William's family to see our grandchildren.

Emma was deeply moved while playing with the little one. As I watched their hustle, I realized this was an irreversible life cycle. The death of one was the life of another. It didn't take long time as Lyell leave to Valhalla, so our old group began to fade away from this life. I saw no evolution by itself in this world anywhere, only decay, disease, and death. I was already starting to be in such poor condition that I could no longer travel anywhere. Accepting the facts, I finished my will. I did not intend to repeat my father's mistake by inciting sisterhood against each other, but I divided my property equally among all my children. My eyes were already in such bad shape that I couldn't read anything, so one of the servants in our house read the letters mailed to me. Most of these came from historians and social theorists. I was not at all interested in their opinions. They focused in their fantasies on things to which I didn't want our doctrine to be attached to. They focused on the possibilities offered by the philosophical side of evolution. They sought justification for the measures proposed by Grant to maintain British superpower status. Inevitably, I had to ask myself, which gates of hell had I opened? They were probably right in their claims, but I did not respond to them.

For the first time in years, I did manual labor work by digging small pits in the soft soil to find worms. While squatting there, I felt a sharp sting on the left side of my chest without warning. I dropped to my knees, gasping for oxygen into my lungs. I fell right to my side. I tried to draw air into my lungs to shout at Emma, but a malicious twinge at my heart blocked my breathing. My tongue felt numb and thick mucus flowed from my mouth. Fear of death took over my mind. I didn't want to die. I was not yet ready to face death. In horror, I thought about what would happen to me after death. I realized I couldn't panic now, or I'd definitely die in this place. I calmed myself down, trying to breathe slowly. I felt how the pain finally eased in my chest. For a moment, I was really afraid I was going to die. I turned carefully on my back.

I tore my shirt open and tried my heartbeat with my right hand. It struck irregularly quickly but weakly. I continued to lie on the grass, breathing gently. I thought of nice things like sunny summer days, nature, the sea, and grandchildren. I tried to get up slowly, but at the same time, I felt that sharp sting in my chest again. I decided to slowly crawl inside the house. As I turned on my stomach, I laboriously pushed myself up and started slowly crawl for toward the back door of our house. In my pain, I wonder how this backyard of ours can feel so big.

As I dragged myself toward the patio, the maid noticed me crawling on the lawn. I said something to her, so she came up to me, asking what was wrong with me. I urged her to ask Emma to the scene. As the servant maid left to run inside, screaming at Emma, I fell unconscious on the stone floor of the terrace. My next memory is of reviving a bitter smell. I lay on the couch in our living room surrounded by a doctor, Emma, and the service staff. The doctor had dipped a piece of clothing into some pungent-smelling substance, making me awake. He explained that I had a worse-than-average heart attack. The doctor ordered me to rest in bed. All physical exertion was prohibited. I would have figured out that even myself without medical education. He could not offer me any other help. There was no use for my money now. How miserable is our medical expertise? Always told only to rest in bed no matter what the illness was. Even the slightest respect for the doctors I still had at the latest now faded away like smoke to the air. Emma had almost invited the priest to our home. I told her in a bitter voice that that guy would have been of no use in my case. I lay helpless on our bed. Emma and our servants took care of me like a baby. The maid read my books, and Emma sometimes played the piano, cheering my mind. At first, my appetite was lost, but little by little, I got stronger and started to feel hungry.

Eating solid food didn't really make me feel better, as it resulted in constipation in my stomach. Emma gave me some drink that softened my stomach. That drink was apparently too effective as it softened my stomach really loose. Because of that, I shit in my pants without being able to do anything about it. I did try to make it to the bucket, but I never got out of bed on time. Every time I pushed myself up out of bed, I felt how diarrhea shit flowed irresistibly from my gut to my legs. I shouted at Emma to place. She helped me get out of bed with the help of two of our servants. The smell of shit in our room was awful. Woe, this feeling of shame! This was so humiliating to my pride. Emma washed me patiently, ignoring the stench. She was mainly amused by this situation. Emma reminded me that she had cared for children all her life and was used to situations like this. How would I have done without Emma? Now I was ashamed of the harsh words I uttered about her when we were young. I planned a gracious death in my mind to free me from this hellish situation. In my most desperate moments, I asked Emma to bring my shotgun, so I could end my suffering, but she didn't even hear such an ungodly request. So, the days crept humiliatingly forward in my life. I wouldn't want to live this way for a month anymore. I was sometimes able to walk inside our house for a while.

That once, I accidentally saw myself in the mirror and was frightened horribly. I didn't almost recognize myself. Was I really that miserable looking? As a result, I told Emma to take all the mirrors far away from me. I wanted to brighten my mind, so I asked the servant staff to move me to our living room. There was more space, and I felt more attached to life. They moved me there and raised the end of my bed so I could see the yard. It was refreshing to see living nature in our backyard. Emma again invited the chamber orchestra to play for me. One of the songs they played remained in my mind. It was Ludwig van Beethoven's piano concerto. As I listened to it, my life went like a series of pictures before my eyes. I lived in my thoughts in the past. I remembered my mother, my failed studies, Fanny, my sailing trip, Annie, and Israfil. It had my achievements and my losses. How much I had experienced and how much I would still have liked to experience. I still missed my daughter Annie.

I soon had another serious heart attack that struck me in the morning. I woke up to it as my chest cramped, as my tired heart pounded asynchronously. In a panic, I instinctively swung my hand and dropped the teacup to the floor that was on the small table next to my bed. The breaking of the teacup woke the servant who was sleeping on the floor.

She came to me asking about my well-being. In my hissing voice, I asked her to wake Emma up and get the doctor. When Emma came to me, I asked her to invite our children home, as I would no longer survive this. Emma burst into tears and hysterically claimed that I would recover. I comforted her to accept the facts and told her to hurry. Emma sent our servants to pick up the doctor and our children. She stayed to sit next to my bed. We looked at each other for a long time without saying a word. The doctor was as helpless as he was last time. He examined me quickly and then chatted further with Emma for a moment. When the doctor came to tell me the results of his examination, I asked him to shut up. I told him I knew my days were numbered, so I told him to go home. Emma escorted the doctor out crying. After that, she came and sat on the edge of our bed again, sobbing. This time I saw in her gaze an awareness that I would not survive this. She had accepted it in her mind. Emma wanted to pray for me, but I stubbornly refused. What would have benefited it? Why pray if not believe? Emma started crying again, saying she didn't want me to go to hell. I told her that I no longer wanted to discuss such a difficult subject in the last hours of my life, but I wanted to spend my last moments with a calm mind. I asked her for a drink, which she also brought.

After drinking it, I told her she was a good wife and the best possible mother for our children. When our children arrived, there was laughter from the grandchildren in the hallway. Emma rose from by my side to receive them. I was left alone in the room. My mind made an exclamation to Emma not to leave me alone, but I didn't dare. As I watched the ceiling of the room, I remembered that Beethoven Imperial Concert again. It felt like another spirit being had come into the room with me. I realized she had come to pick me up. The sunny days of my childhood came to my mind, with no worries or responsibilities. The youth years when I was trying to get a grip on life. How fast those years had gone. I was reminded of John Henslow's biblical counsel years ago: *"My son, remember God in your healthy days of youth, for soon will come the days that do not please you."*

Emma came to the room with our children. Some of them were shocked to see me lying on the bottom of the bed. It was probably a pathetic sight. I said goodbye to them one by one. Our firstborn William came to me last. I wanted him close to me for a longer period of time. I also wanted others to hear how I felt about him. I said goodbye to him with these sentences:

"My dear son William, my life is in the last straight. I might die next night, so I want to speak to you openly. I know I haven't been a good father to you.

Now at an older age, I consciously admit I neglected you. You were welcome and hoped child, but I didn't realize how much time you took from us. I saw from your lovely eyes how badly you had missed me, but I didn't know how to respond to it. I fled your longing of closeness to my own hurries. I wasn't present when you needed me in the difficulties of your life. I didn't know how to be a father to you. We were so similar in many ways, and it annoyed me. William, my dear son, please, could you forgive me?"

At that point, William's chin began to twitch as tears flowed down his cheeks. He pressed his head against my chest and said he would forgive with all his heart. He said now that he loves and respects me more than ever before. Admitting my mistakes had made me a bigger man in the eyes of my son. William said the theory that I came up with showed all of humankind I was a great man. I answered him it is enough for me to be a great man in the eyes of my children. I was no longer so sure about the ingenuity of that theory, for it could make me one of the greatest villains in humanity. I asked with my last strength, the whole family around me. They all grabbed my hands. I told them I loved them more than anything else in the world. Having said that, I felt like my life strength ran out as life began to break away from me.

After the last breaths, I loosened my grip on them and experienced how expressionless they began to separate from me. Slowly but surely, they withdrew from me into another dimension. Or was I the one who separated from them? They were replaced by a glamorous angelic female figure from emptiness. Is that you, Israfil? Am I dying now? If it's your will, then I'll give my life to you, then I can always be in the same place as you, Mom, and Annie are.